RELIGION IN JAPANESE CULTURE

RELIGION IN JAPANESE CULTURE

Where Living Traditions Meet a Changing World

Edited by
Noriyoshi Tamaru and David Reid

KODANSHA INTERNATIONAL
Tokyo • New York • London

NOTE: Except on the cover and title page of this book, Japanese names are presented in the order customary in Japan: first the family name, then the personal name.

PHOTO CREDIT: Inoue Nobutaka, 26, 27.

Distributed in the United States by Kodansha America, Inc., 114 Fifth Avenue, New York, N.Y. 10011, and in the United Kingdom and continental Europe by Kodansha Europe Ltd., 95 Aldwych, London WC2B 4JF. Published by Kodansha International Ltd., 17-14 Otowa 1-chome, Bunkyo-ku, Tokyo 112, and Kodansha America, Inc. Copyright © 1996 by Kodansha International. All rights reserved. Printed in Japan.

ISBN 4-7700-2054-6
First edition, 1996
96 97 98 99 5 4 3 2 1

CONTENTS

CONTRIBUTORS

ARAI Ken
Professor, Komazawa University

INOUE Nobutaka
Professor, Kokugakuin University

ISHII Kenji
Associate Professor, Kokugakuin University

KAWAWATA Yuiken
Priest, Hōbutsuji Temple

MATSUMOTO Shigeru
Professor, Seishin Joshi Daigaku (University of the Sacred Heart)

MIYAKE Hitoshi
Professor, Keiō University

NAKANO Tsuyoshi
Professor, Sōka University

REID, David
Professor, Seigakuin University

SHIMAZONO Susumu
Professor, University of Tokyo

SUZUKI Norihisa
Professor, Rikkyō Daigaku (St. Paul's University)

TAMARU Noriyoshi
Professor, Taishō University

UEDA Kenji
Professor, Kokugakuin University

TRANSLATORS

ABE Yoshiya
Professor, Kokugakuin University

REID, David
Professor, Seigakuin University

PREFACE

More than two decades ago the Agency for Cultural Affairs compiled and published *Japanese Religion: A Survey*. Its main objective was to introduce the general features of religious life in Japan to researchers and interested persons abroad. It was also intended to serve as a practical guide to specific religious organizations with particular reference to their current circumstances.

The present volume emerged from an attempt to revise the earlier book. In the process of preparing new materials, however, it became clear that the new book was relatively independent of its predecessor. The need for revision was obvious. In Japan, as in other industrialized countries in the West, religious life presents a more complicated picture than it did in the 1970s. The Japanese people have shown signs of gradual decline in their commitment to specific religious institutions. At the same time, we have witnessed an upsurge of new, small-scale religious groups together with a growth of interest in spiritual and even occult phenomena. Partly because of its involvement with these developments, the study of Japanese religion, both inside and outside the country, has made great strides and achieved many new insights.

In planning this book our major concern was to present some of the new material and research in a multifaceted and three-dimensional picture of religious life in Japan. The chapters in Part I, mostly borrowed from the preceding volume with slight modifications, describe the major components of Japanese religious tradition, which become the historical and cultural background for the whole. By contrast, the chapters in Part II focus on careful analyses of selected contemporary developments. Of the three appendices, the first deals with Aum Shinrikyō, the new religion linked to the sarin gas attack in Tokyo in March 1995. The second presents a brief analysis of the compilation of religious statistics in Japan, with a summary of recently published data. The third is a chronology of the history of Japanese religion.

We sincerely hope that these chapters will contribute to a deeper understanding of the religion of Japan and its cultural and social relevance in the contemporary situation.

For help in carrying out this project we are indebted to many people and organizations. Thanks are due to the authors who kindly prepared the manuscripts, among whom we are particularly grateful to Prof. Ishii Kenji of Kokugakuin University, who provided basic assistance in planning and organizing the whole project. Kodansha International kindly offered the opportunity for publication. To all we should like to express our heartfelt appreciation.

THE EDITORS
Spring 1996

PART I

A SURVEY

1

INTRODUCTION

Matsumoto Shigeru

Matsumoto Shigeru

• MULTIPLICITY IN THE RELIGIONS OF JAPAN

Many religious traditions coexist in Japan. The most important are: *Shinto*, the indigenous tradition for over two thousand years; *Buddhism* and *Confucianism*, which have profoundly influenced the spiritual and social life of the Japanese people since the sixth century C.E.; *Christianity*, which has exerted a notable cultural and intellectual impact since its introduction in 1549 and its return in the nineteenth century; *new religions*, most of which emerged and experienced their liveliest development during the nineteenth-century transition from the Tokugawa period to the Meiji era as well as during the unstable period after World War II; and, finally, the *folk religions*, centered in the syncretistic religious beliefs and practices that have long been the heritage of the common people. These living traditions, meeting, interacting, and influencing one another, have together shaped religion in Japanese culture.

The complexity of these traditions finds expression in some seemingly contradictory aspects of the contemporary Japanese religious situation. For example, the Japanese people appear to take little interest in religion. Particularly in the modern age, with its industrialization and urbanization, increasing numbers of people commit themselves to no specific religion. But it also appears that the Japanese are very religious, judging from the great number of religious groups, old and new, from the millions of people affiliated with one or more religions, and from the throngs of worshipers who visit famous shrines and temples, particularly at the turn of the year.

Again, a degree of conflict seems suggested by the fact that while the influence of Buddhism on Japanese culture is profound and the number of people classified as "Buddhist" is in the tens of millions, the ancient Shinto tradition remains alive and meaningful in the lives of the Japanese people. There is even a persistent tendency to consider Buddhism an "alien religion." Still another example of apparent contradiction is that the number of followers of the various religions in Japan exceeds the population of Japan. The *Shūkyō nenkan* (Religions yearbook) for 1995, edited by the Ministry of Education's Agency for Cultural Affairs, shows that as of December 31, 1994, over 115 million people were affiliated with Shinto organizations, nearly 90 million with Buddhist, slightly over 1.5 million with Christian, and about 11 million with other religious bodies. The total, over 200 million, contrasts sharply with the 1994 population figure of 125 million.

The multiplicity and complexity of Japanese religious phenomena is related to an assimilative tendency in Japanese culture. Historically, Japan has adopted various cultural and religious traditions and thereby enriched its spiritual life. The newly introduced ideas did not uproot indigenous beliefs but blended into a certain homogeneous tradition, which itself might be called the "Japanese religion." What stands out in this assimilative process is not ideological conflict or discord, but continuity and harmony. One factor that contributes to this cultural characteristic is Japan's geographical situation.

• THE GEOGRAPHICAL SITUATION OF JAPAN

A small country surrounded by the sea, Japan has maintained close contacts with China since ancient times. Japan's geographical position favored the reception of Chinese cultural influences from the mainland, yet it was far enough away from China to be comparatively safe from military invasion and from the political control of the overwhelmingly powerful Chinese dynasties.

The significance of this geographical position becomes clearer when one compares Japan with England. Both are located near a continent and surrounded by water, but when their respective courses of historical development are taken into account, the difference in distance from the mainland assumes critical importance. England, situated about twenty-one miles from Europe, fell prey not only to the Romans but also to the Normans, whereas Japan, separated from China by 115 miles, was conquered neither by the Han dynasty nor by the Mongols. Disturbances within China, whether ethnic or dynastic, did not directly involve Japan. Until the nineteenth century, external pressures came to bear on the Japanese islands only sporadically and for the most part in diluted form. The imported elements never engulfed the existing ones but, like a trickling stream, slowly watered the roots of Japanese culture.

More particularly, the Tokugawa government (1603–1868), in carrying out its isolationist policy, intercepted and controlled the introduction of foreign cultural elements, thus contributing to a process that allowed Japan time to digest and naturalize what it adopted. Owing to its geographical and historical isolation, Japan was able to develop a distinctive culture despite China's proximity and strong influence. For the same reason, Japan has preserved a relatively continuous cultural identity from ancient times to the present. In the religion of the ancient Japanese, the first expression of this cultural identity comes into view.

• RELIGION OF THE ANCIENT JAPANESE: EARLY SHINTO

Before the introduction of Confucianism and Buddhism, the religion of the Japanese was an unorganized, undifferentiated, and unnamed complex of agricultural cult, nature worship, ancestor worship, and shamanism. The social unit of this worship complex was a hereditary group known as the *uji*. Each uji worshiped its own deity, and its members often regarded this deity as their founding ancestor. The chief of the uji was not only a political leader but also a high priest. There was little differentiation between "religion" and "state." This ancient social situation found expression in the archaic word *matsurigoto*, which meant both "government" and "religious rites." Around the fifth century B.C.E., as the Yamato court unified Japan in a single state, previously distinct local cults and traditions gradually became integrated and organized into a religious polity with a nationwide system of rites and myths centered around the sun goddess, Amaterasu.

Shinto, the indigenous religion of Japan, did not originate as a self-conscious tradition. Even the term *shintō* (the way of the kami) entered the language only after the introduction and spread of Chinese culture and religions, serving to distinguish the ancient Japanese customs, rites, and beliefs from Buddhism (the way of the Buddha) and from Confucianism (the way of Confucius). Shinto was not originally a system of moral principles or philosophical doctrines. When it began to express itself as a system of thought, it had to borrow Chinese terms and ideas, both Confucian and Buddhist. Yet in ancient Shinto we can discern the primordial, native expression of a value system that even today remains a basic ingredient of Japanese culture and religion—a value system that functions as a cultural matrix, as it were, for the acceptance and assimilation of foreign elements.

The kami. Shinto deities are called "kami," a term at once singular and plural. The kami are numerous, even innumerable, as suggested by the phrase *yaoyorozu no kami* (myriads of kami). Originally, people applied the word to any form of existence that possessed some extraordinary, awe-inspiring quality. Mountains, seas, rivers, rocks, trees, birds, animals—anything that evoked a sense of mystery or dread was regarded as a kami. The same term applied to human beings who had some extraordinary quality: people like emperors, heroes, uji ancestors, and the like. It will be evident, therefore, that the kami idea held by most Japanese is essentially different from the idea of God found in the Judeo-Christian and Muslim traditions.

Among the various Shinto deities, the kami most highly venerated were those representing the power of productivity or fertility. In ancient myths this power was symbolized in the name *musubi no kami* (the kami of the mysterious generative spirit). This name occurs in the story of Izanagi and Izanami, the divine couple who, according to tradition, procreated both the other kami and the islands of Japan. Central and most important among these ancestral kami was the sun goddess, Amaterasu, traditionally regarded as the supreme ancestress of the successive emperors of Japan.

Japanese people have never conceived of the Shinto kami as absolute or transcendent in relation to human beings or the world—not even in the case of Izanagi, Izanami, or Amaterasu. On the contrary, the constant assumption is that there is a significant continuity between the kami and humans. In sharp contrast to the symbolic dichotomy between the creator and creation in Western religions, the Japanese idea of the relationship between kami and human beings is exemplified in the term *oyako*, signifying the parent-child, or better, the ancestor-descendant relation. The myth that the Japanese imperial line extends in unbroken continuity from Amaterasu to the present emperor gives emphatic expression to the value attached to the oyako relationship.

Purity. The Shinto view of human nature is affirmative and even optimistic. Human nature is accepted as it is; the idea of original sin as found in Christianity does not exist in Shinto. In Old Japanese, *tsumi* (evil) was an undifferentiated concept. It included not only moral transgressions but also natural disasters, physical disfigurements, and disease. Evil was pollution and filthiness, whether physical or spiritual, whereas goodness and purity were essentially one. People took it for granted that human beings were basically clean and pure. Evil was a secondary accretion, a negative entity that could and should be removed by ritual purification (*misogi harai*). This reverence for purity in ancient Shinto, though later combined with Buddhist and Confucian ideas, continues to be a significant element in Japanese culture and religion. It manifests itself not only in religion and morality but also in art, architecture, and many other dimensions of Japanese life.

World view. The Shinto world view, like its view of human nature, is essentially affirmative and this-worldly. It takes the present world as the locus of value. It does not deny the existence of other worlds, but maintains that they have little positive meaning for humans. According to an ancient Japanese myth, the land of Japan is a good land, a land that the kami brought forth, a land that successive heirs of the sun goddess Amaterasu will rule for eternity.

In early Japanese thought one can, it is true, find terms for three other worlds, namely, *takama no hara* (the heavenly world), *yomi no kuni* (the nether world), and *tokoyo no kuni* (the world beyond). None of these ideas, however, implies absolute transcendence over this world or the radical negation of this-worldly values. The first, *takama no hara,* was a resplendent world where the heavenly kami lived, but it was not essentially different from the world we know; it was simply a better version of this world. It should be noted, incidentally, that in contrast to the idea of heaven in Christian tradition or the idea of the pure land in Pure Land Buddhism, *takama no hara* never had any connection with the idea of salvation. The second of these three terms, *yomi no kuni,* identified the place a person's spirit went after death. This place was a dark, polluted, subterranean land, but did not connote retribution for one's conduct in the present world. *Tokoyo no kuni* originally meant "a distant land across the sea." Later the idea of paradise became attached to it, but this idea was devoid of any transcendent reference. The world view of ancient Shinto had its focus in the world we know, and followed from the belief that this is the only world for human beings.

The value pattern underlying ancient Japanese culture and religion shows, then, a sense of continuity between kami and humans, an affirmation of human nature as essentially good and pure, and a positive, this-worldly orientation. The idea of absolute transcendence or negation of this-worldly values is conspicuously absent. The nonexistence of these ideas may be characteristic of the archaic, ethnic religions of the world, but what is particularly striking about Japan is that this basic value pattern survives, with modifications, to the present day.

Into this situation came powerful currents of cultural and religious influence from China. Chief among them were Confucianism and Buddhism.

• BUDDHISM IN JAPAN

Buddhism, first introduced from Korea, was officially welcomed to Japan in the sixth century. The Japanese cultural and religious tradition would be markedly different if Buddhism had never taken root. It should be noted, however, that the Buddhism found in Japan is not the Buddhism that was born in India and raised in China and Korea. At the hands of the Japanese people, Buddhism was consciously or unconsciously "indigenized." Thus even though Buddhism has had a great impact on traditional Japanese values, it has itself been significantly transformed under the influence of this value pattern.

Transcendental world negation. The most important religious and intellectual element that Buddhism brought to Japan was the principle of transcendence and world negation. This principle represented a completely alien value orientation, a perspective that had not existed in the religious ideas of the Japanese people prior to the introduction of Buddhism. It is not surprising, therefore, that at first this new principle was misunderstood. Both supporters and opponents of Buddhism regarded the Buddha merely as a kind of kami, a foreign kami from another land. Those who favored the adoption of Buddhism saw it primarily as a means for the satisfaction of this-worldly interests—and admired Buddhist statues for their exquisite beauty.

Prince Shōtoku (574–622) was the first Japanese to come to a real understanding of Buddhist thought and acquire a deep faith in Buddhism. To him are attributed the words: "The world is false; the Buddha alone is true." This is the first expression of the idea of world negation in Japan. Prince Shōtoku also issued a document known as the Seventeen-Article Constitution. Its moral precepts were largely Confucian, somewhat influenced by the ideas of the Legalists (a school of thought in ancient China which held that social order depended not on Confucian ethical precepts but on the development and application of a body of law). But for his ultimate source of legitimacy, Shōtoku turned to Buddhist teachings. This does not mean that he totally abandoned this-worldly values. As an heir to Japanese traditions and as one with primary responsibility in government, he sought with great dedication to embody his Buddhist faith in secular life. Prince Shōtoku's work marks the first major step in the development of Japanese Buddhism.

Relationship to Shinto. During the seventh and eighth centuries, Buddhism spread rapidly among the nobility and became influential largely because of government backing. The government lent its support to the building of a large number of Buddhist temples and monasteries, and skilled artists produced a variety of excellent Buddhist statues, one of which is the statue of the great Buddha at Tōdaiji temple in Nara. These developments, however, did not entail the abandonment of the indigenous Shinto tradition. Instead, Buddhism and Shinto tended toward a harmonious fusion (*shinbutsu shūgō*), which became one of the primary means for the assimilation of Buddhism in Japan.

One example of such fusion may be seen in a construction known as the "shrine-temple" (*jingūji*). Built within the precincts of a Shinto shrine, the shrine-temple served as a place where Buddhist priests could chant sutras and perform Buddhist rites for the enlightenment of the kami. This custom began in the eighth century and spread to most Shinto shrines during the centuries that followed. It continued until the early Meiji period when, by government order, Shinto and Buddhism were separated.

Ideologically, Buddhist-Shinto syncretism culminated in an elaborate theory called *honchi suijaku* (the prime entity and its manifestations). According to this theory, the Shinto kami are secondary manifestations of certain buddhas or bodhisattvas. During the Kamakura period (1185–1333), this idea found systematic expression in such syncretistic sects as Ryōbu Shinto and Sannō Shinto. Later Shinto scholars turned this theory on its head, insisting that the kami constituted the prime entity or noumenon and the buddhas and bodhisattvas were merely manifestations of the kami. Typical of this approach is Yoshida Shinto, a movement that emerged in the Muromachi period (1336–1573). Arguing allegorically, Yoshida Shinto maintained that "Buddhism may be the flower and fruit of all principles of order (Sanskrit, *dharma*) in the universe, and Confucianism their branches and foliage, but Shinto is their root and trunk."

During the Meiji period (1868–1912), the government decreed the institutional separation of Shinto and Buddhism, but in the beliefs and practices of ordinary people they still exist in harmonious interrelationship. Even today many people keep both a Buddhist altar and a household shrine in their homes. The widespread tendency to have Shinto wedding ceremonies and Buddhist funeral services is also well known. This functional division between Shinto and Buddhism in everyday life expresses the harmonious continuity that most people regard as an ideal characteristic of Japanese culture and religion.

Kamakura Buddhism. The religious reform movements of the Kamakura period (1185–1333) mark another important step in the development of Japanese Buddhism. During the twelfth and thirteenth centuries, four creative Buddhist thinkers appeared: Hōnen, Shinran, Dōgen, and Nichiren. These four leaders laid the foundations for four new Buddhist sects: the Pure Land Sect (Jōdo Shū), the True Pure Land Sect (Jōdo Shinshū), the Zen Sect (Zen Shū), and the Lotus Sutra Sect (Hokke Shū). Together, they made monumental contributions not only to the history of Japanese Buddhism but also to Japanese intellectual history as a whole. They lived in a turbulent age, but in that situation they grasped the essence of Buddhist faith through personal experience. On this basis they opposed the established forms of Buddhism that had largely been devoted to rituals intended to "quell disturbances and protect the country." Their ideas and activities led to a religious awakening in Japan—indeed, even a sort of religious reformation in Japan.

These leaders of Kamakura Buddhism differed from one another in personality, thought, and behavior, but when viewed together and contrasted with previous Buddhist leaders, it becomes evident that they shared two significant characteristics. First, they all emphasized, though in different ways, the moment of transcendence and world negation that properly belongs to Buddhism. Second, all of them represented the object of faith in simplified, purified, and focused form, dedicating themselves unreservedly to this object and to the ordering of human action in its light.

Hōnen (1133–1212) sought a way of enlightenment that all people could understand, a path that would be appropriate to what Buddhism taught was the third and last period of history. (A prominent Buddhist tradition divides human history after the Buddha into three periods: *shōbō*, a period of 500 or 1,000 years during which the way of enlightenment is properly taught, believed, and practiced; *zōhō*, a second period of 500 or 1,000 years during which the way of enlightenment is properly taught, but faith gradually becomes a matter of form and true practice ceases; and *mappō*, a degenerate and degenerating age in which Buddhism survives only as an abstract teaching, not as a way of life or enlightenment. Several eminent scholar-priests, including Saichō, the founder of Japanese Tendai Buddhism, believed the year 1052 marked the beginning of the mappō.) Hōnen came to believe that the single-minded recitation of the *nenbutsu* (the phrase *namu Amida Butsu,* meaning "Praise to Amida, the Buddha of Infinite Life and Light") and the renunciation of all ways of enlightenment based on one's own efforts was "the one way left."

With this faith in Amida and Amida's pure land (*jōdo*), Hōnen founded the Jōdo Shū, or Pure Land Sect.

One of his disciples, Shinran (1173–1262), went even further in emphasizing absolute reliance on the saving power of Amida. He insisted on absolute rejection of reliance on anything in this world, including one's own powers. Shinran carried Hōnen's ideas to their logical conclusion with the insight that the human act of reciting the nenbutsu, and even one's faith in Amida, were not due to innate human capacity or power but were granted solely by Amida Buddha. Shinran's famous statement, "If even the good can be reborn in the pure land, how much more the wicked," is an eloquent expression of faith based on radical self-denial. Shinran marks a decisive departure from the traditional understanding of human nature that gave precedence to the values of continuity, acceptance, and this-worldliness. Not unlike the leaders of the Reformation in Europe, Shinran repudiated the traditional monastic organization, holding that it was not essential to the way of enlightenment. He approved the marriage of priests and himself led a married life while continuing his missionary work. By this example he encouraged a simple, congregational organization of priests and lay people in accordance with the idea of *zaike shinkō* ("a faith for lay believers," that is, for people who do not become monks or nuns but lead a normal family life in the world).

Dōgen (1200–1253) went to China seeking the authentic Buddhist teaching which, tradition said, had been transmitted from one Buddhist leader to another in unbroken spiritual succession since the time of Sakyamuni Buddha. He finally reached the conviction that the practice of *zazen* (sitting cross-legged in concentrated meditation) was the method by which the Buddha himself had attained enlightenment. In contrast to Shinran, who lived a life of profound faith among ordinary people and secular concerns, Dōgen, on returning to Japan, emphasized a secluded, ascetic monasticism with the aim of maintaining as pure a religious life as possible. In keeping with this desire for purity, he rejected not only the idea of compromise with secular authorities but also the idea, current in his day, of working toward the unity of Buddhism, Taoism, and Confucianism. Dōgen provides another example of the emphasis on transcendence and of the tendency toward simplification of the religious life.

Nichiren (1222–1282), after a long spiritual quest, came to believe that the Lotus Sutra (*Myōhō rengekyō*) contained the ultimate teaching of the Buddha concerning enlightenment. He taught his followers to chant *Namu myōhō rengekyō* ("Adoration to the Lotus Sutra") in the belief that invocation of the miraculous power concentrated in the very name of the sutra would lead to illumination. This conscious decision to dispense with "nonessentials" and focus on a single symbolic act again typifies the tendency toward simplification of belief and practice common to the leaders of Kamakura Buddhism.

But Nichiren was unique in his idea of the proper relationship between religion and state. In his view, Japan was by nature and should be in fact "the land of the Lotus Sutra." Because many Japanese disparaged the sutra and since the government would not adopt its teaching, Japan suffered, he held, from natural calamities and social ills. Once having arrived at this position, Nichiren relentlessly drew out its logical implications. He attacked other sects, particularly the Pure Land and Zen sects, and remonstrated against the government as well. Nichiren's position is often regarded as nationalistic. It should be understood, rather, as a prophetic position—extremely rare in the Japanese religious tradition. Nichiren exemplified the fearless proclamation of a judgment derived from faith in a transcendent power, faith that applied to every sphere of life: political, cultural, and religious. Nichiren's sect later split into a number of subsects and also became the source of many new religious movements.

These religious leaders, though differing from one another in their approach to Buddhist truth, were alike in recognizing the significance of the transcendent. In addition, each man in his own way showed a tendency to present Buddhist doctrine and practice in simplified, highly focused form. The result of this tendency was that for the first time in Japanese history Buddhism took root among the people and became a mass movement.

• Christianity

Christianity came to Japan in two waves: Catholicism in the sixteenth century and Protestantism in the nineteenth. By the sixteenth century, both Buddhism and Confucianism had been assimilated into the Japanese cultural and religious milieu. Shinto, Confucianism, and Buddhism, their individual characteristics notwithstanding, had melded into a single, reasonably harmonious cluster within which the spiritual and social life of the Japanese took shape. When Christianity arrived from little-known foreign lands bringing an absolutely different system of thought, it could not avoid clashing with the value system it encountered in Japan.

Initial growth. Though missionary work in this situation was fraught with difficulties, Christianity spread with surprising rapidity. In fact the Japanese seem to have responded to Christianity more readily than people in other Asian countries. One of the main reasons for this positive response appears to be that loyalty to superiors, exalted as the prime virtue in Japanese tradition, was transferred to the transcendent God. In support of this explanation it should be noted that the growth of Christianity was largely due to converts from among the samurai, who placed special emphasis on the virtue of loyalty. This was true in both the sixteenth and the nineteenth centuries.

On both occasions, however, Christianity was eventually suppressed by the political authorities. During the Edo or Tokugawa period (1603–1868), the newly established government prohibited Christianity and persecuted Christians on the ground that the introduction of Christianity was merely a pretext for foreign powers to seek an opportunity to invade Japan. As part of its proscription policy, the government conceived and mandated a temple-registration system (*terauke seido*) that required every Japanese adult to register at a Buddhist temple and to obtain from it each year a certificate affirming that he or she was innocent of association with subversive religion. Again, during the Meiji period (1868–1912) the new government, having made the emperor the pivot of its nationalistic policies, found that Christian loyalty to God made loyalty to the emperor a matter of secondary importance. Christianity was therefore regarded as pernicious, and the government took measures to suppress it.

A threatening way of thought. During both the Tokugawa and Meiji periods the immediate reason for prohibiting Christianity was political, but beyond the political prohibition there seems to have been some degree of outright religious persecution. Its basis is not hard to find. In contrast to mainstream Japanese religious tradition, Christianity involves the idea of a transcendent God, a God whose relationship to the world of human beings includes an assertion of radical discontinuity. From this position it follows that before God all persons are equal and secular human authorities are not absolute. This way of thought threatened the very core of the value system that supported the Japanese social order of the time. Assessments of this kind led to official and unofficial attacks on Christianity not only during the Edo and Meiji periods but also during World War II.

Christianity since World War II. Defeat in war at last put a halt to the policy of suppressing Christianity because of doctrines believed to jeopardize absolute loyalty to the emperor. Christianity then had a most favorable opportunity for development. But the growth of Christianity since 1945 is far from remarkable. Though millions of people have joined the new religious movements that flourished after the end of the war, adherents to Christianity still comprise a mere one percent of the total population.

One reason Christianity is not more generally accepted may be that to the Japanese religious consciousness, with its orientation toward family or household religion as opposed to a religion of individual choice and commitment, and its almost instinctive inclination to affirm an essential continuity between the divine and the human, Christianity simply seems utterly alien.

The influence of Christianity, however, is considerable, particularly in the cultural sphere and in the area of social concerns. The achievements of Christians in such fields as education, social work, the labor movement, etc., have been significant.

• RELIGION AND SOCIETY IN MODERN JAPAN

Under the Tokugawa shogunate, Buddhism became a de facto state religion and an instrument for the control of the masses. The Meiji government reversed this policy in the sense that it removed Buddhism from its favored position, but continued it by substituting Shrine Shinto in its place. The guiding principle of the new government may be summed up as the restoration of imperial rule and, with reference to Shinto, the unity of religion and state (*saisei itchi*).

In order to realize this goal the government determined to separate Shinto from Buddhism, despite their long history of mutual involvement, and to free Shinto institutions from the administrative control of Buddhist priests. The "pure Shinto" idea behind this policy had taken a particularly aggressive turn under the inflammatory pressure of Hirata Atsutane (1776–1843) and his school of Shinto restorationists. During the early Meiji period, it led to a brief anti-Buddhist iconoclastic outburst that resulted in the destruction of many art objects and treasures.

Controlled change. Eventually, however, it proved impossible to realize in the modern age the old ideal of a state based on the integration of government and religion. On the one hand, Western nations were demanding abolition of the legal prohibition of Christianity that had stood for two and a half centuries. On the other, some Buddhists, caught up in the spirit of modernization, were joining Christians in demanding not only separation of religion and state but also freedom of religious belief, thus putting internal pressure on the Meiji government to move toward religious tolerance.

For a time the government was unable to choose between restoration and innovation, but in 1889 it promulgated the Imperial Constitution of the Great Empire of Japan, otherwise known as the Meiji constitution. In Article 28 it declared that "Japanese subjects shall, within limits not prejudicial to peace and order, and not antagonistic to their duties as subjects, enjoy freedom of religious belief." This article guaranteed not only freedom of worship but also the freedom to propagate one's faith. These freedoms, bestowed by the emperor, became the legal privileges of Buddhists, Christians, and the adherents of "Sect Shinto" (*kyōha shintō*)—a government classification for Shinto-oriented groups that had been taking shape since the closing years of the Edo period. These freedoms, however, were subject to the vague but significant limitation that religious liberty must not be construed in such a way as to interfere with the duties of the subjects of "the sacred and inviolable emperor."

The following year, 1890, saw the issuing of the Imperial Rescript on Education. In strongly Confucian terms it enjoined the ideals of social harmony and loyalty to the emperor. This rescript served as the basis for a system of moral education that affected every child in Japan and exerted great influence on Japanese moral consciousness for over half a century. When Uchimura Kanzō (1861–1930), a leading Christian thinker, refused to bow before the imperial rescript and was accused of lèse-majesté, his action and the immediate reaction, both of which took place in 1891, portrayed in taut dramatic form the conflict between imperialistic nationalism and religious freedom.

New religious movements such as Tenrikyō, Konkōkyō, and Kurozumikyō were kept under particularly strict control by the Meiji government. These movements, deriving from the religious experience and personality of their respective founders, appealed to many who were no longer satisfied with the traditional religions. The new groups offered something original both in doctrine and ritual, but the Meiji government refused to recognize them as independent religions and therefore did not permit them the freedoms enjoyed by other groups. On the contrary it compelled them, by direct and indirect intervention, to make their teachings and rites conform to those of State Shinto (*kokka shintō*). Only when they had donned a Shinto cloak did the government permit them to exist, calling them "Sect Shinto" organizations.

New religions and latently religious people. Political pressures of this kind ended with the cessation of hostilities in 1945. At this juncture a host of new religious groups made their appearance. During the 1950s, because of rapid industrialization and urbanization, many people moving to metropolitan centers were cut off from the traditional forms of religion they had known in their native villages. Seeking spiritual support, they flocked to the new religions. Many of the new groups faded out of existence soon after their birth, but some have grown at an explosive pace. Among them are Reiyūkai, Risshō Kōseikai, P.L. ("Perfect Liberty") Kyōdan, Seichō no Ie, Sekai Kyūseikyō, and Sōka Gakkai.

Stimulated, if not threatened, by these new movements, some of the more traditional religious organizations have begun to seek a new role in Japanese life, a role that will make them less dependent on habit and convention. They are trying to rationalize their doctrines and improve their organizational structures so as to respond to contemporary needs. On the whole, however, most of the traditional groups are still groping for the right answers.

One problem that Japanese religious groups, old and new, are encountering at the present time is religious apathy. Statistical surveys show that adults who claim to believe in or belong to a religion form only thirty to thirty-five percent of the population sampled. Yet of those who admit to no religious affiliation, over seventy percent affirm that religious sentiment is important. This suggests that many Japanese people today are living with religious needs that have not been satisfied either by the traditional or by the newer religious groups. To respond to these latently religious people may be one of the most significant tasks now confronting the religions of Japan.

2

SHINTO

Ueda Kenji

- INTRODUCTION

It is difficult to capture Shinto in a definition, for it had its beginnings in the shadowy, prehistoric period when human beings first lived on the Japanese archipelago. It has changed much during its long history, and to the present day includes not only religious but also socio-cultural dimensions. Assuming that any culture possesses an undergirding value orientation, and that the uniqueness of Japanese culture is attributable to such an orientation, I would tentatively identify what may here be called "basic Shinto" with the fundamental value orientation of the Japanese people. Accordingly, Shinto, in the most comprehensive sense of the term, represents the value orientation of the Japanese people in the various forms it has taken and the developments it has undergone throughout Japanese history—including contact with foreign cultures.

Basic forms. As a religious system, contemporary Shinto has four main forms: the Shinto of the Imperial House (*kōshitsu shintō*), Shrine Shinto (*jinja shintō*), Sect Shinto (*kyōha shintō*), and Folk Shinto (*minkan shintō*).

The first, centering in rites for the spirits of imperial ancestors and observed at imperial institutions, is distinguished from other forms of Shinto partly because the emperor himself performs its ceremonies, and partly because it retains the most archaic styles of Shinto worship. This form of Shinto, though of intrinsic interest, is not open to the public and will be omitted from this survey.

Shrine Shinto is characterized not only by a general system of beliefs but also by the importance it attaches to shrine rituals and festivals held in honor of the kami. Shrine Shinto will be treated in more detail below.

State Shinto, a political creation that had its beginnings in the Meiji period, may be understood as a combination of Shrine Shinto and the Shinto of the Imperial House. Faced with the collapse of Edo-period feudalism, the need to negotiate with unknown foreign powers, and the problem of widespread civil discontent, the newly formed Meiji government had to modernize both the polity and the economy. The government felt these goals could best be achieved on a foundation of clear national and cultural identity.

Believing that an emperor-centered Shinto would provide the natural symbolic means for consolidating and mobilizing the nation, and having determined to integrate Shinto into the structures of power by giving its priests and institutions privileged status and financial support, the government promulgated such measures as the separation of Shinto and Buddhism, the revival of the ancient Department of Shinto Affairs (*Jingikan*), and the appointment of propaganda officials. Though it took shape over a period of years, State Shinto was defined in a way that distinguished it from every other form of religion. It was legally identified as a government institution and its priests as government officials. From a legal point of view, therefore, State Shinto was not a religion, and the values it inculcated came under the heading of moral instruction, not religious teaching.

About the same time, in response to pressure from Western governments, the Meiji government formally bestowed religious freedom on Japanese citizens "within limits not prejudicial to peace and order, and not antagonistic to their duties as subjects" (Meiji constitution, Article 28). In practice this meant that religious groups needed government authorization to exist within the law; their doctrines and rituals, moreover, were subject to government regulation.

Thus it was that a sense of national identity centering in devotion to the emperor became, through State Shinto, the official foundation of the new order and the touchstone by which all religious organizations were judged. This was the general policy the government maintained until the end of World War II. It is against this background that the term "Sect Shinto" becomes understandable.

The government classification "Sect Shinto" refers to thirteen religious organizations that came into existence during the closing years of the Edo period and the early years of the Meiji period. Until the end of the Edo period (1868), the only religions to which the government paid serious attention were Buddhism, to which it gave place of honor, Shinto, which it largely ignored, and Christianity, which it prohibited. With its decision to exalt Shinto, the Meiji government disestablished Buddhism and, acceding to foreign pressures, gave Christianity the legal right to exist. With Shrine Shinto now transformed into State Shinto, the question arose as to how to regulate the new religious organizations. The government did not wish to incorporate them into State Shinto, despite many points of convergence, but it did want to make them conform to the doctrinal and ritual standard of State Shinto. The solution was to create a new classification: Sect Shinto. The government eventually recognized each of the thirteen sects as an offshoot of Shinto tradition—though in the case of Konkōkyō and Tenrikyō the classification proved to be a procrustean bed, a difficult fit for those obliged to comply with it.

The Sect Shinto classification, which still exists today, is not entirely precise, but the groups brought together under this heading do show certain common characteristics. All but one, Shinto Taikyō, were founded by charismatic personalities. The kami of Sect Shinto, with the exception of the deities of folk origin worshiped by Konkōkyō and Tenrikyō, are the same as those of traditional Shinto, e.g., Izanagi, Izanami, and Amaterasu —kami whose names appear in the Shinto classics. As for the practice of faith in daily life, the first obligation is dedicated effort that, however minutely, benefits the imperial house and the nation. The expectation is that such effort will contribute to the advancement both of the individual and of human life generally. Believing in the continuity between humanity and divinity and in the essential oneness of the visible and invisible worlds, Sect Shinto is more concerned with life in this world than life in the next. Consequently, it teaches and encourages simplicity, purity, honesty, diligence, and selfless service.

Like other religious organizations of the traditional type, the Shinto sects are heavily dependent on the structures of agrarian communities. Confronted by the wave of changes that accompany modernization and urbanization, they are in the throes of working out more effective programs and more appropriate structure (see chapter 9).

The names of the thirteen sects and their founders, listed in order of the year of government recognition, are given in Table 1.

Folk Shinto, the fourth main form of present-day Shinto, is a catchall term for the amalgam of superstitious, magico-religious rites and practices of the common people. Unlike Buddhism and Christianity, Folk Shinto cannot be represented in terms of doctrine, canon, or membership. Its basis of support is to be found, rather, in the popular acceptance of Shinto customs and perspectives in daily life. (For a detailed introduction to Japanese folk religion, see chapter 5.)

Shinto has, then, four main forms, the most representative of which is Shrine Shinto. The balance of this chapter will be devoted to an interpretive account of this phenomenon.

TABLE 1

SECT SHINTO SECTS

Name	Founder	Recognition
1. Kurozumikyō	Kurozumi Munetada	1876
2. Shintō Shūseiha	Nitta Kuniteru	1876
3. Fusōkyō	Shishino Nakaba	1882
4. Izumo Ōyashirakyō	Senge Takatomi	1882
5. Jikkōkyō	Shibata Hanamori	1882
6. Ontakekyō	Shimoyama Ōsuke	1882
7. Shinshūkyō	Yoshimura Masamochi	1882
8. Shintō Taiseikyō	Hirayama Seisai	1882
9. Shintō Taikyō	———————	1886
10. Misogikyō	Inoue Masakane	1894
11. Shinrikyō	Sano Tsunehiko	1894
12. Konkōkyō	Kawate Bunjirō	1900

• SHRINE SHINTO

State Shinto was abolished following the issuance of the Shinto Directive by the Occupation authorities in December 1945. With the formation of the religious organization known as the Jinja Honchō (Association of Shinto Shrines) in February 1946, Shrine Shinto was divorced from the state and began a separate existence as an explicitly religious entity.

Basic principles. The Jinja Honchō, a voluntary liaison organization that includes most of the Shinto shrines in Japan, formulated a useful summary of the principles of Shinto faith. This statement, though in no sense binding on Shinto adherents or organizations, was published in 1956 under the title *Keishin seikatsu no kōryō* (General characteristics of a life lived in reverence of the kami). Each person who lives according to Shinto is enjoined:

1. To be grateful for the blessings of the kami and the benefits of one's ancestors, and to be diligent in the observance of Shinto rituals, performing them with sincerity, cheerfulness, and purity of heart.
2. To be helpful to others through deeds of service without thought of reward, and to seek the advancement of the world at large as one whose life mediates the will of the kami.
3. To bind oneself with others in harmonious acknowledgment of the will of the emperor, praying that the country may flourish and that other peoples too may live in peace and prosperity.

In order to make this statement of belief clear, it is best to approach the subject not through commentary on its technical terms but, more concretely, by examining macrocosmically how Shinto faith manifests itself in its shrine context.

Since the shrines of Japan differ widely in historical background, in the kami they enshrine, in particular beliefs, and in the position they occupy in the lives of the people, the proper procedure, strictly speaking, would be to examine them one by one. It should be noted, therefore, that the approach employed here is not optimal, for it necessarily entails generalization. With this warning in mind, we begin with a consideration of the Shinto shrine setting.

Naturalness. A shrine is not just a worship facility. Neither is it solely a place in which to keep the ashes of the dead or to store works of art. With its grounds and auxiliary buildings, a shrine is a place for the veneration of the kami. As such, it is a sacred place. In accordance with the belief that the kami once possessed human form, it is also legitimate to consider the shrine the dwelling of the kami.

In ancient times, when there were no fixed shrines, people believed that the kami lived in remote places and visited human society on special occasions. Shortly before an important rite or festival, people would prepare a temporary enclosure, or *himorogi*, a symbolic square of space with a sprig from a sacred tree at its center, distinguished from secular space by a shoulder-high boundary of straw rope. Alternatively, they would build a somewhat more permanent enclosure known as an *iwasaka*, a sacred space marked by a rock border. They then invoked the kami and carried out the rite or festival. Vestiges of this ancient form of worship still exist in some shrine rituals. With the passage of time, however, temporary sacred enclosures gave way to permanent structures. Eventually, people came to believe the kami dwelt in these buildings. Thus it is that to the present day Shinto shrines are constructed in the shape of a house.

The Japanese understanding of sacred space involves more than the shrine itself. It includes the natural surroundings as well. Many shrines are far removed from human habitation. They are located in the natural landscape: sometimes on a mountain, near a waterfall, or on a remote island. In such situations nature itself may be viewed as a kami symbol. Even where cities and towns have grown up around previously distant shrines, or where shrines have been established in populated areas, the general rule is to provide a natural setting, at least symbolically. A pond with miniature mountains and a pathway often suggests the beauty and mystery of nature. From the importance attached to the natural world, it may be inferred that it is in the bosom of nature that the Japanese people have for centuries experienced most profoundly the sense of communion with the kami. To infer that Shinto is nothing more than nature worship, however, would be to draw a hasty conclusion.

This high valuation of naturalness and simplicity has an impact on shrine construction. The dominant principle is the use of plain lumber and the avoidance of superfluous decoration. Two places that exemplify this principle are the Grand Shrines of Ise and the Grand Shrine of Izumo, both known for their venerable and highly authoritative traditions. It is true that as history brought Shinto into contact with such mainland influences as yin-yang dualism, Buddhism, and Confucianism, some shrines were painted and adorned with carvings. The original ideal never dropped out of sight, but Chinese influences did contribute to the architectural heterogeneity evident today. Modern building materials and methods have also made an impact, and in present-day Japan shrines constructed of reinforced concrete are not unusual. Traditionally, however, simplicity, purity, and harmony with nature are the values of highest priority in shrine construction.

Shinto includes the belief that the kami are revitalized with the coming of each new year. Expressions of this belief can be found not only in Shinto rituals and folk religion but also in the tradition of dismantling the shrine and building it anew at regular intervals. Mainly for economic reasons, this tradition has largely fallen into disuse, but in the reconstruction of over a hundred shrines at Ise every twenty years, and the regular rebuilding of several other shrines, the tradition survives to the present day.

Forms of worship. Shinto lays particular emphasis on ritual. Unlike religions that start from dogmas and creeds and try to work out as logically as possible the principles by which human life should be governed, Shinto stresses inward mystical experience and consequently attaches high value to mystically oriented rites. In shrine worship three categories of rites may be distinguished.

As the first two come under the general heading of purification, we should begin with a word as to how purification is regarded in the Shinto world. According to Ise Shinto teachings dating to the thirteenth century that have found general acceptance among Shinto adherents, purification rituals have a twofold reference: external and internal. In kami worship, purification of the body is accompanied by inward purification, a restoring of the heart to its original uprightness. During purification rites, the body represents the spirit in such a way that physical purification may become a symbolic, spiritual purification as well.

Of the three categories of mystical shrine rites, the first in order of observance is that which emphasizes the external: the rites of preliminary purification (*kessai*). This category embraces a cluster of observances ranging from avoidance of all foods not prepared over a ritually pure fire to complete immersion of the body in a sea or river. Since extensive rituals of this kind eventually proved impossible for most people to incorporate into their daily pursuits, the custom arose, particularly in connection with major festivals, for the households in a community to perform religious duties in rotation (the *tōya* system). This is still a widely practiced custom, especially in rural areas. Alternatively, a few members of the community may be assigned the task of performing the rituals of preliminary purification so as to travel to a distant shrine and worship the kami there as representatives of the community (the *daisan* system).

Rites of preliminary purification entail taboos on death and flowing blood. Menstruating women and persons with a recent death in the family are expected to refrain from shrine worship. Today, however, perhaps as a consequence of urbanization and rapid social change, these preliminary rites are more frequently honored in the breach. For the most part Shinto priests are the only ones who observe all the rituals of preliminary purification. Other people content themselves with a symbolic rinsing of mouth and hands when they visit a shrine.

The second category consists of a single rite: the internally oriented rite of exorcism and purification (*harae*). This ceremony, normally performed only by a Shinto priest, entails the passing of a purification wand (*haraegushi*) over the worshipers or the object to be purified. A highly symbolic act, it effects, according to Shinto teaching, an inward cleansing from all sin and pollution. Whether the rite should be viewed as magical or religious can best be determined by the attitude of the individual participants, but the point to be stressed is that Shinto attaches great importance to spiritual purification that frees the body and spirit from all uncleanness and reveals the heart in its pristine beauty and integrity.

After external and internal purification, the worshiper is ready for the third stage: the rites of dedication. They begin with the offering of sprigs of the sacred *sakaki* tree. This gesture originated as a symbolic dedication of the first fruits of the harvest, and today, complemented by offerings of rice, saké, and other products, it continues to be a vital part of public worship. The Shinto way of honoring the kami on festival occasions is to serve the kami as one would an honored guest. Thus the worship includes the offering of festive foods and the performance of music and dance. Throughout, the worshipers' reverence and gratitude are manifest. The prayers (*norito*) read on such occasions are highly stylized and rhetorical, but permeated with praise of the kami, petitions for protection and blessing, dedication to the divine will, and vows to persevere diligently in this life.

The aim of these three types of worship, then, is to help people return to original purity and uprightness and live a life of reverence for the kami.

The kami and the shrines. At a place of honor within the shrine sanctuary is a kami symbol or emblem. Occasionally, because of Buddhist or Hindu influence, a kami may be represented as a statue or an image before which people worship, but as a general rule, the object of veneration is not an image in human form.

The mirror is the most frequently found kami symbol. According to the ancient myth of Japan's creation, Amaterasu, the kami who founded the imperial line, bestowed upon her descendants a mirror representing herself. The mirror, therefore, has for centuries been regarded not only as a symbol of authority but also as a representation of the presence of the kami. Other symbols include the sword, articles of apparel, and other items specific to particular kami.

Since the object of worship is a spirit, what symbolizes this spirit is merely a representation. At the same time, however, since the symbol represents the presence of the spirit, it is treated with the same reverence as the kami.

The beliefs of the early Japanese concerning the nature of the kami have not changed greatly with the passage of time, but it may be worthwhile to examine the relationship between the kami concept and Shrine Shinto. For this purpose, it is convenient to begin with a general definition of the kami as set forth by the renowned scholar and Shinto restorationist Motoori Norinaga (1730–1801).

> The word "kami" refers, in the most general sense, to all divine beings of heaven and earth that appear in the classics. More particularly, the kami are the spirits that abide in and are worshiped at the shrines. In principle human beings, birds, animals, trees, plants, mountains, oceans—all may be kami. According to ancient usage, whatever seemed strikingly impressive, possessed the quality of excellence, or inspired a feeling of awe was called kami.

Perhaps no other definition has caught so accurately and concisely the chief characteristics of the Shinto idea of the kami. But when it comes to the kami worshiped at the shrines, one can discern a certain selectiveness. The tendency is to restrict enshrinement to the following: Amaterasu as the mythical head of the imperial line; the kami who appear in the myth of the origin of Japan; the ancestors of emperors and famous clans; the kami of food and productivity, of land and profession; and finally, historical figures who have made an outstanding contribution to society.

Though Motoori is correct in saying that any forceful manifestation of life or power that has a bearing on human existence is at least potentially a kami, it does not follow that all kami are enshrined as objects of worship. The kami recognized in flora and fauna, some of whom interfere with or even bring harm to humans, do need to be appeased and pacified with religious rites, but they are not incorporated into the shrines. Thus, for example, when work on a house or other building is about to begin, the people in charge will ask a Shinto priest to perform an outdoor ceremony called a *jichinsai* on the construction site to conciliate the kami of the land with offerings of rice, saké, lengths of cloth, or money. The same ceremony is also intended to appease the evil spirits that lurk in nearby rivers and mountains. But the only kami introduced into shrine worship are those with human characteristics. Even the fox shrines (*inari jinja*) are no exception, for according to Shrine Shinto, *inari* comes from *ine nari* or rice harvest, and refers to the spirit of the grain. Rice is a life-giving power and a symbol of life-giving kami. (At the popular level, a different view prevails. There *inari* is identified with the fox, or *kitsune*. People regard the fox as the messenger of the gods, and approach the gods through their messenger.) Other divinities, classified as spirits (*mi*) or demons (*mono*), rank below the anthropomorphic kami.

According to Shinto belief, therefore, all forms of existence are spiritual entities. The idea that material objects might exist in and of themselves does not even arise. This point of view is fundamental to Shinto ontology. Within this general frame of reference, Shinto belief further holds that the kami who created the land bless and sustain life in this world. Human participation in and advancement of this life is at once the realization of the will of these deities and the fulfillment of the meaning and purpose of individual existence.

The character and spiritual authority of the kami are evaluated in terms of their contribution to human happiness. This is the reason that the kami idea includes distinctions of rank. Not only is there a distinction between enshrined and unenshrined kami, but differences in status also exist among the enshrined deities—and, by extension, among the shrines.

The kami as powers. At the level of intellectual cognition, kami faith can be understood from one perspective as belief in life-giving powers. The myths preserved in the classics, speaking of the emergence of the various kami, do not present them as beings who transcend the world. On the contrary, as entities constituted from the nuclei of things in heaven and earth, they come into view as beings in and through whom life is generated, grows, and advances. Many tokens of this understanding of the kami appear in rituals transmitted across the centuries and in the religious practices of ordinary people. With this idea in mind, it will be easier to understand other kami attributes and characteristics.

The life-giving and life-promoting powers that the Japanese people have encountered in religious experience are perceived and conceptualized in particularistic terms. In their origin, human beings and nature are, as it were, blood relatives, common offspring of the kami who brought Japan into existence. In their essential being both nature and humankind are kami. Individual forms of existence are revered in all their individuality, for through them the kami exercise their particular functions. In this sense Shinto is a polytheistic religion: it offers its adherents the possibility of believing in many kami.

Interrelated in terms of function and descent, the Shinto kami, taken as a whole, maintain harmony in the evolution of life. This is not to say, however, that they are all of equal standing. There are, as mentioned above, distinctions of rank. This is why Shinto is sometimes described as a hierarchically organized polytheism with Amaterasu at its head.

Some people charge that Shinto is nothing but a politically contrived ideological myth, created to justify governmental authority in the name of the emperor, who is exalted as the direct descendant of the allegedly absolute Amaterasu. This judgment, however, is a political one that ignores Shinto's character as a religion. The fact is that in the early centuries of Japanese history, as previously autonomous clans pledged allegiance to the imperial house, the same general pattern of worship unfolded among all the clans. Never has the leading position occupied by Amaterasu meant that she was absolute. Amaterasu is believed in and worshiped as head of the pantheon, yet at the same time pays her respects to other kami. Ordinary people, without ceasing to revere Amaterasu, believe in other kami as well, and when they have a request to make, they go to the kami whose functions relate most directly to their particular concern.

The affirmation that the evolution of life-giving, life-promoting powers is to be understood in terms of particularity may also be expressed by contrasting it with other principles. From a Shinto perspective it is clear that the essential value of existence is to be discovered not in an absolute, a priori rational principle (the Greek *logos*), nor in a universal norm or law (Sanskrit, *dharma*), but in the possibilities inherent in concrete forms of existence. Accordingly, Shinto is a religion of the relative—in the positive sense that it is committed to reality in the endless process of becoming. This is the reason that Shinto places such high value on the birth of new life and on the transmission of life through successive generations.

Human existence is undoubtedly finite and relative. Yet precisely through its vertical and horizontal interrelationships with ancestors, kin, and descendants, with family and work, with ethnic, local, and national communities, with the human race as a whole as well as with plants, animals, nature, and all conceivable forms of being, human existence maintains its function and character as one form of existence among others. In doing so it becomes a part of life that is infinite and inexhaustible. This is why the Japanese people believe in and worship ancestral kami, household kami, occupational kami, the kami of local and national communities, food kami, plant and animal kami, the kami of nature—a countless host of kami. Fellowship with these kami is effected through traditional rituals. In such worship people realize the boundlessness of life and attain spiritual security.

Some people, not yet understanding Shinto, criticize it as a religion whose primary interest is in this-worldly benefits. From a Shinto perspective, however, an interest in tangible benefits that will promote life in this world is a perfectly natural consequence of its esteem for the kami that bestow and enhance life. What is difficult to understand is why such a concern should be deprecated.

Another dimension of kami belief, one that may seem, at first, to contradict the positive attributes affirmed above about the kami, is the idea that kami power has a negative, destructive aspect. Thus, for example, belief in kami that inflict calamities (*tatarigami*) and in vengeful, malevolent spirits (*goryō*) has long occupied an important place in Shinto. Illustrations of this type of belief appear in the earliest myths. Since the ninth century (the early Heian period), rituals designed to avert catastrophe and conciliate the kami who cause them have been a notable part of the body of rites carried out by the imperial court. Even today rituals for this purpose are regarded as indispensable both in Japanese folk religion and in Shrine Shinto. Historically, the role of Buddhism was of great significance as it mingled with Shinto and influenced the development of belief in destructive, harmful deities. But the point to note here is that from a Shinto standpoint these vengeful, destructive kami are the source of all sin and impurity.

As a matter of doctrine, the question of the exact relationship between these kami and the evils associated with them has been disputed since the nineteenth century. One school of thought claims these kami merely make people aware of certain evils. The other argues that they actually bring these evils on people. This problem has never been conclusively resolved, but judging from the existence of exorcistic elements in the rite of purification (*harae*), the central rite of Shrine Shinto, the evidence seems to favor the latter position.

It is important, however, to distinguish between the ethical and religious components. Despite the negative nature of what these kami do, a positive assessment emerges when they too are considered as manifestations of a power of life. Even when implicated in events that appear disastrous from a human standpoint, they are worthy of reverence and worship. The power that promotes life is no less a power when it destroys. Inextricably associated with the positive manifestations of the power of life, even the pernicious kami have their place in the Shinto pantheon. Human beings, through the observance of rituals in their honor, come into contact with eternally creative and evolving life.

Matsuri. With the single word *matsuri*, the Japanese language designates two separate but related phenomena: communal festivals and the personal practice of faith in daily life. In its first meaning, matsuri signifies attending to the kami as the guest of honor at a sacred banquet. People give ritual expression to a sense of awe and thankfulness, presenting prayers not only for divine favor and tangible blessings but also for exemption from accident and misfortune. They celebrate the joy of life in song and extol the virtues of harmony and fruitfulness among all forms of existence that share in the fellowship of life. This is matsuri in the sense of communal worship addressed to a kami and offered in the presence of the deity.

In its second meaning, the word matsuri suggests transmission of the will of the kami in the personal sense of individual participation in the activities that make the universe vibrant with life. It suggests realization of one's true self, and awareness that the gift and power of life depend on the kami. This is matsuri in the sense of putting faith into daily practice.

These two meanings, though logically distinguishable, are inseparable in reality. It is only fair to point out, however, that as generally used the term matsuri refers only to the communal festival; most people are unaware that it also implies the practice of faith in daily life. This blind spot is probably due to the conspicuousness of the ceremonies that take place at the shrine, and also to the fact that Shinto does not propound an authoritative creed. Its adherents are free to determine their own courses of action.

The two situations in which these meanings of matsuri find their most natural and concrete expression are the home and the shrine.

Traditionally, the Japanese home has, in a place of honor in the living room, an altar for the worship of the kami (*kamidana*). Since the end of World War II, the number of homes with such altars has declined as a result of waning religious consciousness, increasing westernization in residential construction, and a tendency for multigenerational families to be replaced by nuclear families. But kami altars still exist in many Japanese homes, including cramped apartments, for which small-scale *kamidana* are now available.

At the center of the kami altar is a miniature shrine before which the family members offer their worship (matsuri). On the altar one often sees talismans of various kinds and other kami symbols. Every day someone in the family, generally the wife, presents offerings of cooked rice, water, fruit, etc., and those who wish to do so pay homage to the kami, usually in the morning and evening. The archaic, rhetorical prayers (norito) that priests offer at shrine festivals have no place in family worship, but some people use set prayers for purification and blessing.

Particularly widespread is the custom of showing reverence to the ancestral spirits through ritual presentation of offerings of food and drink, sometimes at the family grave but more often in connection with the worship rituals that take place in the home. Most people perform their ancestral rites before the household Buddhist altar, but families dedicated to Shinto and its rites erect a separate Shinto altar for the ancestral spirits.

Essentially, the faith-informed worship of the kami before the miniature household shrine is identical with that offered at the large community shrine. But the two previously discussed meanings of the word matsuri become particularly evident in the individually offered acts of worship in the home. This holds true not only in terms of context but also in terms of subjective awareness.

The Shinto shrine, the second locus of matsuri observance, bases its festivals on a calendar that starts with New Year's Day. Most shrine observances are public and liturgical prayer rites. But with the development of a professional priesthood and, more particularly, with the practices established during the period of shrine nationalization, many people take the attitude that these rites are primarily a priestly preserve. Except for delegates from the parish council, participation by parishioners is uncommon. On the other hand, just as each shrine traces its origin to particular kami that people revere and believe in, so too each shrine, in honor of the kami it enshrines, holds regularly scheduled major festivals (*reitaisai*). These are frequently spectacular occasions, colorful and gay, in which people participate with enthusiasm, whether as parishioners, believers, or ordinary citizens. When Japanese people hear the word matsuri, it is this image with its joyous, heartwarming associations that generally leaps to mind.

Common to most festivals, despite distinctive local traditions and customs, is the performance of certain time-honored rites by the priest or priests, members of the parish council, and selected representatives from the households affiliated with the shrine. There are also many festivals conducted exclusively by lay people, festivals in which the priests take no part whatever. But apart from rites in which participation is minimal, two forms of ritual behavior attract great crowds of people at every major festival: the deity's symbolic tour of the parish (*shinkō*), and the special performances and general merrymaking that contribute to the entertainment of the kami (*kami nigiwai*).

In the symbolic tour, the spirit of the kami is first ritually installed in an elaborate portable shrine borne by a team of young men from the parish. Then the kami makes a circuit of the district, usually following the same fixed route. This is a rite of considerable significance, for in it the kami encounters people at the places where they live and work, purifies the parish as a whole, and enriches its people with fresh strength and vitality.

Public performances of dance and song in the midst of festal revelry are also indispensable features of the major matsuri. In addition to entertaining the kami, the performances and joyous atmosphere serve to unite members of normally separate groups with the kami in an exaltation of spirit that transcends everyday concerns. This is the setting in which religious orgies sometimes occur, here understood as the inversion or violation of normal rules of behavior. The groups people belong to are essential to their existence as human beings. Yet group life, no matter what kind of membership principles or rules of order it relies on, always involves certain contradictions, frictions, and antagonisms. The matsuri relieves people from these strains and tensions by bringing their energies to white heat in the religious context. Perhaps for this reason, though seemingly contrary to expectation, the communal festival makes a contribution to group solidarity by its orgiastic overturning of normal standards of behavior. Thus the observance and violation of ordinary conventions are two sides of the same coin. Both suggest that the Shinto kami are primarily gods of the group and of the community.

It hardly needs mentioning that Shinto leaves room for individual faith as well. This comes out most clearly in petitions for tangible blessings. When it comes to the holding of festivals, however, the smallest viable social unit is not the individual but the family. This is one of the most fundamental Shinto principles. Earlier, it was suggested that the term matsuri has two meanings: worship in the presence of the kami at community festivals, and the personal practice of faith in daily life. Personal faith does not contradict the principle that assigns priority to the family. The Shinto belief is that diligent endeavor in daily life is at once the will of the kami who brought this land into being and the fulfillment of their will. The kami bestow their blessings on the people with the hope that their lives will be productive and fruitful. To accept these blessings and live in grateful awareness of the kami who bestow them is to become aware of one's identity as a member of an entire people. This is what it means to become a *mikoto mochi*, a person who mediates the will of the kami in daily life. Individual existence finds fulfilment only as one realizes that personal life is inseparably bound up with the task of passing on and enhancing the life of the whole community one belongs to. This is not to say, however, that the people whose welfare one seeks must be those of a specific culture or nation. Shrine Shinto is essentially a religion that honors the uniqueness of the particular. It does not seek to win converts, and the central role it assigns to the Japanese emperor means that it will probably never be exported, except to communities of Japanese expatriates. But when it comes to identifying the people whose welfare it is to seek, Shrine Shinto is not limited to the Japanese. Eventually, the horizon

3

BUDDHISM

Tamaru Noriyoshi

• DISTINCTIVE FEATURES OF JAPANESE BUDDHISM

Ever since Japan entered history as a unified state, Buddhism has been an important influence in the religious life of the Japanese people. So pervasive is its influence, not only in the area of religion but in Japanese culture generally, that any attempt to comprehend these dimensions of Japanese life would be impossible if it did not take Buddhism into account.

Two contrasting aspects. Buddhism has planted deep and penetrating roots in Japanese society. Buddhism is also, however, a religion of foreign origin, and came to Japan bearing foreign skills and ideas. Thus on the one hand, Japanese Buddhism is part of a world religion and as such possesses a universal, international orientation. On the other hand, it took shape within the social climate and traditions of Japan, and therefore bears within itself distinctively Japanese characteristics. In considering the phenomenon of Japanese Buddhism it is essential to keep these two contrasting aspects in mind.

Whether one perceives Japanese Buddhism primarily as a special form of the world religion of Buddhism or as a distinctly Japanese religious phenomenon depends largely on one's angle of vision. An interest in Buddhism as a system of thought and as an agent in the diffusion of culture tends to emphasize the universal, whereas attention focused on Buddhism as a historical institution and as an influence on human action in society tends to stress the particular. In reality these are of course inseparable, but it is useful to distinguish between them for the purpose of conceptual clarification. An approach that confines itself to Buddhism as a system of thought and a cross-cultural intermediary will be directed to what Japanese Buddhism has in common with the Buddhism of India, China, and other countries. Conversely, an approach focused on Buddhism as a social reality will highlight what distinguishes Japanese Buddhism from the Buddhism of other countries and regions: what makes Japanese Buddhism Japanese.

When Buddhism first came to Japan, it was accepted, like other cultural imports, primarily as a complex of objects and ideas (sutras, statues, doctrines, etc.). The imported religion was clearly Buddhist but hardly Japanese. Yet during the process of assimilation and creative reproduction, a Buddhism that is unmistakably Japanese was born.

Sources of Japanese Buddhism. Founded in the fifth century B.C.E. by Siddhartha Gautama, Buddhism originated as a Hindu reform movement that advocated the practice of meditation as a means of attaining enlightenment and, ultimately, Nirvana or emancipation from the wheel of rebirth. Since it denied the authority of the Vedas, Buddhism stood opposed to Brahman orthodoxy. In the Indian context it was regarded as revolutionary, though its world-denying, mystical character shows that it remained under the influence of Indian ways of thinking.

By the time of King Aśoka's reign (c. 268–232 B.C.E.), Indian Buddhism had split into several groups generally referred to as Theravada schools. Around the beginning of the Christian era, Mahayana Buddhism arose, being distinguished from Theravada Buddhism primarily by its enlargement of the bodhisattva ideal. According to this ideal, certain compassionate beings or bodhisattvas defer their emancipation in order to save others. This enlarged bodhisattva ideal had a doctrinal consequence: enlargement of the offer of enlightenment. The offer was now available not only to those who entered monastic orders but to all who trusted in a bodhisattva. For several centuries Buddhism continued to evolve in India, developing in interaction with the various Indian religions and philosophies, but after the Islamic invasion of the thirteenth century it ceased to exist in the land of its birth.

During the centuries between its birth and disappearance in India, Buddhism spread beyond Indian borders. It developed as it went, and at length became a world religion comparable to Christianity and Islam. In contrast to Theravada Buddhism, which took root in Sri Lanka, Myanmar (formerly Burma), Thailand, and other countries located for the most part in South Asia, Mahayana Buddhism made its way via Central Asia to China and various countries of East and Southeast Asia.

The Buddhism that Japan first encountered came from Korea in the sixth century C.E.—552 according to the *Nihon shoki,* or *Nihongi* (720), but 538 according to the earlier *Jōgū Shōtoku hō'ō teisetsu.* Later, in cultural waves of varying size and duration between the sixth and sixteenth centuries, Japan acquired its knowledge of Buddhism directly from China. Since Buddhism came to Japan by the northern route, Japanese Buddhism is frequently classified as Mahayana. It is true that when contrasted with Theravada Buddhism, which has its center in the monastic community or *sangha*, Japanese Buddhism is clearly of a different cut. But it is important to recognize that the Buddhism that came to Japan across the years also includes various forms of Theravada Buddhism—forms ranging from some of the earliest examples of Indian Buddhism to the developments of much later centuries. The scriptures, teachings, and rituals of nearly every period and culture that Buddhism passed through are preserved, studied, and kept alive in Japan. Just as the islands of Japan served, both geographically and chronologically, as the terminus of the Buddhist journey, so too Japanese Buddhism may be thought of as a recapitulation of the developments that have gone into the shaping of Buddhism as a whole.

Buddhism underwent many important changes as it moved from India through Central Asia and China to Japan. What reached this country sometimes possessed a form that would not have been recognized as Buddhist in the land of its origin. In some cases it contained in developed form what had existed embryonically in primitive Buddhism; in others it included elements taken over from different religious systems. To complicate matters even more, sometimes what had once been peripheral now stood in a position of central importance. The result was a radical change of emphasis. A good example of this kind of shift may be seen in the idea of salvation proclaimed by Pure Land Buddhism, namely, salvation through faith in Amida Buddha. Another example is the belief in quasi-magical formulae and techniques so pronounced in Tantric Buddhism.

All in all, Buddhism tended to become increasingly complex in the course of its travels. This complexity is worth noting, for it is against this background that the subsequent development of Buddhist schools of thought within Japan needs to be understood.

Differentiating features of the appropriation process. As suggested above, what is distinctive about Japanese Buddhism is more readily apparent in its practical adaptation to Japanese society than in its contributions to Buddhist thought.

In the sixth century C.E., when Buddhism received its official introduction from the continent, Japan was in the midst of fashioning a new social order, unifying previously independent clans under the aegis of the imperial house. Culturally, the young nation was at a low stage of development, for it was still preliterate. Buddhism, as the vehicle of an already highly developed Chinese culture represented particularly by the Chinese system of writing, made an incalculable contribution to Japanese culture and education. It continued to act as a medium for the transmission of Chinese culture until the importation of Zen Buddhism during the medieval period.

Buddhism's entry into Japan had behind it the authority and eminence of Chinese culture and its imperial form of government, gaining leverage, as it were, from the superior position of China. This played a decisive role in determining the character of Japanese Buddhism. To the political and cultural leaders of Japan, Buddhism appeared as an advanced form of culture. The first Japanese to accept and align themselves with Buddhism came from the imperial family and influential noble houses. Not till the medieval era (the Kamakura period, 1185–1333, and the Muromachi period, 1336–1573) did Buddhism begin to penetrate deeply into the lives of the common people. Sociologically, therefore, the movement was from the upper strata of society to the lower, or from the center to the periphery. In this it differs from primitive Christianity, for example, which first took root among people of humble birth and later spread upward. Thus the first trait to be noted in the appropriation process is that Japanese Buddhism began as a religion of the aristocracy and only gradually made its way into the ranks of people of low degree.

A second distinguishing feature, a frequently noted corollary of the first, is the close bond between Japanese Buddhism and the state. For the government, this relationship involved both patronage and control of Buddhists and Buddhist organizations. From the Buddhist side it entailed receiving certain emoluments and providing moral and spiritual support for the state—on occasion compromising its own principles. This bond, to be sure, constituted only one element in the process by which Buddhism was appropriated in Japan. Besides this element there was always an undercurrent of popular Buddhism that grew stronger with the passage of time. On the whole, however, when Japanese Buddhism is contrasted with the Buddhism of other countries, it is this tie with the state that is singularly conspicuous.

During two periods of Japanese history, the Nara period (710–794) and the Tokugawa period (1603–1868), the close relationship between Buddhism and the state appears with particular clarity. The Nara government promoted Buddhism, but strictly controlled the status of priests and nuns according to a comprehensive administrative and penal code known as the *ritsuryō* system. Later centuries saw, for a while, an increase in the autonomy of Buddhist institutions, but the Tokugawa period brought the imposition of even tighter controls. The shogunate drew up regulations that affected every Buddhist temple, and every adult was required by law to register at some temple. These steps resulted in the formation of a network of government-initiated parish-like organizations; it also resulted in the incorporation of the temples into the feudal administrative system. Thus began a peculiarly Japanese institution known as the *danka seido*, a system that required every household to be affiliated with a Buddhist temple. The law establishing the *danka seido* was rescinded in 1871, but to this day many households continue to feel that they have a special relationship with and obligation to a particular temple. This tie provides an important social support for long-established Buddhist organizations.

The third point that stands out when one considers how Buddhism was adopted in Japan is the strong link between Buddhism and the family, traditionally regarded as the basic unit of Japanese society. Bound to families and clans through ancestral rites, Buddhism gradually reached a point where services for the dead became one of its most significant functions. A tendency in this direction existed even during its first centuries in Japan, but as time went on, it became increasingly important. Eventually, with the increase of adherents among the common people during the medieval period, the conducting of requiem services came to be thought of as Buddhism's raison d'être. Another reason for this development is that Buddhist temples and institutions without the benefit of state support or aristocratic patrons looked to ordinary people for economic help by handling their funerals and other mortuary rites. This makes it easier to understand why, even today, most Buddhist temples hold for their supporting families not only funerals but also the prescribed series of mortuary rites—and why many priests consider it an essential duty to supervise and maintain the temple graveyard. From this perspective there is warrant for calling Buddhism "a religion of the dead."

Rites for the dead did not occupy such a central place in early Buddhism. In India, ceremonies for deceased members of the religious community were held, to be sure, but the main purpose of the religion was clearly to attain enlightenment. As Buddhism made its way across China and into Japan, however, death-oriented rites gradually grew in importance and degree of elaboration. Thus the bond it established with the family through assimilation of pre-Buddhist Japanese usages resulted in a change in Buddhism itself. Despite efforts by advocates of Shinto to promote Shinto funerals, especially from about the end of the Tokugawa period, Buddhism continues to hold a virtual monopoly in this field.

Fourth in the cluster of traits that describe Buddhism as it came to be adopted in Japan is the role it allows to magic. Human petitions that look toward essentially magical solutions are generally more concerned with this-worldly problems than with death and the afterlife. In terms of objectives they range from individual or family desires for recovery from illness, avoidance of adversity, attainment of prosperity and the like, to public concerns such as peace for the nation or victory in war. At work in such petitions is a credulousness which supposes that the recitation of sutras, the performance of rituals, and the observance of spiritual disciplines, not to mention the use of magical formulae together with special objects like amulets and the relics of saints, will produce a supernatural result.

Magical ways of thinking and acting are generally regarded as vestiges of primitive belief, usages that antedate the rise of higher religion. Logically, therefore, Buddhism, at least in its original form, should have been free of magical elements. In fact, however, traces of magic appear to have existed even in the earliest period of Indian Buddhism. With the passage of time and the emergence of Mahayana Buddhism, especially that branch of the Mahayana stream known as Tantric Buddhism, Indian folk beliefs and practices merged with Buddhism to an even greater degree, and magic came to play a more important part. In the case of Japan, the position assigned to magic is particularly prominent in the schools affiliated with Tantric Buddhism, notably the Shingon sects and certain of the Tendai sects.

With regard to the roles Buddhism has played as it put roots down in Japanese society, reference has been made to its starting at the top, its ties with the state, its involvement in family mortuary rites, and the scope it allows to magic. It is not claimed that these points provide a complete portrait of Japanese Buddhism, nor that they admit of no exceptions. In connection with the final point, for example, it is widely known that the Pure Land groups take a firmly antimagical position. Again, since parallels for each of these points can be found in other religions, it may be going too far to call them differentiating traits. In combination, however, this complex of traits can be taken as a general guide to the character of Japanese Buddhism.

• MAJOR SCHOOLS OF JAPANESE BUDDHISM

Pre-Nara debut and Nara period developments. An important era in the history of Japanese Buddhism began with the official introduction of Buddhism in the sixth century and reached its culmination in the Nara period (710–794). During this time, Buddhism found acceptance among influential clans and nobles and gradually secured a footing in Japanese society. Of exceptional importance among those who accepted the new religion was Prince Shōtoku (574–621 or 622), second son of Emperor Yōmei and regent for Empress Suiko.

Coming to power before the various clans had been unified, Prince Shōtoku pursued two complementary goals. He sought, on the one hand, to establish a single, centralized government under the authority of the emperor and, on the other, to raise the cultural level of Japan through government patronage of the newly arrived religion. So successful were his efforts on behalf of Buddhism that he is frequently called the father of Japanese Buddhism. He established Hōryūji temple in 607 as a center for Buddhist studies; it still stands as one of the oldest Buddhist buildings in Japan. Of his own accord, he also studied and even wrote commentaries on three sutras (the Lotus Sutra, the Discourse on Ultimate Truth by Vimalakīrti, and the Book of Earnest Resolve by Śrīmālā), seeking in this way to digest and appropriate Buddhist ideas. Interestingly, the commentaries attributed to Shōtoku manifest not only a surprisingly accurate understanding of Buddhist principles but also a typically Japanese tendency to adapt Buddhist ideas to this-worldly interests. Even at this early date there was a clear inclination to keep Japanese values intact and modify Buddhism in their favor.

The zenith of government support for and promotion of Buddhism during this early period came in the eighth century. Particularly noteworthy is the decision of the emperor Shōmu (r. 724–749), proclaimed in 741, to build a state-subsidized provincial temple (kokubunji) in every district and to have a gigantic bronze statue of the Vairocana Buddha cast and enshrined in the parent institution, Tōdaiji temple, in Nara. Completed in 749 after years of painstaking labor, this Vairocana Buddha at once symbolized the magnitude of the universe and the power of the centralized state.

Nara Buddhism consisted of six schools: Sanron, Hossō, Kegon, Jōjitsu, Kusha, and Ritsu. These schools or sects derived not so much from distinguishable groups or interests in Japanese society as from different doctrinal emphases and areas of study. The priests of that day generally took their training at more than one school. The first three schools belonged to the Mahayana tradition and the other three to the Theravada. The six together allowed Japanese scholar-priests to investigate all the major currents of Buddhist thought. It should be emphasized, however, that this function was carried on only in monastic communities. Outside the monastery walls, the primary role of Buddhism in Nara society was the performance of certain rituals believed to contribute to the peace and security of the government, and the offering of prayers and chants for the realization of this-worldly goals on behalf of aristocratic patrons.

Of these six schools, three still exist today: the Hossō school, with Kōfukuji temple as one main temple and Yakushiji temple as another; the Kegon school, with Tōdaiji temple at its head; and the Ritsu school, also associated with Tōdaiji temple. Adherents to these schools come almost entirely from temples and monasteries. Because their lay followers are few, none of these schools has made much of an impact on Japanese society. Taken together, however, they represent the embryo from which Japanese Buddhism has grown. As prototypes preserved to the present day, they have an influence and significance none the less real for being intangible.

The Heian period (794–1160) and the Buddhist syntheses. The transfer of the capital from Nara to Kyoto in 794 marked a turning point not only in government affairs but also in the history of Buddhism. In the early part of this period two extraordinary men, Saichō (767–822, generally known by his posthumous title Dengyō Daishi) and Kūkai (774–835, usually called by his posthumous title Kōbō Daishi), separately established near Kyoto two new schools of Buddhism: Tendai and Shingon. Despite their disagreement on many fine points of doctrine, these schools exhibit a number of fundamental similarities.

To begin with, the leaders of both schools went to China (then under the T'ang dynasty) to acquaint themselves directly with the latest theoretical and practical developments in the world of Buddhism. In doing so they joined a long and distinguished tradition dating from the early history of Japanese Buddhism.

A second prominent feature of both schools is their comprehensive and harmonizing character. In the preceding era, as we have already seen, scholarly priests in Japan studied the various forms of Buddhism that took shape in India and China, but for the most part they simply lined them up and examined them one after another. The Tendai and Shingon thinkers, however, refused to stop there. Following the orientation of their schools, both groups sought to work out a system of thought in which every point of view, Buddhist and non-Buddhist, would receive an assigned place in an all-embracing synthesis. As these schools grew in strength and influence, the structures of thought they created served as the ideological foundation for the fusion of Shinto and Buddhism that later took place.

Tendai is the Japanese form of the Chinese *t'ien-t'ai*, at once the name of a mountain in China, a temple situated on that mountain, and a sect founded at that temple by Chih-i (538–597). It was there that Saichō studied and from there that he returned to Japan to found the Tendai school. Among the many Mahayana sutras, the Tendai school attaches particular value to the unquestionably important and popular Lotus Sutra. But in contrast to its Chinese model, it also accords a place of honor to other influential Mahayana teachings such as those of the Kegon school, the idea and practice of concentrated meditation (*zen*), and Tantric Buddhism. According to Saichō, these various teachings, though distinguishable, were only superficially contradictory. At bottom they were simply different manifestations of a single, ultimate truth.

Advancing this claim, Saichō soon found himself in trouble with representatives of the more rigid Nara schools. Returning to Enryakuji, the temple-monastery compound that he had built on Mount Hiei a short distance northeast of the capital, he sought to establish the Tendai school there as an independent sect. During his lifetime, however, this goal remained unrealized. Hierarchically, he was dependent on the hostile Nara sects for ordination of his disciples, and legally, his group, like all other Buddhist groups, could not exist as an independent body without the permission of the state. Because of repeated remonstrances from the Nara schools, the government withheld this permission for many years, finally granting it on Saichō's death. Since then, the Mount Hiei Tendai center has grown to become one of the largest and most important places in Japan for the study and practice of Buddhism. One indication of its influence is that all three of the Buddhist schools formed during the Kamakura period—Pure Land, Zen, and Nichiren—had some connection with Mount Hiei.

The Tendai sect, like the Shingon, made use of esoteric rites of an essentially magical nature, but its chief contribution to Japanese Buddhist history has been in the area of doctrine and philosophy. Central to Tendai thought is the theory of *hongaku hōmon*, the idea that enlightenment is not to be achieved through the gradual elimination of attachment to ultimately illusory phenomena, but is to be discovered as innately given. Elaborating the idea of "emptiness" (Sanskrit, *śūnyatā*; Japanese, *kū*) propounded by Nagarjuna, a man of the second or third century C.E. generally acknowledged as one of the greatest Mahayana philosophers, the *hongaku hōmon* theory involves an ontology of absolute monism or nondualism. This way of looking at things holds that though a person cannot avoid dualistic antitheses such as those between life and death, deluded blindness and spiritual understanding, ordinary life and the enlightened life, etc., one can, by simply opening one's eyes, discover the ineradicable, naturally given enlightenment that transcends these polarities. More fundamentally, this original enlightenment (*hongaku*) cannot be found if one adheres either to the seeming reality of the dualistic realm or even to ontological nondualism. Thus this philosophy involves the rejection of all phenomenal realities, including the philosophical premises of this rejection, only to turn again and affirm them with an absolute affirmation.

The word *shingon* is a translation of the Sanskrit term *mantra*, meaning the embodiment in sound of a divine power that can effect spiritual and temporal results. This stream of Buddhism, introduced by Kūkai, derives from the Tantrism that arose during the last period of Mahayana development in India. It may be characterized as a blend of abstruse metaphysical teachings and rituals deeply imbued with magic.

As a young man, Kūkai applied himself to Confucianism and philosophical Taoism but, still unsatisfied, turned to Buddhism at the age of eighteen and immersed himself in the Nara schools. Thus began a quest for enlightenment that lasted many years. At the age of thirty-one, he crossed the sea to China, went to the T'ang capital of Ch'ang-an, and devoted himself to studying the Tantric Buddhism then in vogue. Here he found what he had long sought. On returning to Japan three years later, he received permission from the imperial court to propagate Tantrism, and he established as the chief centers of his work two temples: Kongōbuji temple on Mount Kōya, south of Nara, and Tōji temple in Kyoto. Kūkai was a man of many talents who excelled in the fields of literature and art. As a result, the sect he founded came to include many elements of an artistic and literary nature.

Of particular importance among his many writings is the *Jūjūshin ron* (Treatise on the ten stages of spiritual development). In this work he set forth in systematic form the basic principles of Shingon teaching. Joining both Buddhist and non-Buddhist teachings into a comprehensive synthesis, he classified them on an ascending scale of ten stages, ranging from the rudimentary religious consciousness that depends on the phenomena of nature to the perfected state of being realized in Tantric Buddhism. According to Tantrism, absolute truth is symbolically present in all phenomena, of which three are singled out as especially important: the already introduced *mantra* (Japanese, *shingon*), the *mandala* (Japanese, *mandara*), and the *mudrā* (Japanese, *inzō*). The concept of mandala as used by Kūkai refers to a schematic representation of the true order of the universe in the form of Buddhist statues or something that stands for them. *Mudrā* is a designation for various series of ritual gestures symbolic of religious truth. Together, these Tantric ideas and forms have exercised a determinative influence on Japanese Buddhist iconography.

The corpus of Shingon teachings left Kūkai's hands in so complete a form that little remained to be done. His successors therefore devoted their energies not so much to the refinement of doctrine as to the performance of intricate and elaborate rituals. In its ritualism Shingon Buddhism is constantly at risk of degenerating into magic, a danger to which it has not infrequently succumbed.

New movements of the Kamakura period (1185–1333). With the establishment of the Kamakura shogunate in 1185, Japanese history entered a new phase, commonly identified as the beginning of Japan's medieval period. Political authority passed from the hands of aristocrats at the imperial court in Kyoto to the newly ascendant military class, thus initiating the first stage of Japanese feudalism. At this juncture several developments occurred in Japanese Buddhism. Most important among the new movements taking shape at this time were the three touched on above: the Pure Land, Zen, and Nichiren schools. At times they fought among themselves, but each pursued its own course—and continues to do so today.

These three movements arose within the Tendai orientation, only later becoming independent schools. What they did, in effect, was to select, from the range of teachings included in the harmonizing approach of an earlier day, one motif and give it the sole place of honor. Pure Land Buddhism chose the way of salvation through faith in Amida Buddha; Zen, the way of concentrated meditation; and Nichiren Buddhism, the way of dedication to the truth of the Lotus Sutra. All three, in contrast to the synthesizing perspective of Tendai and Shingon, were selective, uncompromising, and sectarian in outlook.

Historically, each movement has a distinctive background. Among the three, Zen is somewhat unusual, for it alone came to Japan as an innovation—then popular in Sung China. The practice of meditation (Sanskrit, *dhyāna*; Chinese, *ch'an*; Japanese, *zen*) goes back, of course, to the time of primitive Buddhism. Even then it played a central role. But the practical, nonspeculative Chinese people saw in it a means of maintaining inner poise in the midst of worldly turmoil, and thus it became not merely a form of spiritual training of which all schools made use, but a separate school in its own right. Pure Land Buddhism, on the other hand, cannot be found in primitive Buddhism. It first appears as a component of Mahayana Buddhism. The fact that it rose to prominence so suddenly during the late Heian and early Kamakura periods has to be understood in relation to the historical situation. This need for contextual comprehension holds true for Nichiren Buddhism as well. In contrast to the Zen and Pure Land schools, both of which trace their origin to China and India, Nichiren Buddhism has no foreign prototype. Of the three, it is the most markedly Japanese.

The first school to be considered in more detail is the Jōdo or Pure Land school. The most important figure is Hōnen (1133–1212, also known as Genkū). Hōnen divided Buddhism into two categories: one in which people seek to attain enlightenment through disciplined effort, and one in which people seek to be reborn in the pure land, the spiritual state of oneness with ultimate reality, through reliance on the mercy of Amida Buddha. Of these two, his choice, he declared, was for the latter. Hōnen was the first person in Japan to pose the problem in such a way as to call for an either-or choice. Underlying the choice he made was both a belief in the absolute saving power of Amida Buddha and the conviction that humankind was deeply enmeshed in sin. Accepting the Buddhist teaching that this was the final period of history (*mappō*), a degenerate period in which Buddhism survived only as a doctrinal shell, not as a way of life, Hōnen held that in this period people simply did not have the capacity to achieve enlightenment by their own efforts (*jiriki*, one's own strength). The only way left, he believed, was to rely on the strength of another (*tariki*), that is, on the merciful compassion of Amida Buddha. This pessimistic view of history and of humankind is undoubtedly tied to the profound social changes of the early feudal period. Because of this outlook, Hōnen was led to abandon meditation, ritual, and all the traditionally prescribed means of attaining enlightenment, and to urge, instead, the one way that remained: calling on the name of Amida. Emphasizing, as it did, not lofty doctrines or elaborate and costly rituals but simple faith, the Pure Land Sect (*Jōdoshū*) established by Hōnen appealed strongly to the common people of Japan.

Hōnen's teachings reached a new stage of development at the hands of his most famous disciple, Shinran (1173–1262), founder of the True Pure Land Sect (*Jōdo Shinshū*). Shinran focused on a teaching of Hōnen's which, though fundamental, had been only one among others in Hōnen's thought. Shinran made the idea of the compassion of Amida the pivot and criterion of all his teaching and conduct. Because of this idea, he even rejected Hōnen's distinction between *jiriki* and *tariki*, returning, as it were, to the position of the absolute affirmation of phenomenal reality previously encountered in the *hongaku hōmon* teaching of the Tendai school. What led him to take this position was the belief that Amida's compassion and saving intention were absolute and that Amida had, in fact, already accomplished his purpose. All people, regardless of their condition, were already saved—though they might be unaware of the fact. Shinran held, therefore, one form of the doctrine of predestination. Applying this faith to daily life, Shinran maintained that there was no real difference between the monastic life and life in the secular world, so he himself married and raised a family. Other Buddhist sects, before and for some time after Shinran, adhered to the traditional idea that Buddhism required a celibate, monastic organization. The step Shinran took in getting married brought into being a new model of Buddhist life: *zaike bukkyō* (devotion to Buddhist ideals while living a married life in the secular world). Spreading throughout Japan, particularly among farming people, the organization founded by Shinran grew in size and influence and remains one of the largest Buddhist sects in Japan today.

Zen Buddhism, the second of the Kamakura period schools, also marked a break with traditional Buddhism since it rejected elaborate philosophical problems and formalistic rituals in favor of bringing Buddhism into daily life—to this extent agreeing with the Pure Land sects. This point of view finds focused expression in such Zen slogans as "transmission that does not depend on teaching" *(kyōge betsuden)*, "written words are useless" *(furyū monji)*, "direct communication that goes straight to the heart" *(jikishi ninshin)*, and "to discern one's true nature is to attain Buddhahood" *(kenshō jōbutsu)*. In contrast to Pure Land Buddhism, however, which sought salvation from without, Zen took its stand on the idea of enlightenment through personal effort.

Zen, after achieving considerable popularity in Sung China, was introduced to Japan in more than one form and by more than one person. Rinzai Zen was introduced by Eisai (1141–1215), a Japanese monk who went to China in 1187, devoted himself to Zen, and returned to Japan in 1191. With the patronage of the Kamakura shogunate, Eisai built Jufukuji temple in Kamakura and Kenninji temple in Kyoto, thus laying the foundation for the dissemination of Zen in Japan. The bond established between Zen and the emergent samurai class is especially noteworthy. In part this relationship was a function of the political antagonism between the Kyoto-based court aristocrats, who clung to traditional Buddhism, and the Kamakura-based samurai, who had committed themselves to a new course and were ready for a new spiritual orientation. At a deeper level, however, this bond seems to have resulted from a natural correspondence between the simple, robust character of Zen and the ethos of the samurai.

Not long afterward, Dōgen (1200–1253), another Japanese monk, introduced Sōtō Zen. Whereas Rinzai employs question-and-answer techniques, stories about past Zen masters, and logically insoluble conundrums as aids to enlightenment, Sōtō concentrates exclusively on meditation practiced while sitting erect in a cross-legged position (*zazen*). Dōgen coined a pithy phrase: *shikan taza*, that is, entertain no vagrant thoughts, "just sit" in earnest contemplation. Seeking to develop a pure form of Buddhism, Dōgen kept his distance from those in positions of power, shut himself up in Eiheiji temple in the mountain fastnesses of remote Echizen Province (now part of Fukui Prefecture), and dedicated himself to the training of his disciples.

As time went on, Rinzai and Sōtō developed in remarkably different directions. Whereas Rinzai sought adherents primarily among the high-ranking samurai who now held the reins of power, Sōtō worked mostly among provincial samurai and commoners. Thus arose the saying *rinzai shōgun, sōtō domin* (Rinzai for the shogun, Sōtō for the peasants). Perhaps for this reason, Sōtō Zen, more than Rinzai, merged with indigenous folklore to such an extent that mortuary rites and essentially magical incantations gradually came to occupy a position nearly as important as the spiritual exercises that had belonged to it in the beginning. The incorporation of funeral ceremonies and rituals for the dead into Buddhism began, it is true, with the Pure Land sects, but the subsequent elaboration that took place was largely due to Sōtō Zen.

Among the new Buddhist movements of the thirteenth century, the last to appear was the one that bears the name and impress of its founder, Nichiren (1222–1282). A man of prophetic character, Nichiren involved himself deeply in the historical situation of his day and passionately sought to reform Japanese society.

The controlling idea of Nichiren's life and thought is epitomized in the phrase *risshō ankoku*, that is, to establish true Buddhism and on this basis to reform the country and make it secure. Troubled by persistent doubts, Nichiren reflected on the natural disasters and social unrest that plagued his period and concluded they stemmed from a decay in Buddhism. Until true Buddhism made its appearance, he believed, the country could never become what it should. This true Buddhism Nichiren believed he had found in the Lotus Sutra, and he harshly and continuously denounced the Ritsu, Shingon, Zen, and especially the Pure Land sects for their devotion to fallacious teachings. To the Kamakura shogunate he presented a memorial urging the reform of Buddhism and the government in accordance with the teachings of the Lotus Sutra. Not only was his advice rejected, he himself was persecuted for his presumptuousness and his activities repeatedly suppressed until at length he was exiled to the distant island of Sado. This was not the end of his life, but it did mark the virtual end of his efforts at direct reform. Throughout a career marked by frequent persecution, Nichiren displayed a dauntless spirit of resistance that undoubtedly derived both from his strong sense of mission and from his belief that the nation was in a period of crisis.

During the years after Nichiren's death, followers of his sect increased in number despite the obstacles in their path. By the latter half of the medieval period, most of the sect's supporters came from the merchant class in Kyoto and other cities. As with other sects, winning adherents from the common people entailed compromises with the popular demand for tangible benefits and led to an increase in the magico-religious elements presumed effective in producing these results.

Two significant developments since the Meiji Restoration (1868) may be summarized briefly. One is the alliance of Nichiren Buddhism with nationalism. This development, though linked to Nichiren's strong concern for the nation, involved a failure to recognize that his teachings also imply a critical stance toward the state. The second and perhaps more important development is the proliferation of new religious movements of Buddhist origin that have sprung up during the twentieth century. Such powerful organizations as Reiyūkai, Risshō Kōseikai, and Sōka Gakkai are all associated in one way or another with Nichiren Buddhism. This fecundity stands out as a distinctive characteristic of the Nichiren school.

• BUDDHISM IN JAPANESE LIFE

Buddhist contributions to Japanese culture. During the fifteen hundred years since it entered Japan, Buddhism not only introduced certain changes in Japanese life but also underwent changes itself. In considering what Buddhism introduced, it is important to distinguish between elements that properly belong to Buddhism and those that later became attached to it. For by the time Buddhism reached Japan, it was already a composite phenomenon. Within the framework of this distinction between the essential and the peripheral, some attention should also be given to the way the Japanese apprehended Buddhism. Even though people can quickly pick up the material elements of culture and the skills requisite to their use, adopting a new world view and learning to think on the basis of a new set of values are slower processes that involve interaction and mutual modification.

With regard to elements peripheral to Buddhism through which Buddhism has exercised (and continues to exercise) influence on Japanese life and culture, one may begin with what is fundamental to any civilization: its written language. It has already been mentioned that Chinese ideographs, whose role in Japanese culture is incalculable, came to Japan with Buddhism. In addition, the Japanese syllabaries were probably modeled on a Sanskrit prototype transmitted through Buddhism; the syllabary mnemonic i-ro-ha, known to all Japanese people, was written as a poem exemplifying a Buddhist view of life. Besides these systems of writing, the number of ordinary Japanese words and phrases that depend on Chinese translations of Buddhist sutras is almost beyond reckoning.

Buddhism has also played an important role in the field of education. From the time Buddhism entered Japan, its temples served not only as religious institutions but also as centers of learning. Until the Meiji government established a system of public education, most elementary education in Japan was handled by schools (terakoya) affiliated with Buddhist temples. Printing techniques, the use of the almanac, and the rudiments of Chinese medicine were among the skills disseminated through the agency of Buddhism. Even the custom of drinking tea came to Japan with Zen, tea being regarded as a kind of tonic.

Buddhist influence on the arts has been even more pronounced. Japanese painting and sculpture began with the idea of portraying objects of worship in visible form for use in the temples. Music too, both instrumental and vocal, was adopted for use in Buddhist rituals. In postmedieval drama, especially Noh, Buddhist themes are very evident. Again, such typical and widely practiced art forms as the tea ceremony and flower arrangement owe their popularity to the fusion between secular culture and the Buddhist spirit that took place after the mid-nineteenth century.

Turning now to elements intrinsic to Buddhism, we immediately encounter a more problematic situation. For whereas the borrowing or adopting of cultural elements is a somewhat superficial thing that can be analyzed with relative facility, the influence that takes place at a deeper, spiritual level is more diffuse and difficult to trace. But it is possible to point out two elements that have exercised this kind of influence.

One is the speculative, metaphysical way of thinking that enlarged and enriched the naive, restricted outlook of the ancient Japanese. Ideas from the Buddhist (or Indian) worldview that played a role in this development include transmigration, karma, and the rule that the chain of cause and effect holds good through past, present, and future.

The other element is the world-denying, transcendental value orientation that gave the Japanese people a sense of the transience of human life and an awareness of more universal values. This element usually expresses itself in ways that center in the idea of evanescence. For example, in the mid-eighth-century anthology known as the *Manyōshū*, there are some poems, though only a few, devoted to the theme of the frailty of human life. Again, the early eleventh-century *Tale of Genji* is the source of a pithy saying that has become classic in Japan: *mono no aware*, a poignant expression evoking the stab of desolate pathos people sense in the face of beauty they know will decay. In both cases the ideas involved are almost certainly due to the influence of Buddhist thought. In a development that is perhaps typical of Japan, though, it often happens that the themes of transience, evanescence, impermanence, and the like are used to express aesthetic more than religious feelings. Even today a sensitivity to *mono no aware* still plays a quiet but influential role in the Japanese view of life.

Modification of Buddhism in Japan. The transformation of an originally religious sensibility into an aesthetic brings us to the second half of the problem: how Buddhism has changed as a result of its encounter with Japanese culture and the spiritual outlook of the Japanese people. The result of this encounter, to put it in somewhat extreme form, is the conversion of Buddhism from a world-denying to a world-affirming religion.

Originally, Buddhism required that its adherents, if they were in earnest, reject the life of ordinary society and devote themselves to the pursuit of inner, personal enlightenment. This entailed abandoning one's family and renouncing participation in political and cultural affairs. In this sense primitive Buddhism was a religion that transcended the present world.

In Mahayana Buddhism the attitude toward life in this world became ambivalent, and as Buddhism journeyed across China and into Japan, its attitude was increasingly affirmative. The emphasis swung from individual enlightenment to the amelioration of social conditions and paved the way for the acceptance, by Japanese Buddhism, of a multitude of secular values.

Prince Shōtoku's tendency to attach considerable importance to matters bearing on life in Japanese society has already been noted. The same tendency, it should be added, runs through many schools of Japanese Buddhism discussed above: Shingon, with its affirmation that the person who engages in spiritual training can attain Buddhahood in the immediate present (*sokushin jōbutsu*); the True Pure Land Sect, with its paradoxical affirmation of life in the secular world; Zen, with its realistic attitude toward life; and Nichiren Buddhism, with its interest in the welfare of the nation. Thus the Japanese propensity for placing a high value on the things of this world functioned, on the one hand, to change the inner character of Buddhism and, on the other, to provide people with a vantage point from which they could, as occasion arose, criticize Buddhism from outside. The latter consequence becomes particularly evident in the anti-Buddhist ideas of Japanese Confucianists during and after the seventeenth century.

The this-worldliness found in Japan is not unique to this country. It may be that this phenomenon, characteristic of modern secular cultures generally, is a manifestation of a worldwide tendency toward secularization.

- BUDDHISM IN MODERN JAPAN

A different world. The modernization program that started with the Meiji Restoration involved a change of milieu for all Japanese people and institutions, including Buddhism. We can distinguish two major periods when extensive social changes took place. One began in 1868, when Japan embarked on a course leading to the creation of an absolutist state, the other in 1945, when this process came to an end. Both periods had largely negative effects on the traditional Buddhist organizations. But these changes did require the established bodies to work out new ways of coping with the demands of the situation—and led to the rise of several new organizations.

If one contrasts the situation of Buddhism in the feudal period with its status in the modern period, the most pronounced difference will be seen in its relation to the state. The Meiji government, in pursuit of its goal of mobilizing the nation under the authority of the imperial house, not only gave priority to Shinto but also, for a time, deliberately sought to suppress Buddhism. This policy did not last long, but the government patronage Buddhism had previously enjoyed was over. Today, since the establishment of laws based on the separation of religion and state, Buddhism is simply one tradition among others in a religiously pluralistic society.

Though not enacted with Buddhism in mind, two other legal developments that have exerted no small influence on Buddhism are the land reform of 1945–1946 and the family law written into the Civil Code in 1947. The land reform greatly weakened Buddhist temples, particularly in rural areas, by depriving them of their title to lands formerly rented to tenant farmers. This undercut a major source of temple income. The family law, by recognizing the nuclear family rather than the traditional system of interlocked households (*ie seido*), weakened the *danka seido* system that had tied households to a particular Buddhist temple and guaranteed its financial support. True, the act mandating this system had been rescinded as early as 1871, but the law continued to recognize interlocked households as corporate entities with legal rights to property, thus ensuring the de facto continuation, until 1947, of the old temple support system.

Again, the relationship between temples and adherents, centering in the ancestral rites which priests perform when families request their services, has become even more unstable because of the rapid urbanization of recent decades. It remains true, though, that most people still look to the Buddhist temple for funeral and post-funeral ritual services despite this threat to their traditional role.

Another traditional temple function, the offering of ritual and essentially magical incantations for people seeking tangible benefits, seems to be losing its attraction for those raised in enlightened, secular circumstances. But practices of this sort are still in demand at many temples. This fact serves as a reminder that deep-seated magical traditions survive even today in the spiritual outlook of the Japanese.

New directions. Confronted by this battery of changes, many of which seem detrimental to Buddhism, the traditional Buddhist organizations are seeking ways to cope with the new situation.

Under the heading of organizational reform, one conspicuous feature is a new and more enterprising attitude toward educational and social programs. Buddhist priests have had centuries of experience in these areas, but now, making use of the new techniques that have become available, such as counseling, many sects are redoubling their efforts to promote this kind of work. Some temples have adapted by opening their doors to tourists, by starting real estate businesses, and generally by diversifying their activities. There are also a few sects which, in response to the legal abolition of the traditional household system, have undertaken to establish themselves not on the basis of the household with its religious practices, but in relation to the individual with religious faith.

Another area in which Buddhists have made remarkable advances since the beginning of the modern era is that of scholarly research into Buddhism. Materials dating back to the earliest period of Buddhist history are available in Japan. This favorable circumstance, combined with the introduction of modern research methods from the West beginning in the 1890s, has made it possible to maintain rigorous standards of scholarship in documentary and historical studies—which continue apace. It should be noted, though, that these are strictly academic studies and have no direct bearing on the practical concerns and activities of Buddhist organizations as such.

The traditional Buddhist organizations, despite their adoption of new methods and techniques, generally tailor their various adaptations so as to preserve the status quo. But many new movements have appeared on the fringes or outside the framework of the established groups. Since they do not come under the traditional hierarchical structures, they may be somewhat loosely described as lay Buddhist movements (*zaike bukkyō undō*). Some are small groups made up of a handful of people devoted to spiritual cultivation and study or perhaps to the application of Buddhist principles in contemporary society. Others have in the last few decades become mammoth organizations, comparable in size and influence to the long-established sects. This latter group, deriving primarily (though not exclusively) from the Nichiren stream, forms one class of what are generally called "new religions," a subject considered in some detail in chapter 6 of this book.

4

CHRISTIANITY

Suzuki Norihisa

• DISTINCTIVE FEATURES

Foreignness. The feeling that Christianity is a "foreign religion" is still strong among the Japanese. Buddhism too is a religion of foreign origin, but when Christianity arrived in 1549, Buddhism had already existed in Japan for a thousand years.

The time factor, however, is only one of the reasons the Japanese regard Christianity as alien. They have both intrinsic and extrinsic reasons for this assessment. The intrinsic reasons are related to elements within Christianity itself, the extrinsic to certain features of the Japanese social milieu. This distinction, however, is easier to make in the realm of logic than in the dimension of history. In practice they are inextricably intertwined.

There were three periods when Christianity made rapid progress in Japan: the period of the civil wars (1482–1558), the early Meiji period (1868–1891), and the postwar Occupation period (1945–1952). These were years of rapid social change and value upheaval, years marked by an imperative demand for a new order. During these periods, Christianity's foreignness became one of its greatest assets. People turned to Christianity precisely because it represented something new. This sense of foreignness was reinforced by the missionary conviction that Christianity should be proclaimed in "pure" form—which in effect meant a presentation of Christianity that had few points of contact with Japanese culture. Thus demand and desire coincided, and Christianity came to have a more exotic flavor in Japan than in Europe or America.

The sense of foreignness associated with Christianity has a close relation to the Japanese sense of cultural identity. From its earliest history Japan has maintained a certain cultural homogeneity. Its geographic isolation, on the one hand, and its closed society, on the other, led to a pronounced inclination to distinguish sharply between things foreign and things domestic. Of the foreign, anything that looked useful and assimilable was promptly adopted, but the Japanese were quick to sense and reject whatever appeared likely to cause confusion and discord within their relatively integrated society. This sensitivity was particularly keen during times of unrest and anxiety when the stability of the preceding era had faded and the demand for a new order had not yet coalesced. Any historian of Christianity in Japan is aware that such betwixt and between periods coincide exactly with the times when Christianity was prohibited or Christians persecuted. The persecution of Catholicism by Toyotomi Hideyoshi and the Tokugawa shoguns, the attack on Christianity after the lèse-majesté incident occasioned by Uchimura Kanzō, the police pressures on Christians and Christian organizations during World War II—all happened at times when the demand for unity and a sense of cultural identity was especially strong. Japan's political leaders then spoke with renewed emphasis of Japan as "the land of the gods" (*shinkoku*), and Christianity as a "subversive creed" (*jakyō*).

It was not that these times threw a spotlight on elements of Christianity that, otherwise obscure, called for decisive repudiation. They were times, rather, when it was felt that the unity of the nation needed to be reinforced. Christianity, representing a foreign threat to this unity, was made to serve as a scapegoat. As the next section shows, elements in Christianity that collided with this desire for cultural identity and national unity were blown out of all proportion and seized on as reasons for mistrusting Christianity and Christians. From these encounters between Christianity and the governments of these particular periods arose the feeling that Christianity was, and is, an alien religion.

Heterogeneity. Foreignness and heterogeneity are not necessarily the same, for the one merely indicates an alien origin whereas the other suggests incongruity. Christianity, it appears, has had to bear both burdens.

The status of Christianity in Japan is remarkably similar to that of Marxism. Both have enjoyed a degree of popularity, particularly among intellectuals, but most people find it difficult to relate to either one. People in positions of power and influence hold both at arm's length.

The primary reason for this reaction appears to be connected with the fact that both Christianity and Marxism, with their self-contained, global systems of thought, involve an ideal they seek to realize through transformation of the social order. Christianity is oriented toward the hope of a world order it calls "the kingdom of God." Despite differences of interpretation among the several churches and denominations, Christianity in the modern Western world manifests a general unanimity of perspective as to what must go into the shaping of this order. Christianity rejects the idea that people may pick and choose among the elements that constitute this kingdom, sensing that this would result in an intolerable loss of meaning. It demands of those who choose a Christian life that their commitment to Christianity include the kingdom of God as an undivided whole.

Japanese culture, for its part, though often characterized as openly embracing contributions from other cultures, has not been able to assimilate Christianity. This intolerance is a reaction to the organic unity of the Christian religious system and its resultant international character. The openness of Japanese culture is an openness with fixed limits, the boundaries being those of the nation or body politic. Whatever threatens these limits is not tolerated but excluded.

Christianity has never been so unlike the other religions of Japan as to have nothing in common with them. But once brought to this country, certain elements were abstracted and held up as irreconcilable. Japanese polytheism with its idea of continuity between the divine and the human as opposed to Christian monotheism with its emphasis on discontinuity; an optimistic view of human nature as opposed to the Christian idea of humans as sinful beings; a cyclical view of time as opposed to a view of time as rectilinear and eschatological; a group-oriented ethic aiming at social integration as opposed to an inner ethic oriented to the individual who stands alone in the presence of God; a particularistic value orientation as opposed to the universalist value orientation of Christianity—these contrasts are by now well known. Yet supporters of Christianity and supporters of Japanese social tradition have both exaggerated these differences. The very elements once advanced as reasons for accepting Christianity later become reasons for rejecting it. More appropriate than the interpretation of these differences as incompatible polar opposites is the suggestion that their presence exposes Christianity on every side to strains and collisions with Japanese society.

Attractiveness to people not bound by natural communities. The problem of how Christianity would be received began the moment the first missionary arrived in Japan. When Protestantism was introduced and Roman Catholicism reintroduced to Japan in 1859, Shinto and Buddhism were already long established. Christianity, as the newcomer, was hard put to win acceptance among the people. Particularly resistant to its spread were the ubiquitous local and kinship communities, for these had their religious and integrating center in Shinto and Buddhism. Converts to

Christianity tended, therefore, to be people who were relatively free of community constraints and obligations.

Among the first to embrace Christianity were unmarried students in urban centers. They studied English and other foreign languages, attended Christian schools, and thus came into frequent contact with Christianity. Upon graduation, they became teachers, physicians, and other professionals in the new middle class. Even today most Japanese Christian laypersons belong to the urban middle class.

In rural areas during the 1870s and 1880s many progressive farmers, particularly landowning entrepreneurs of the upper middle class, were attracted to and accepted Christianity. In these cases entire families entered the Christian faith with the head of the household. But this state of affairs did not usually endure. Only among women and children—that is, among people who had fewer obligations in the local and kinship communities and therefore found it easier to maintain a private faith—did conversions to Christianity continue. Yet they too usually dropped away from the church before long.

Apart from the northern Kyushu area where converts to Catholicism among the lower classes are comparatively numerous, Christians are rarely found either in the lower or the upper class. Protestants of the early Meiji period were, to a remarkable degree, bureaucrats of the samurai class who had served under the feudal domains affiliated with the fallen shogunate. This contributed to the development within Japanese Christianity of a certain aloofness from the establishment. This distance did not necessarily mean these Christians were antiestablishment, for even though they sought to realize a mental or spiritual revolution in Japan, they did so without any thought of overthrowing the government. Their aloofness suggests, rather, that many Japanese found it no simple matter to transcend the perspectives of the state.

Once a body of believers had been drawn from the urban middle class, and once these people had organized and established churches, they promptly made of their churches miniature closed societies. People of other classes, coming into contact with these cliques, felt rejected. Aware they constituted a suspect minority group, church people saw their churches as citadels protecting them from a hostile administration. Accordingly, they developed close-knit ties among themselves. In the process they brought into play the conscious distinction between insiders and outsiders typical of Japanese groups. Their churches became even more tightly closed societies.

The acceptance of Christianity by the urban middle class in these circumstances allows one to form some idea of the norms at work in the adoption process. Those who moved toward Christianity came to it as social outsiders and were attracted by the ethical ideals it offered for a relatively isolated life. In addition Christianity then had a certain fascination as a religion identified with Europe and America: in a word, with modernity. This self-identification with supposedly modern ideas led Christians to conceive and initiate many projects for the improvement of society, but to what extent Christianity was accepted as a religion remains an open question.

In thinking about how Christianity has been received in Japan, it is important not to stop short with those who constitute the active membership of the churches. If one considers the people who have received their education in Christian schools and those who attended church in their youth, perhaps even going as far as to accept baptism, the number of people involved increases immensely. Any account of the influence of Christianity in Japan should include not only those counted as communicant church members but also these latent believers.

• CHRISTIAN CHURCHES AND GROUPS IN JAPANESE HISTORY

The Roman Catholic Church. The history of Christianity in Japan, apart from the incidental communication of the principles of Christian faith by Portuguese traders, began in 1549 with the arrival of three Jesuit missionaries: Francis Xavier, Cosme de Torres, and Juan Fernandez. During the sixteenth and seventeenth centuries, the number of converts to Christianity grew rapidly, the total number of Christians in 1614 amounting to about three hundred thousand. The term used to describe the Catholicism of that period is *kirishitan.* As compared to the present percentage of Christians in Japan (1 to 2 percent, depending on whether one is counting registered members or asking people what religion they belong to), the ratio then was about ten times as high. For reasons that have already been suggested, however, opposition to Christianity began to take shape.

In 1587 the powerful regent Toyotomi Hideyoshi (fl. 1582–1598), who had previously displayed a friendly attitude toward Christianity, suddenly issued a series of edicts banning the Jesuits (the only Catholic order the pope had then authorized to work in Japan) and ordering all Japanese Christians to recant on pain of exile or death. Neither order was enforced to the letter, but the handwriting was on the wall. Ten years later, at Hideyoshi's command, twenty-six Christians (twenty Japanese and six missionaries) were crucified at Nagasaki. In 1614 Tokugawa Ieyasu, first of the Tokugawa shoguns, issued and enforced an edict aimed at the complete eradication of the Christian church in Japan. He did not fully succeed, but the dwindling of Christian believers due to torture-induced recantation and death, and the near total absence of new converts, meant that for all practical purposes Christianity in Japan was annihilated.

But why was it that so many Japanese people, on encountering Christianity as transmitted to them by men from faraway Portugal and Spain, became converts to this faith? Even today the answers are not complete, but some points are clear.

When Christianity first arrived, Japan had just gone through two centuries of civil wars. The old social order had collapsed, and the surviving feudal barons were engaged in a desperate struggle for power. Trying to adapt to this situation, people sought a new value system that would provide them with some sense of meaning and enable them to live through these times. The traditional religions of Japan, however, were powerless in the face of this demand. This spiritual vacuum seems to have made people receptive to Christianity. In addition people were amazed and fascinated by the advanced medical knowledge, techniques for the organization of mutual assistance, and other social and cultural contributions brought from the West and thought of as related to Christianity. Their understanding of Christian teachings, however, was extremely superficial.

The Catholic missionaries, for their part, especially those of the recently founded Jesuit order, were filled with zeal for evangelism, a heritage of the Counter-Reformation. Moreover, in their approach to the people of Japan, they made a cautiously ambitious attempt to adapt themselves to Japanese customs, a policy they had not adopted in other countries. They also brought with them, as gifts for people in high positions, muskets, clocks, richly bound books, and other items, which brought them into contact with feudal lords interested in importing Western products and using the technological and cultural knowledge of the West to their advantage. To the extent that they succeeded in converting the leaders of society, the missionaries also gained large numbers of converts from among their retainers.

All this was wiped out, however, by the edicts of Toyotomi Hideyoshi and the Tokugawa shoguns. Their goal was to consolidate the war-torn country under a single political authority. Christianity, which placed loyalty to God before loyalty to one's lord, was banned as a "subversive creed." As a pretext for this decision, it was also charged that the Western countries supporting the Christian missionary endeavor were secretly planning to invade and colonize Japan.

During the shogunate of Tokugawa Iemitsu (fl. 1623–1651), a series of orders was issued forbidding Japanese ships or citizens to leave the country without authorization, establishing the death penalty for Japanese citizens abroad who attempted to return, and designating the Japanese ports that foreign vessels would be allowed to enter subject to government control. Originally, these orders were issued with the intention of bringing into shogunate coffers the trade revenues of Iemitsu's rivals, the feudal barons of southwest Japan. To justify his actions, however, he made it appear that his real objective was to exclude Christianity.

In this connection Iemitsu established the system known as the *danka seido*, which required the head and adult members of every Japanese household to register as supporters of a Buddhist temple. Simultaneously, Buddhism was made a de facto state institution. In consequence of this development, Buddhist lay people soon sensed their contributions and participation were less important than before, and their relationships with the temples became increasingly nominal. Buddhism turned into a "household religion" *(ie no shūkyō)*, and since people came to rely on it primarily for mortuary rites for their ancestors, it gradually came to be known as "funeral Buddhism" *(sōshiki bukkyō)*. But while Buddhism received special status as an organ of the state, Christianity was condemned as a subversive religion. To some extent, this feeling about Christianity persists even today.

During the Tokugawa period, while vigilance against Christianity was still intense, officials sometimes discovered pockets of believers who had successfully concealed their faith: the "hidden Christians" (*kakure kirishitan*). In the late 1850s Japan reopened its ports and again allowed Christian missionaries to enter the country. Father Bernard Petitjean of the Société des Missions Etrangères de Paris was the first to make contact with a group of these hidden Christians. His "discovery of the Christians" took place in Nagasaki in 1865. These underground Christians had transmitted their faith from generation to generation for over two centuries, camouflaging it with Shinto and Buddhist symbols. They were sustained by a strong internal organization, the power of simple conviction, and the hope that one day they could reveal their faith in public.

With removal of the need for concealment, many of those who had survived by disguising their faith returned to the Roman Catholic fold. Others, however, continue to this day to mask their faith as before. The phrase *kakure kirishitan* in its present-day sense applies particularly to this latter group.

During the many years when camouflage was deemed imperative, the faith of these people merged with indigenous folklore to such an extent that today it can hardly be recognized as Christian. The veneration they felt for the forebears who had enabled them to survive by teaching them the techniques of concealment led to the incorporation of ancestor worship into their Christianity.

The hidden Christians have long been most numerous on the chain of islands immediately west of Nagasaki and in other remote, isolated areas. Their numbers are decreasing, however, as young people migrate to the big cities. This form of Christian faith appears to be approaching extinction.

A glance at the distribution pattern of Roman Catholics in the modern period shows that they tend to concentrate in northern Kyushu and in big cities like Tokyo. Their density in northern Kyushu is not unrelated to the hidden Christian tradition that sprang up there. This background, plus direct evangelization, has meant that in terms of social stratification, Roman Catholics in northern Kyushu tend to come from the lower classes. By contrast, Catholics in the major metropolitan areas are products of modern education and tend to come from the upper and upper middle classes.

Nowadays positions of Catholic hierarchical authority and leadership in Japan are mostly occupied by Japanese priests, but the proportion of foreign priests among Roman Catholics is much greater than that of foreign clergy among Protestants. In the same vein, the Roman Catholic Church has generally been more conservative than the Protestant churches and has tended to avoid confrontation with the government. Reforms by Japanese Catholics to keep the church abreast of changes in society are almost invariably one step behind the innovations of the Roman Catholic Church in the West.

Catholic educational institutions, run primarily by religious orders, tend to specialize in elementary and middle school education. As for social work, hospitals and other social welfare institutions have constituted an important part of the Roman Catholic mission ever since the return of missionaries to Japan in 1859.

The Holy Orthodox Church in Japan. Since its founding by the monk Nicolai in 1861, the Russian Orthodox Church has maintained close relations with the mother church in Moscow and introduced Japanese society to many aspects of Russian culture. Church membership, however, has not increased noticeably since the latter part of the Meiji era. At least part of the reason for this is the suspicion engendered by the Russo-Japanese War of 1904–1905 and the Bolshevik Revolution of 1917. It should also be mentioned that relations between the Orthodox Church of Japan and the Russian Orthodox Church were severed in 1947 at the instigation of the Allied occupation. The churches later resumed their former relationship.

Protestant Christianity. Japan's encounter with Protestant Christianity began in the mid-nineteenth century after Commodore Matthew Perry pried open Japan's sealed doors. Before long, all the major denominations of Protestantism were represented in Japan, mostly by American missionaries. These missionaries, products of the pietistic revivals then sweeping America, were committed to the propagation of the Christian faith in a particular form: an austere Puritanism. The spirit and outlook of men like Captain Leroy Janes in Kumamoto, James Hamilton Ballagh and Samuel Robbins Brown in Yokohama, and William Smith Clark in Sapporo were carried on by those they taught. It is no exaggeration to say that Japanese Protestantism took shape at their hands.

Most of the early converts were inspired by the hope of becoming persons whose services would benefit Japan. Many of these people, however, came from clans that had supported the fallen shogunate and thus could find no openings in the new Meiji government. In lieu of direct political service, they tended to think of conversion to Christianity as a means to the formation of disciplined character and as an avenue to Western skills and the English language, all of which, they hoped, would benefit the nation in the long run.

The converts of later generations were of a different stripe. Coming largely from the new urban middle class that sprang up with the emergence of industrial cities, these people were attracted by Protestant Christianity's modern, bourgeois ethic with its emphasis on freedom, equality, and charity. Also attractive were its austere moral demands for industriousness, sincerity, honesty, and abstinence.

Reflection on the nature of the interest these two types of converts showed in Christianity suggests that they accepted Christianity mostly for ethical reasons. This characteristic is typical of Protestant Christianity in Japan, and it has led to a certain social activism among Japanese Protestants.

Other noteworthy characteristics include a tendency to deny the importance of differences between denominations and an emphasis on administrative and economic independence from foreign churches. Both characteristics find concrete expression in the United Church of Christ in Japan (*Nihon Kirisuto Kyōdan*). Formed during World War II partly under government pressure and partly in response to long-standing Christian desire, the United Church of Christ in Japan took shape primarily under

Congregational and Presbyterian leadership and embraced nearly all the Protestant organizations in Japan. After the war, when religious freedom was restored, several groups withdrew, but the United Church remains the largest single Protestant body in the country. During the confusion and financial misery of the postwar years, the United Church was dependent to some extent on economic assistance from churches in other countries, notably North America. This economic dependence, however, has now been phased out. Administratively, the body was autonomous from the beginning.

Postwar secessions from the United Church, together with the birth of new groups, have led to the present situation. Today more than a hundred Protestant denominations and sects exist in Japan. Some of the main ones, besides those already mentioned, are Lutheran, Baptist, Anglican, Salvation Army, Unitarian, Christian Science, and Mormon organizations.

One group that has attracted some attention is the Fellowship of the Way (*Dōkai*) founded by Matsumura Kaiseki. This group is unique in that it represents a syncretistic blend of Confucianism and Christianity, but numerically it is quite weak.

In recent years a movement with the unwieldy name of The Holy Spirit Association for the Unification of World Christianity (*Sekai Kirisutokyō Tōitsu Shinrei Kyōkai*) has been introduced from Korea. Generally known in Japan as the First Principles Movement (*Genri Undō*), as opposed to the West where it is sometimes referred to as the Unification Church, the hallmark of this group is its aggressive anti-Communism.

The Nonchurch movement. Perhaps the most distinctive of Japanese Protestant groups is the Nonchurch movement (*Mukyōkai*) founded by Uchimura Kanzō (1861–1930). Uchimura held that the most essential element of Christian faith is radical dependence on the gospel, and that baptism, communion, and other sacraments are not necessary. His aim in so teaching was not to oppose the existing churches but to develop for Christian people a form of Christianity that would incorporate the spirit of the Protestant Reformation at a clearer, deeper level. The consequence, however, has been the development of a movement that quite literally rejects the churches. Under the influence of this orientation, present-day adherents of the Nonchurch movement hold lectures, Bible classes, discussions, and prayer meetings at private homes or rented halls. The Nonchurch movement has become, in effect, one sect or denomination among others.

Leaders of the Nonchurch movement come almost without exception from the intelligentsia; many are university professors. Their followers also belong to the intellectual strata of society, often as students and white-collar workers.

This movement's emphasis on radical simplification and its strong sense of independence qualify it as one model for understanding how Christianity becomes indigenized in Japan.

- CHRISTIANITY IN MODERN JAPAN

The principle of religious freedom. Just as Japan was emerging from two centuries of seclusion, an event occurred which stimulated a major change in Japanese laws regarding religion. In 1867 the shogun-appointed governor of Nagasaki discovered that many inhabitants of a northern Kyushu village called Urakami were secretly practicing the Christian faith. He ordered their arrest, but before the order could be carried out, the shogunate fell. The new Meiji government, having determined to achieve national solidarity through the inculcation of State Shinto doctrines and the mandatory observance of rites intended to reinforce belief in the divinity and authority of the emperor, continued the Tokugawa ban on Christianity. Acting on government orders, the new officials in Nagasaki arrested more than three thousand Urakami villagers and exiled them to scattered domains.

Christian diplomats from the West rose up as one man in protest against this action, contending that religious freedom was a basic human right. When Iwakura Tomomi and his delegation visited several Western countries in 1871 in a futile attempt to obtain revision of the unequal treaties inherited from the shogunate, he and his colleagues were inundated with remonstrances. On the home front, Nakamura Keiu, in his "Memorial Addressed to the Tenno" (1871), and Mori Arinori, in a book entitled *Religious Freedom in Japan* published in America in 1872, spoke out for the principle of religious freedom and urged the government to adopt it. Responding to these pressures, the government ordered the removal, in February 1873, of the public notices proscribing Christianity. In the following month it revoked the sentence of exile passed on the Urakami villagers.

It should be noted, however, that removal of the signs prohibiting Christianity did not mean that Christianity was no longer forbidden. Officially, the explanation was that people were already so well acquainted with the prohibition that the signs had become unnecessary. But in practice the removal of the notices meant that the government tacitly permitted Christianity to exist.

This tacit permission was not a result of lobbying by Christian lay people or the expression of a national consensus favoring recognition of religious freedom as a basic human right. Just as the shogunate's ban on Christianity was motivated by interests of state, so too the Meiji government's decision not to interfere with Christianity had its origin in national interests—particularly the desire to obtain more favorable treaty revisions with Western countries.

The Christian view that faith is a matter between the individual and God has repeatedly come into conflict with the indigenous tradition that religion is essentially a concern of the community. The lèse-majesté incident triggered by Uchimura Kanzō in 1891, the outcry against Christianity during World War II when some Christian students and teachers refused to worship at Shinto shrines as required by the government, not to mention innumerable local clashes between Christian believers and supporters of the community religion—such encounters have a continuous, long-standing history. The Meiji constitution legally guaranteed religious freedom in 1889, but the conditions it attached to this freedom, namely, that citizens might enjoy it "within limits not prejudicial to peace and order and not antagonistic to their duties as subjects," show that this legal guarantee was still weighted on the side of community controls. Not until 1946, with the promulgation of the present constitution, was authentic freedom of religion incorporated into Japan's legal structures. Even today, however, it would be difficult to say that religious freedom is firmly established in daily life.

Christian influences on Japanese society. The second wave of Christian missionaries and the Meiji government's introduction of a comprehensive program of industrial, military, legal, and educational modernization struck Japan simultaneously. Converts to the new faith, eager to realize their vision of the kingdom of God, awakened to the fact that social conditions were far removed from their ideal. Thus as the Meiji oligarchs sought to modernize Japan by westernizing its material civilization, Christians tried to modernize Japanese society ethically and spiritually.

In the field of general education, Christianity provided a much-needed complement to the limited number of government-supported schools. Even during the years when open preaching of the gospel was not permitted, some missionaries built private schools and gave instruction in the Bible and the English language to the young people who flocked to them. When at length the government lifted the ban on the dissemination of Christian teachings, mission groups working with Japanese Christians established Christian educational institutions in every area of the country. Christianity's contribution to Japan's modernization, especially with regard to women's education, was highly significant.

At the level of higher education, in contrast to the government universities, which tended to emphasize coldly intellectual instruction and specialized in the training of future bureaucrats and government leaders, the Christian universities laid great stress on educating the whole person and on developing students who would devote themselves to the service of humankind. Today, however, due to the growth in the number and quality of public schools and institutions of higher learning, the role of Christianity in the Japanese educational world is diminishing.

Christians also opened the field of social work. To people who had previously been neglected and even despised in Japanese society, Christians extended helping hands. Believing in human equality and in charity toward all, they led the way in social welfare by establishing and supporting institutions to care for the destitute, lepers, the physically handicapped, the mentally retarded, delinquents, prostitutes, and other people in need. Gradually, as the government assumed responsibility in this area and organized public facilities to care for such people, the influence of Christianity waned. Nonetheless, the social work programs of groups like the Salvation Army are still pointed to as models for the organization of social welfare.

The socialist movement in Japan also owes its beginnings to Christianity. As Japanese Christians began to consider the teachings of human equality and love for one's neighbor in relation to existing economic disparities, many came to think of socialism as a means for expressing and applying Christian ideals. They became leaders of Japan's first labor movements. Japanese Christian socialists have tended to rely on humane, nonviolent methods to achieve their goals. Toward the end of the Meiji period they withdrew from the more militant, revolutionary Marxist groups and are now more important for historical reasons than because of their present influence.

The impact of Christianity on Japanese society has also been evident in such activities as the demand for parliamentary government expressed in the "movement for freedom and people's rights" (*jiyū minken undō*), the campaign for abolishing concubinage in favor of monogamous marriage, the movement for total abstinence from smoking and drinking, the mobilization of support for the antiprostitution law, and similar undertakings.

The early converts to Christianity learned through hard experience that adherence to the faith placed them in a state of tension with the society of their day. But the more Japan becomes modernized, the less conversion to Christianity causes tension within society. Some people have therefore begun to wonder about the early Meiji converts, asking whether the Christianity they adopted was actually a religion or, perhaps, a religiously tinted system of what were, for that time, novel ethical values.

Christianity and other religions. It is well known that the Shinto restorationist Hirata Atsutane (1776–1843) read Christian literature in Chinese translation during the years Christianity was still prohibited, and that the Christian understanding of God had no little influence on his thought. In modern times as well many leaders of the Sect Shinto bodies and the new religious movements have studied Christianity closely and incorporated Christian elements into their doctrines, organizational structures, and methods of propagation. Buddhist social work and Buddhist Sunday School programs have also found much of their inspiration in Christianity.

On the Christian side, however, apart from the short-lived example of Shinto-Christian syncretism in the 1930s and 1940s called "Japanese Christianity" (*Nihonteki kirisutokyō*), which sought to legitimize Christianity by reference to Shinto classics, there is little evidence that Christianity has adopted anything from other religions. This is probably due, on the one hand, to a tendency in Christian thought toward exclusiveness with regard to the non-Christian religions and, on the other, to a conversion mentality that inhibits attempts to understand them. Recent reflection on this matter seems to suggest that the Christian failure to take other religions seriously is one of the main reasons Christianity has been unable to speak meaningfully to present-day Japanese society.

Indigenization. In 1959, Christianity commemorated its first century of existence in Japan since the reopening of the country. Taking this celebration as an occasion for reflection, Christians gave considerable thought to the issue of indigenization. They noted that despite recent urban population growth (a circumstance they once thought would prove advantageous for church growth), the number of converts to Christianity remained at much the same level as before. Conversely, the new religions, primarily urban phenomena, were gaining adherents right and left.

Against this background, people proposed varying definitions of indigenization and arrived at different conclusions as to whether Christianity was really becoming indigenized. There was general agreement, however, that a reassessment of Christian methods of evangelism was imperative.

Through these deliberations, Christians learned they needed to pay more attention to an area they had previously neglected: the study of Japanese society and of Japan's spiritual and cultural traditions.

During the last twenty-five years, Christian involvement in Japanese society has become increasingly important. The movement among university students in the late 1960s and early '70s that began as revolutionary action for social reform had a direct impact on the churches, especially in the Protestant stream. Church leaders divided into a "social faction" (*shakaiha*) which put a premium on active participation in social justice issues, and a "gospel faction" (*fukuinha*) which insisted on the primacy of the biblical message. Differences between these factions continue to influence the Christian world. Two theological departments, one at Aoyama Gakuin University, the other at Kantō Gakuin University, have been shut down because of difficulties with social faction "troublemakers." Christian involvement with social justice issues is especially evident in three areas: relationships between churches on the main islands of Japan and churches in Okinawa, relationships between Japanese churches and the churches of Koreans resident in Japan, and efforts to end discrimination against an oppressed Japanese ethnic group known as the *burakumin*. In each of these areas some church leaders are working to correct unfairness and form institutional relationships that respect human dignity. Others are seeking ways to combat pollution and destruction of the environment.

Another noteworthy development of the last quarter-century is the dramatic decline in the number of foreign missionaries. In 1970 the Catholic Church had 2,268 missionaries; today it has between 800 and 900. The situation is a bit more complex in the Protestant world. The foreign missionary figure for 1970 was 1,081; today the figure is 1,793. But this statistical increase conceals the fact that mainstream Protestant denominations are no longer sending missionaries to Japan. Experienced missionaries from these denominations have largely retired. New missionaries come mainly from conservative and fundamentalist Christian groups in the United States. This change does not affect most Japanese Christians, but to the extent that foreign missionaries or mission boards control these conservative and fundamentalist bodies, it implies a continuing difficulty for indigenization.

Yet there is some evidence that indigenization is to some degree already under way. Two striking phenomena show that large numbers of Japanese people are already standing at the entrance to Christianity. The first is that a number of Christian writers are creatively at work in the field of modern literature. The fact that Endō Shūsaku and Miura Ayako, to mention only two, have thousands of readers suggests that whether a writer is Catholic or Protestant, there is considerable appreciation among the Japanese for the spiritual heritage of Christianity. Second, annual events of Christian origin—not only Christmas but others ranging from Valentine's Day to Halloween—are observed almost as much as traditional events like New Year's and Bon. Weddings too are important, for over half of the young people on the threshold of marriage choose to have a Christian wedding.

Christianity's indigenization in Japan, then, is near but not too near, far off but not too far off.

5

FOLK RELIGION

Miyake Hitoshi

• FOLK RELIGION AMONG THE RELIGIONS OF JAPAN

For most Japanese people, the religious life involves more than what goes on in Shinto, Buddhism, Christianity, or other religious organizations. In real life, the religious practices the Japanese have developed and maintained in response to daily needs, practices generally called "folk religion," occupy them even more than the institutional religions.

Folk religion *(minkan shinkō)* is essentially indigenous primitive religion into which elements from Shinto, Buddhism, Taoism, yin-yang dualism, Confucianism, and other religions have been grafted. It differs from Shinto, especially Shrine Shinto, in that it has no classic texts like the *Kojiki* or *Nihon shoki,* and lacks the hierarchical structure of an organization like the Jinja Honchō (Association of Shinto Shrines). Overlapping at many points with Folk Shinto, it is a multilayered phenomenon. Folk religion, unlike the institutional religions, has neither doctrines nor organization; it neither seeks to win converts nor to propagate a faith. It is, rather, something transmitted as a matter of custom among people bound together by community or kinship ties. With its festivals, cycle of annual observances, rites of passage, ceremonies of exorcism and the like, folk religion puts the greatest emphasis not on ideas but on rituals. Among its rituals, particularly numerous are those that serve the aim of securing tangible benefits such as fertility, growth, prosperity, protection from danger, healing from disease, etc.—immediate, concrete benefits in this world. Perhaps because of rituals like these, Japanese folk beliefs and practices have a distinctly magico-religious character.

What folk religion involves may be presented more concretely. The ordinary Japanese person offers obeisance at the family Shinto and Buddhist altars, before the kami of the kinship group (*dōzoku*), and before the stone pillar erected in honor of the kami who stands guard at the entrance to the village and drives away misfortune. To each a prayer is offered for protection in daily life. At stated times the ordinary person participates in services for the ancestors, in ceremonies to obtain a good harvest, and in other rituals of the yearly round. At special times he or she takes part in various rites of passage connected with birth, coming of age, marriage, and death. To allay anxieties about the future, a person may request the services of diviners, and in time of illness ask for ritual prayers and charms that will drive out bad fortune and attract good. All this belongs to folk religion.

Folk religion and other religions. It is true, of course, that weddings and festivals are usually Shinto affairs and that funerals and other mortuary rites are usually Buddhist. In these and other ways the organized religions participate in the customs and usages of folk religion. More to the point, it is within the frame of reference provided by folk religion that the organized religions have made their way into Japanese society. Only as they accommodated themselves to folk religion and its implicit norms did the institutional religions find acceptance and begin to exercise influence on people in daily life. Any attempt to understand the role of Shinto, Buddhism, and other religions in the lives of Japanese people must come to terms with folk religion.

In historical perspective, folk religion has been the source of many new religious movements in Japan. Not only the various Sect Shinto groups but most of the so-called new religions sprang from the soil of folk religion. Besides providing a foundation on which the other religions of Japan could take root, folk religion also has a close connection with the Japanese national character and ethos. In view of these considerations it will be evident that no student of the religions of Japan can afford to neglect Japanese folk religion.

• The World View of Early Japanese Folk Religion
Kami and spirits. The primitive, indigenous religion that still forms the core of Japanese folk religion saw spiritual power in wind and rain, fire and water, thunder and lightning, rocks, forests, mountains, and other phenomena of nature, as well as wild animals and people of unusual character or attainments. In the presence of objects and beings like these, people felt a sense of natural awe that caused them to discover kami and spirits in anything strange or impressive. They believed these kami or spiritual powers influenced human life as bestowers of both good and ill. The primitive world view was, in a word, animistic.

Of no little importance among the kami and spirits were those that resided in objects with which people came into frequent contact: water,

stones, trees, forests, mountains, and the like. In addition people venerated the kami of soil and locale, of the household and kinship group, of
the village entrance and the village as a whole, etc. As might be expected
in agricultural communities, the kami of the rice fields and the kami of
the harvest, because of their direct connection with life, were particularly
important in the overall scheme.

The human spirit or soul had a special name: *tama.* The belief was that
human life began with the receiving of a tama at birth, and ended with
the departure of the tama at death. The tama of existing people were
called "living souls" (*ikiryō*), and those of deceased people "dead souls"
(*shiryō*). For the repose of the dead souls, living relatives held memorial
rites at some time during the Feast for the Dead, during the New Year
season, during the days set aside for ancestral observances about the time
of the spring and autumn equinoxes, and at other stated periods. A soul
for whom living kin performed the proper rites over a prescribed number
of years (thirty-three or forty-nine depending on the locality) then became
one of the "ancestral kami" (*sosenshin*).

Ancestral kami were thought to reside in different places at different
seasons. During the winter, they stayed in the mountains, symbols of the
other world, and were regarded as mountain deities (*yama no kami*). But
in the spring they returned to their homes and became rice-field kami (*ta
no kami*), gods of fertility and productivity. There they remained until
autumn, watching over the work of the farm during this critical season.
Then, having received the gratitude and veneration of the household at
the harvest festival, they made their way back to the mountains. Some say
that these ancestral kami were the predecessors of the kin-group kami
(*ujigami*) that later played a prominent role in Japanese religious history.
Be that as it may, this brief sketch may suffice to show the centrality of
ancestor worship in Japanese folk religion.

In addition, folk religion appropriated objects of worship from the
organized religions. From Shinto, it adopted Hachiman, the god of war,
Kumano, the mountain god, and Tenjin, the god of learning. From
Buddhism, it borrowed the bodhisattva Fudō, the destroyer of evil, Kannon,
the beauteous goddess of mercy, and Jizō, protector of the helpless spirits
of dead children. From Taoism, it took over the sun, moon, and stars.
From any religion that happened to be convenient, it claimed deities to
protect people from plagues, etc. It often happened, moreover, that these
borrowed deities coalesced so completely with the kami and spirits mentioned above that they became practically indistinguishable.

Divine chastisement and protection. Folk belief held that if a taboo were broken or if people failed to give the deities the worship that was their due, the kami of nature, the kami of the soil, the kami of fertility, the ancestral kami and others would become angry and chastise those responsible with great severity. Besides these normally well-disposed kami, there were also evil kami (*yakushin*), animal spirits, and a host of other malevolent kami and spirits (*jashin jarei*) that brought harm and trouble to humans. Particularly fearful were the spirits of people who had died filled with resentment, animosity, and a desire for revenge—spirits called *goryō*. Their malignancy caused earthquakes, epidemics, and other catastrophic chastisements. Thus evils and misfortunes were explained as a result of the wrath of usually well-intentioned kami or again as a result of the spite and ruthlessness of malicious kami and spirits.

The anger of the benevolent kami and the malice of the malevolent were not, however, irreversible. By honoring them with carefully and respectfully performed ceremonies of worship, people could moderate their rancor and ward off afflictions. For the rest, people trusted their clan kami and particularly powerful deities from other religions to keep the scourge-wielding kami and spirits under control.

It also happened that malevolent kami and spirits, won over by rites of appeasement, not only ceased to castigate people but switched sides and became their protectors. The *goryō*, in particular, precisely because their visitations were so calamitous, became especially powerful guardians. The malicious kami brought under the control of clan kami were given the status of clan kami "princes" (*wakamiya*), and the malicious kami governed by the various buddhas and bodhisattvas were assigned to these princes as protectors. The belief was that both types of kami thus became protectors of the humans they had once sought to injure.

Early Japanese folk religion, then, is a form of faith in which the ancestral kami played a leading role. People prayed to well-disposed and presumably powerful kami and divinities for protection from the calamities inflicted by malevolent kami and vengeful spirits, hoping in this way to live secure, trouble-free lives.

• PRESENT-DAY RITES AND PRACTICES
Worship and taboos. Worship in which people make offerings to the kami and communicate with them is by no means limited to the organized religions. It is fundamental to folk religion rituals. The context in which such worship takes place ranges from the privacy of the home to the inclusiveness of the community festival. More explicitly, worship offered before

the family Shinto altar (*kamidana*) and Buddhist altar *(butsudan)*, before the shrines of the household and kinship group, before the stone pillar of the kami who guards the entrance to the village (*sai no kami*, or *dōsojin*), etc., normally takes the form of a folk religion ritual. It has no connection with institutional religion.

In correlation with worship, particularly with community festivals, goes a strong belief in taboos. The taboo idea is generally associated with that of impurity, causing people to avoid whatever might render them ritually impure. At festival times this involves suspending the normal activities of daily life. Since birth, death, and menstruation are considered sources of defilement, a person connected with any of them is supposed to refrain from participating in the festival.

Taboos are prominent at festival time, but they influence people at other times as well. Some of the most commonly observed are: the geomantic directional taboos that prohibit situating a house entrance or toilet on the northeast corner, the unlucky quarter known as the "devil gate" (*kimon*); the taboos relating to unlucky days, dictating, for example, that a marriage should not be scheduled on a day called *butsumetsu* ("Buddha's death") or a funeral on one known as *tomobiki* ("a friend will follow"); and the place-taboos, which reduce the price of residential lots bordering a graveyard.

The yearly round of observances. During the course of the year, many Japanese people, when planning their activities, still rely on an almanac. The almanac predicts good and bad fortune for all kinds of undertakings, depending, for example, on the direction an activity involves and the time it is to begin. Following a time-honored astrological scheme, people believe that kami of various kinds, both gracious and menacing, propitious and malignant, make a circuit of the heavens and take turns controlling the points of the compass. If the direction one proposes to travel in is one then governed by Toshitokujin, the kami of the virtue of the year, the prospects are highly favorable; if, on the other hand, the direction is governed by the dread Konjin, whose wrath can cause seven members of a family to die, one ought to reconsider. Again, some days are auspicious and others not. A *tai-an* ("great tranquillity") day is full of good promise for weddings, journeys, and almost any undertaking, whereas a day designated as *butsumetsu* ("Buddha's death") bodes ill for any enterprise. All told, there are six kinds of days, each with a proclivity toward bane or blessing that may switch at the noon hour. The almanac classifies each day of the year as one of these six. For many people it is still important to take these matters of direction and timing into account.

The almanac also lists many rituals whose practice has become a matter of custom. These rituals make up the yearly cycle of observances (*nenjū gyōji*). Over the centuries, some rites have dropped out, some have changed their character, and a few new ones have made their way into the almanac. But of the rituals observed today, those described below are the most important. (The dates of starred items follow the lunisolar calendar, presently about one month ahead of the Western calendar used in Japan since 1873.)

1. New Year (*shōgatsu*), approximately one week beginning January 1. In preparation for the New Year, people give their houses a thorough cleaning, decorate the entrance with braided rice-straw (*shimenawa*, a symbol of the sacred), and toward the end of the year welcome at a specially erected altar the kami of each year's rice harvest (*toshigami*). During the New Year's season, the family enjoys a festive food known as *zōni*, a stew of vegetables to which cakes of pounded rice have been added; people make their first visit of the year to a Shinto shrine or Buddhist temple; and students call on their teachers, employees on their employers, adult children on their parents, etc., to present greetings and renew ties.

*2. The Little New Year (*koshōgatsu*), approximately one week ending January 15. According to the old lunisolar calendar, the new year began on what is now January 15, and many people observe both New Year's days. Families observing the Little New Year begin, from January 7, by avoiding anything that might make them impure. On the evening of January 14, they light a bonfire as a sign of welcome to the kami whose munificence provides people with rice each year. The next day, they engage in ritual activities that may generally be characterized as anticipatory celebrations of the arrival of spring and as ways of divining whether the new year will be a year of plenty or a year of want.

3. Turn of the Seasons (*setsubun*), February 3. Though February 4 is considered the first day of spring, the rituals connected with the coming of spring are held on February 3, the last day of winter. On this day people celebrate briefly, frequently in the early evening with children joining in. Participants throw toasted soybeans from the house into the garden while crying "*oni wa soto*" ("out with the devil"), and from the garden into the house while calling out "*fuku wa uchi*" ("in with good fortune").

4. Doll Festival (*hina matsuri*), March 3. An event for girls, the Doll Festival involves a tiered display, in the main room of the house, of dolls costumed in varying degrees of splendor depending on the family finances.

The dolls represent the ladies and nobles of the ancient imperial court. On this day families celebrate their daughters' growth and advancement by drinking a toast of sweetened saké. Originally, the dolls (then much simpler) appear to have served as scapegoats onto which people symbolically transferred their sins and impurities, then cast them into a stream to be carried away.

*5. Spring Veneration of the Local Tutelary Deity (*haru no shanichi*). The day (*nichi*) set aside for veneration of the local tutelary deity (*sha*) in the spring (*haru*) is selected according to the yin-yang cosmological scheme. This school of thought holds that the universe is composed of five basic elements: fire, water, wood, metal, and earth. Each element, moreover, has two aspects: the male, associated with light, warmth, dryness, movement, etc., and the female, associated with darkness, cold, moisture, passivity, and so on. The Japanese almanac calls the yang or male component *e*, meaning "elder brother," the yin or female component *to*, or "younger brother." The ten classifications resulting from this combination of five elements and two aspects are assigned sequentially to each day of the year. *Haru no shanichi* falls on the "elder brother earth day" (*tsuchi no e*) closest to the vernal equinox, thus on March 22 in 1996. Most people who follow this custom know little of the cosmology, but they maintain the tradition of honoring the tutelary kami of their area on this day with rituals and offerings intended to keep the deity well-disposed.

6. Spring Equinox (*haru no higan*), approximately one week including the day of the equinox, March 23. *Higan*, a word used to designate the equinox, is also a Buddhist term meaning "the other shore." Mindful of this association, people return to their home towns and villages at the equinoctial period and visit the family grave, making offerings of pounded rice cakes, saké, incense, and the like.

7. Flower Festival (*hana matsuri*), April 8. On the festival (*matsuri*) of flowers (*hana*) those who preserve the custom climb to the top of a nearby hill, eat and drink together, gather wildflowers, and return home. Originally, the belief appears to have been that the mountain deities (*yama no kami*), who are really ancestral kami, followed the flower-bearing people and returned to their homes to become rice-field deities (*ta no kami*). Even today many people regard April 8 as the day set apart for welcoming the rice-field kami, and during April, rituals in honor of the kingroup kami are held in many parts of the country. This day also commemorates the birth of Gautama the Buddha and is celebrated by pouring sweetened tea over an image of the Buddha.

8. Boys' Day (*tango no sekku*), May 5. In earlier years the timing of the Boys' Day festival was a matter of astrological calculation. As mentioned above, the almanac still classifies each day of the year as belonging to one of the five elements, either in its superior (*e*) or subordinate (*to*) form. But in addition to these ten primary classifications (*jikkan*), it is now necessary to point out the twelve secondary classifications (*jūnishi*): mouse, ox, tiger, hare, dragon, snake, horse, ram, monkey, bird, dog, and wild boar. In fact, therefore, the classification process involves combining the ten primary and the twelve secondary classifications. The title *tango no sekku* means the annual festival (*sekku*) held at the beginning (*tan*) of May on the day of the horse (*go*). This is the day on which families with boys celebrate their sons' growth and advancement with a display of dolls representing armored fighters, a carp streamer flown from a tall pole in the yard, etc. Originally, the purpose of this festival was to pacify the malevolent, vengeful spirits (*goryō*) whose visitations were so catastrophic. The armed dolls were set up at the gate to ward off spiritual danger, only later making their way into the house as decorations.

During April and May, incidentally, people observe many ceremonies relating to rice production, among them the Rice-Planting Festival (*ta ue matsuri*) and the Drumming Out of Noxious Insects (*mushi okuri*).

9. June Observances. The first important rite in June is the Water Kami Festival (*suijin sai*), held on June 15. This festival seeks to enlist the aid of the water kami, the deity who controls all agricultural productivity, in averting disease or other harm that might be inflicted by the *goryō*. Typically, the summer festivals held in urban areas, usually toward the end of June according to the premodern lunisolar calendar, aim at the prevention of plagues.

On June 30 a special ceremony is held at the shrines of local tutelary deities in every corner of Japan. This is the rite known as the Grand Purification (*ōharae*), a ceremony in which people symbolically transfer the sins and defilements accumulated during the preceding half year to a paper doll which they bring to a Shinto shrine, where a priest performs a ceremony of group exorcism and purification.

Because June is heavily loaded with ceremonies that call for avoidance of whatever might make one ritually impure, people sometimes call it a "month of taboos." July marks the beginning of the latter half of the yearly round of observances.

*10. Star Festival (*tanabata*), July 7. The ideographs used to write ta-nabata mean "the evening of the seventh." Tradition has it that the night of July 7 marks the time when two stars, Vega and Altair, personified respectively as a weaver woman and her lover, hold a rendezvous in the heavens. In their honor, and with a prayer for self-improvement in arts and crafts requiring manual dexterity (calligraphy, for example), people compose short poems on gaily colored strips of paper, fasten them to bamboo leaves, and float them away on a nearby stream. Originally, it was from this day that people began to observe certain abstentions in preparation for the next major holiday, the *bon* festival.

*11. Feast for the Dead (*bon*), July 13–16. The word *bon* means a tray or platter for food, and the *bon* festival is essentially a time for families to welcome the ancestral spirits back to their homes with gifts of food and other offerings. As the *bon* period approaches, families prepare for it by tending the graves of their ancestors, trimming the shrubbery and rinsing off the gravestones. They erect a special altar (*bon dana*) inside or outside the house on which to present their offerings. On the evening of July 13, people build a small fire (*mukaebi*) just outside the gate as a sign of welcome to the returning spirits. Sometime during the next two days, a Buddhist priest may be invited to come to the house and chant a sutra before this altar. In the evenings, people participate in community folk dances (*bon odori*) intended to gladden the hearts of the spirits and keep them well-disposed. On July 16 family members carry the offerings to a stream and float them away on the current, and in the evening they light at the gate another small fire (*okuribi*) to see the spirits off.

*12. Moonviewing (*tsukimi*), August 15. The evening of August 15, according to the old lunisolar calendar (mid-September according to the present calendar), is when people hold parties to enjoy and admire the beauty of the full moon. Originally, this was a festival when people offered thanks for the first fruits of rice. In token of gratitude, they presented white, spherical dumplings called *tsukimi dango*. Today, these gatherings are for the most part only vestigially religious, but a sense of gratitude and appreciation is not entirely absent.

The eighth lunar month, it should be added, is the month of typhoons, so it is also the month of Wind Festivals (*kaza matsuri*). These festivals are intended to propitiate the wind kami and prevent storm damage.

From the middle of August to the beginning of November according to the lunisolar calendar, the dates varying with the locality, people hold rice-harvest festivals, variously called the Reaping Festival (*kariage matsuri*), the Harvest Festival (*shūkaku sai*), the Festival of First Fruits (*niiname sai*), etc. The Festival of First Fruits falls on the day the rice-field kami return to the mountains. Autumn festivals in honor of the kami of the kinship group take place in every corner of the country.

*13. Autumn Veneration of the Local Tutelary Deity (*aki no shanichi*). Like its spring counterpart, this festival is held on the "elder brother earth day" (*tsuchi no e*) closest to the autumnal equinox, therefore on September 18 in 1996. The purpose of this festival is, as before, to keep the territorial guardian kami (*sha*) peaceable and beneficent.

14. Autumnal Equinox (*aki no higan*), like the Spring Equinox, approximately one week including the day of the equinox, September 23. Sometime during this period, people make an effort to visit the family grave and pay respects to their ancestors on "the other shore" (*higan*) with offerings of incense, flowers, cakes of rice, fruit, and the like.

15. Water Kami Festival (*suijin sai*), December 1. As in the festival of the same name held in June, the purpose of the December festival is to ward off the potentially calamitous thunderbolts of the vindictive *goryō* through appeal to the water kami.

December, like June, is known as a "month of taboos." From about the middle of the month people go over their houses, cleaning and making necessary repairs, hanging at the entrance the previously mentioned straw rope (*shimenawa*) symbolic of the sacred, and otherwise preparing for the New Year.

The last night of the year, sometimes called *joya* (generally translated as New Year's Eve but literally "night of expulsion"), is similar to the last day of June in that this too is a time when people go to a Shinto shrine to have the sins and defilements of the preceding half year "expelled" through the ritual of Grand Purification (*ōharae*).

Reflection on the yearly round of observances presented above suggests the various rites and ceremonies may be classified under three headings. New Year and the Feast for the Dead are ancestral festivals; the Little New Year with its divinatory elements and anticipation of blessings to come, the Flower Festival with its symbolic welcoming of the rice-field kami, the Rice Planting Festival together with the Reaping and Harvest Festivals when people bid farewell to the rice-field kami are all agricultural rituals; and the Turn of the Seasons Festival, the Doll Festival, Boys' Day, the Water Kami Festival, the June and December rituals of Grand Purification, the Star Festival, the Drumming Out of Noxious Insects, the Wind Festivals, etc. are rituals of exorcism and purification.

Again, when we consider the yearly round of observances as a whole, it is important to note that it falls into symmetrical halves. Whereas the first half of the year includes such agricultural rites as the welcoming of the rice-field kami and ceremonies in anticipation of harvest blessings, the second half encompasses the harvest thanksgiving festivals and the seeing off of the rice-field kami. In the same way, just as the New Year's season and the summer Feast for the Dead are preceded by rituals intended to expel malignant spirits and by purificatory abstentions and taboos, so the spring ritual to eliminate destructive insects has its counterpart in the autumn ritual to avert typhoon havoc.

Rites of passage. The stages of a person's life are formally introduced by certain rites of passage. The chief rites of passage in Japan are six.

1. Birth (*tanjō*). An infant is born, according to Japanese folk belief, when the deity in charge of birth (*ubugami*) grants it a soul. One week later, in the evening (called *shichiya* or "seventh night"), the child is named and introduced to its relatives. On the thirtieth day after the birth, the taboos are lifted, and the parents take the infant to the local shrine. There the parents introduce the child to the tutelary kami of the area and offer worship. At the child's first festival (*hina matsuri* for girls, *tango no sekku* for boys) and again at its first birthday, there is a special family celebration.

2. Three, Five, and Seven Years of Age (*shichi go san*). November 15 is a gala day for children of three, five, and seven. On this day the parents of three- and five-year-old boys and three- and seven-year-old girls take their children to the local shrine to pray that the kami will watch over them as they grow. From this time the children are formally under the care of the local guardian deity.

3. Coming of Age (*seijin shiki*). During the feudal period, the coming of age period for boys was sometime between the ages of thirteen and nineteen. On coming of age, a boy went through a special rite called *genpuku* ("first clothes," i.e., the clothes of manhood). At this time the sons of high-ranking samurai, in an official ceremony, received a new name and a special cap symbolic of their new status. From their families, in a separate rite, they received a new loincloth. (This latter part of the "first clothes" rites was called *fundoshi iwai*, or loincloth celebration). Sons of lesser samurai and commoners, in a family and kinship-group ceremony, received only the loincloth.

For girls, the sign of maturity was the menarche, or first menstruation. At the ceremony that followed, the family and kinship group, whatever their social rank, presented the daughter with a *koshimaki*, or underskirt.

Today, the coming of age rite is a civic ceremony held on January 15 for all those of both sexes who have turned or will turn twenty during the calendar year. After this ceremony they are considered adults and may legally marry without parental consent.

4. Marriage (*konrei*). The folk rituals connected with marriage in present-day Japan include more than the wedding ceremony. The first is the rite of engagement, confirmed by betrothal gifts from fiancé to fiancée. Then comes the wedding rite in which the couple make an implicit pledge, through the ritual exchange of nuptial cups in the presence of the kami, to be husband and wife to one another. This ceremony is usually followed by a banquet in which the newlyweds are introduced to relatives and friends as husband and wife, and all present ratify their mutual ties with toasts of saké.

5. Years of Peril and Years of Celebration. According to the almanac, each person, depending on the date of birth, must face certain years of peril (*yakudoshi*). At these times evil influences threaten and one must take careful precautions. Among them the one year that is particularly ominous for women is the thirty-third year of life, for men the forty-second. This is called the *daiyaku*, the year of great peril. During these hazardous years, one is well advised to take an active part in shrine festivals and to make use of spells and amulets to ward off evil.

Balancing the years of peril are the years of celebration (*toshi iwai*). The sixty-first year of life, which marks the beginning of a new sexagenary calendrical cycle, and again the seventieth year, traditionally regarded as a rare attainment, are both years to celebrate.

6. Mortuary Rites (*tomurai*). Japanese folk belief has it that death occurs because of the soul's departure from the body. Accordingly, when death is imminent, people cry out to the soul of the dying person and beseech it to remain with the body. Once it is certain the person is dead, the family places a bowl of cooked rice by his pillow to sustain him in the spirit world, and provides him with a sword or other edged tool (a razor, for example) so that he may protect himself against malevolent spirits. The night before the funeral those closest to the deceased stay up all night with the corpse. The next morning the body is cleaned with warm water, dressed in white, and placed in a coffin. Buddhist priests conduct the funeral service, which includes words of counsel to the deceased. Then the family, relatives, neighbors, and associates accompany the dead person either to the cemetery or to the crematorium.

One week after death, on the day called *shonanuka* ("seventh day"), a priest gives the deceased a posthumous name for use in the spirit world. The bereaved family is in mourning for forty-nine days. On the forty-ninth day, a rite is held in honor of the dead person, and from this time the taboos are lifted. Subsequently, mortuary rites for the deceased are held at the first Feast for the Dead *(bon)* and on the first, third, seventh, thirty-third, and in some districts the forty-ninth anniversaries of the person's death. With the conclusion of these observances, the last of which is called *tomurai agé* ("completion of the mortuary rites"), the spirit of the dead person is believed to lose its individuality and become one with the ancestral kami. There is also the belief that the ancestral spirit, led by the kami in charge of birth *(ubugami)*, may be reincarnated in a newborn child.

Considered as an integrated whole, these rites of passage give expression to a discernible belief structure. Life begins with the receiving of a soul, and under the care and protection of kami and spirits, this soul develops and advances as the person, passing from stage to stage, grows to maturity. At death the soul leaves the body, but when honored by surviving family members with the proper rituals, it continues to rise in status, at first being no more than an ancestral spirit but eventually becoming a kami.

Also noteworthy is the symmetrical relation between the rites associated with birth and growth, on the one hand, and those associated with death and mortuary rites on the other. One thinks, for example, of the parallel between the seventh night after birth *(shichiya)* and the seventh day after death *(shonanuka)*, each of which involve the bestowing of a name. The lifting of birth taboos can be balanced against the termination of death taboos; the celebration of the first birthday has a counterpart in the mortuary rite held one year after death; the periodic rituals of the third, fifth, and seventh years of life parallel the ongoing series of mortuary rites; the coming of age ceremony corresponds to the ceremony of mortuary rite completion, etc. From this symmetry it may be inferred that in the view of many Japanese people, the souls of the living and the souls of the dead go through similar processes of development.

Superstitions. Even though one observes the taboos, participates in the festivals, attends to the yearly round of observances, and fulfills all responsibilities connected with rites of passage, there still remains some anxiety about the future. The possibility of unexpected sickness and unpredictable calamity can make anyone apprehensive. To overcome this anxiety, people make use of omens and divination; to avert threatened misfortune, they turn to magic and prayers of supplication.

"A piece of stem floating upright in your tea? You're going to have good luck." "A broken comb? Someone's going to die." Examples like these show that omens are deemed to foretell events in such a way that there seems to be a causal relation between the portent and what is predicted. Divination, on the other hand, has a closer relationship to religion. Though it too may forecast an event or seek to determine the cause of an affliction, divination depends primarily on man-made techniques or shamanistic inspiration. Man-made divinatory techniques include drawing lots, counting how many beans enter a length of reed during the cooking of bean gruel, and others derived from yin-yang magic, such as physiognomy, palmistry, astrology, etc. In shamanistic divination the medium, often a woman, attempts to become possessed by her tutelary kami and to convey a message from the deity. Alternatively, the medium may become possessed by the spirit of a dead or even a living person; or she may listen to the voices of malignant kami and find out what is angering them or what they desire.

The prayers of supplication mentioned above are essentially petitions addressed to one or more objects of worship. These petitions have to do not only with the realization of desires but also with the elimination of chastisements and afflictions caused by evil-intentioned kami and spirits. Petitions of the latter kind may be addressed to powerful, friendly kami, asking them to intervene. They may also be addressed directly to the interfering kami, asking them to stop. In presenting a petition a person may bring a votive offering, often a picture of a horse (*ema*) to a shrine or temple; he may take an oath to abstain from a favorite food or drink for a time; or he may submit himself to some austerity, such as worshiping at a temple or shrine for a thousand days in succession, or perform other sacrificial acts to prove his sincerity. In addition it is not uncommon for people to present their supplications in communal gatherings, particularly when drawn together by a matter of common concern such as praying for rain (*amagoi*). More exceptionally, communal prayers may be offered for individuals, that they may recover from illness or receive other kinds of help.

The Japanese word *majinai*, roughly approximated by the English word "magic" (but more positive in connotation), embraces the whole range of rites, talismans, and spells by which people seek to manipulate supernatural powers for such purposes as attaining happiness, protecting themselves from spiritual slings and arrows, or driving off malicious spirits. This magic takes many forms. To attain happiness, one may chant supplicatory words while performing certain operations with magical objects. To banish malign kami and spirits, a person may suspend from the eaves of his residence, or at the entrance to his village, fetishes believed to possess preternatural power. There is magic to exorcize spiritual visitants who come to inflict punishment (*tatari*) or harm (*sawari*). There is magic to intimidate with fire or sword the baneful spirits that, obsessed with human affairs, cause all manner of accident and misfortune. As a rule, *majinai* involves not only the use of amulets, charms, and other magical objects but also the incantation of allegedly potent formulas.

These and related superstitions show, then, that there are people in Japan who believe the afflictions they suffer are the chastisements of malicious kami and spirits. They believe that through divination they can discover both causer and cause. They believe that in order to rid themselves of the problem, they can rely not only on their tutelary kami, to whom they address prayers of supplication, but also on manipulatory magic. Of course this does not exhaust the subject. People also use divination to plot their future course, and rely on magic and supplication to attain goals or prevent misfortunes. But the material presented above may afford a general idea of the place and nature of superstition in present-day folk rites and practices.

• FOLK RELIGION AND JAPANESE SOCIETY

Folk religion and units of social organization. Folk religion is a phenomenon engendered and cultivated in response to the needs of mutually dependent families of fixed residence living in a largely agricultural community. Its organizational foundation is to be found, therefore, not in a separate, visibly religious structure, as in the institutional religions, but in the agricultural community itself. More concretely, folk religion draws its support from the household, kin-group households, neighboring households, the village or town as an organizational unit, and so on.

The traditional Japanese household (*ie*) may be characterized as a group with a consciousness of common lineal descent in which the members, united under the authority of the father as head of the house, work cooperatively at farming or another occupation and together administer the estate. The household is not only the basic unit of group production but also the primary locus of security for its members. Because this is the group to which members look for ultimate support, the household has need of guardian powers to give it special protection. It relies, for example, on the kami of the Shinto altar, the ancestral spirits of the Buddhist altar, and the kami of the household and kinship group (*yashikigami*). It is the household, moreover, that constitutes the basic social unit of the various agricultural rites, ancestral ceremonies, and rites of passage.

A single household, however, cannot satisfy all the demands of life. To cope with these demands, households band together in various ways. Those united by ties of blood, marriage, adoption, etc., and possessing an awareness of connection with a common forebear, have given rise to the *dōzoku*, an institution comprised of one main household (*honke*), directly descended from the founding ancestor, and one or more collaterally related branch families (*bunke*). In addition neighbors form themselves into various kinds of *kumi*, groups of neighboring households or community households joined for purposes at once secular and religious. Like the household proper, the *dōzoku* and *kumi* are important sources of support for folk religion.

The *dōzoku*, or kinship group, which has a small shrine of its own, is a social unit that not only offers worship to its ancestral kami but also draws its member households together for cooperative observance of several agricultural rites. Ceremonies connected with coming of age, the New Year, the Feast for the Dead, etc., are commonly performed by the assembled kinship group. Birthdays, celebrations for children of three, five, and seven, marriages, funerals, and other rites of passage are also organized by this kinship group.

The *kumi*, which are of many kinds, also have their own shrines and meeting places. They care for these places cooperatively and worship together there on occasion. The age-group *kumi* are perhaps the most important for present purposes. These groups participate as support units in the festivals and yearly round of observances. The children's group, for example, plays a major role in the driving away of noxious insects, the youth group in weddings and coming of age ceremonies, and the old people's group in the association (*Nenbutsu kō*) that gives special place to the rite of chanting the name of Amida Buddha.

The villages, towns, and other administrative units embracing the household, kinship group, and kumi also provide important organizational support for folk religion. Observances by these corporate organizations include not only holding festivals for the kami who guards the entrance to the village and the guardian kami of the area (*chinju*) but also praying for rain, driving off harmful insects, and many other activities. Thus by drawing people together for observance of the various rites of Japanese folk religion, the comparatively large units of village, town, and the like, with the smaller groups they embrace, give their members a sense of emotional security and, in addition, reinforce each group's internal solidarity. Some members may move to a big city, but these supportive ritual groups endure, with city members returning for special occasions.

The rise of explicitly religious organizations. Beyond what it evolved to meet the needs of people living in primarily agricultural communities, folk religion also absorbed, however fragmentarily, a number of ideas and rites from the institutional religions, notably Shinto, Buddhism, Taoism, and yin-yang dualism. Of these adopted elements, the greater part were introduced by people who, though they might settle down and live in one place for a time, were generally wayfarers: wandering Buddhist monks, men of profoundly religious character, mountain ascetics, female shamans, obscure Shinto priests, yin-yang diviners, blind exorcists who entertained people with songs and stories, and others. When the local inhabitants got together for one of the yearly observances or for a rite of passage, these itinerant religious specialists took part. (Sometimes they took advantage of the unsophisticated countryfolk who believed in magic, divination, and other superstitions.) Participating in the planning and carrying out of community rituals, they brought new and exotic ideas, adapted and inter-preted them to fit the local situation, and in this way introduced some completely new rites and beliefs.

A wayfaring religious specialist connected with a great religious center like Kumano, Ise, or Kōya would, on occasion, conduct a party of vil-lagers to his center on pilgrimage. This kind of experience, or the decision of likeminded people to meet together even without making pilgrimages, led to the formation of explicitly religious groups called *kō* (associations). Many of these *kō* had their animating center in the personality and lead-ership of an itinerant adept. *Kō* membership did not, to be sure, entail dropping out of other groups. On the contrary, in a society where institu-tions like the *dōzoku* and *kumi* played such an important role, it was nat-ural and even essential that members of these groups should continue in them even as they formed and participated in their *kō*. Perhaps because of this circumstance, it not infrequently happened that even though a *kō* leader died or failed to return, and even though the tie with a major reli-gious center was severed (if it ever existed), the *kō* continued to function because of the unaided efforts of members already deeply rooted in the structures of their communities.

Japanese folk religion, even today, depends primarily on units of social organization such as the household, the linked household kinship group, the *kumi*, and the community. It draws its support, then, from the forms of corporate life within which Japanese people carry on their daily activities. The one specifically religious group that people participate in voluntarily because of shared religious interests, the *kō*, is an exception in appearance only, for even this group has to accommodate itself to the organizational structures through which the needs of life are met.

People sometimes say that folk religion is merely a vestige of the past. It is true that with economic growth and modernization some people's attitudes toward folk religion are changing. They regard it not as a round of ritual observances in which their participation is expected, but as an object of nostalgia.

One cannot say, however, that this form of religion is by any means a lifeless shell. In households, kinship groups, neighborhood groups, and institutional religions, not to mention national holidays, it is part and parcel of people's lives. The ideas and beliefs of folk religion are often decried as superstitious. Yet nearly as often, its rites and world view, taken up into the new religions or other religious groups and there decked out in new garments, continue to sustain people who hope for and count on concrete solutions to the immediate problems of everyday life. The substratum of all other religions in Japan, folk religion lives on today.

6

NEW RELIGIONS

Arai Ken

• BACKGROUND

The religious life of the common people. Reform movements among the long-established religions, not to mention the arrival of Christianity in Japan, can undoubtedly be considered new religious movements, but neither has had much effect on the general public. Far more influential in this respect, with the single exception of State Shinto, are the various so-called "new religions" that sprang up during the modern period. These were popular in origin, and arose against the immediate background of popular religious convention.

One of the features long typical of the religious life of ordinary people in Japan is simultaneous adherence to two or more forms of religion. For many years Shinto and Buddhism maintained a syncretistic coexistence, and most people could hardly distinguish a Shinto kami from a Buddhist bodhisattva. There did exist, however, a vague but discernible functional distinction between Shinto, Buddhism, and folk religion. In broad outlines this distinction still exists today.

Buddhism is the religion of the household. People venerate their ancestors in accordance with Buddhist rites. The family tomb is located on temple grounds, and the mortuary tablets (*ihai*) of deceased family members are kept in the household Buddhist altar and honored with daily offerings. It is still customary to ask a priest to chant a sutra on the occasion of a funeral or the anniversary of a family member's death.

Shinto is the religion of the local community. Agricultural rites, exorcistic rites to drive away plague and disease, and the festivals celebrated annually by the village or parish are held at Shinto shrines under the direction of Shinto priests. Shinto is also related to certain rites of passage: young children are taken to the shrine shortly after birth and again for festive ceremonies during their third (both boys and girls), fifth (boys only), and seventh years (girls only).

Folk religion, though difficult to categorize, may for present purposes be thought of in terms of community age-group associations. Traditionally organized rural communities, though dwindling in number, have several types of age-group associations that still provide organizational models for many groups in metropolitan areas. The first type is the *kodomo gumi*, or children's association. This group brings together children between seven and fifteen years old for special events such as the New Year, the Star Festival, the *bon* festival, etc. From the age of fifteen or so, young people belong either to the boys' *wakamono gumi* or to the girls' *musume gumi*. This age group forms a kind of labor pool: the boys assist their elders in preparing for, carrying out, and cleaning up after festivals and in other tasks, while the girls, less strictly organized, join needlework groups, *bon odori* dance groups and the like.

The next age group, the *chūrō*, consists chiefly of married men. Their primary responsibilities are to oversee arrangements for community rites and festivals and to act as advisors to the *wakamono gumi*, of which their own association is often a part. Women of this age group usually belong to voluntary or quasi-voluntary associations called *kō*, such as the *Nenbutsu kō*, an organization for repetition of the sacred name of Amida Buddha, or the *Kōshin kō*, a group that periodically holds all-night vigils, ostensibly for protection from the heavenly chastisements said to threaten those who sleep at these times. The final group is usually called the *toshiyori gumi*. New members enter this group at about the age of sixty-five. This group is not universal, but where it does exist it may consist of men only, women only, or sometimes both men and women. Their chief responsibility is to perform community rituals, whether of Shinto, Buddhist, or folk religion provenance.

It should be noted, however, that in most cases these religious activities are carried out as a matter of custom or convention. People aware of the faith behind these activities are few and far between. Most people simply hold a vague expectation that conduct of this kind will keep their family and community under divine protection.

In times of emergency such as dire illness or bankruptcy, people tend to go outside their normal range of religious activities in search of divine assistance. Appeals and vows are made indiscriminately to kami and bodhisattvas with a reputation for miraculous efficacy. If it seems necessary, the sufferers turn to people known for magico-religious power, people like the mountain ascetics (*yamabushi* or *shugenja*), entreating them to say prayers and perform rituals on their behalf. But once their prayers have been answered, the relationship with these religious specialists seldom continues. In the exceptional instances when a lasting relation is established it frequently takes the form of a religious association that makes pilgrimages to well-known shrines and temples or climbs sacred mountains and performs religious austerities.

Against this background it will be readily apparent that it was the *kō*, or voluntary religious association, that became the seed from which the new religious movements grew.

It sometimes happened that a person going through a critical illness or other calamity had a special kind of religious experience: a sense of being invaded and possessed by a divine spirit. On the strength of this inspiration the spirit-filled person often assumed the role of a faith-healer, conceived and proclaimed unique religious doctrines, and gradually attracted adherents. Many of the new religious movements trace their origin to this kind of development. Ordinary people, feeling little in common with the lofty teachings of Buddhism and Christianity, here found an understanding of the divine with which they were already familiar in the context of Folk Shinto. The new religion provided them with concrete solutions to immediate needs, and they, touched and grateful, gave it their support.

Socioeconomic factors. A second set of circumstances contributing to the birth and growth of new religious movements was the high rate of economic productivity and attendant increase in urbanization that began around 1960. Throughout most of the modern period the population of Japan was overwhelmingly rural, but since 1960 urban residents outnumbered the rural by a ratio of seven to three. The ratio today is, if anything, even more pronounced.

The rapid growth of the cities dealt severe blows to Shinto and Buddhism alike, both of which had taken for granted the stability of the social units on which they relied: the community and the household. With urbanization, their basic units of support began to crumble. Rural areas, drained of inhabitants, could not even muster enough citizens to hold the annual Shinto festivals. Conversely, urban areas became so densely overcrowded that festivals had to be canceled because of the danger of traffic accidents if great numbers of people filled the streets. Migrants to the cities, taking up new jobs and new positions in society, naturally developed new interests that frequently left them with little time or inclination for the religious activities of a community and shrine to which they felt little attachment. Consequently, these shrines had to make do with the same small number of supporters they had had before the urban population explosion.

The rural Buddhist temples, formerly able to depend on the support of a relatively fixed number of households, had no way of maintaining contact with families that moved to the cities. Moreover, people who made this move often left their Buddhist altars behind, in effect weakening their ties with the temple where their ancestors were buried, so they felt no need to affiliate themselves with any other temple.

Thus the cities became gathering places for many who had cut their traditional religious ties and lived in a spiritual vacuum. Christianity, abstruse and alien, offered no attraction. It was in this situation that the new religions, fired with missionary zeal, spoke to the needs of the common people.

• THE NEW RELIGIONS AND THEIR GENERAL CHARACTERISTICS

Toward a definition. The term "new religions" is rather ambiguous. In ordinary use the term designates religious organizations that have come into being outside the framework of the established Shinto, Buddhist, or Christian bodies and maintain an independent existence. But this generalization says little about the new religions themselves. Unfortunately, no clear and generally accepted scholarly definition yet exists, but a survey of the literature suggests that scholarly uses of the phrase "new religions" tend to take one of three forms. The first limits the term to religious organizations that have emerged since the end of World War II. The second broadens the definition to include groups that appeared during the Taishō period (1912–1926) and the first two decades of the Shōwa period (1926–1988), for example, Ōmoto and Hito no Michi. The third takes in groups that had their beginnings in the closing years of the Tokugawa, or Edo, period (1603–1868) and experienced much of their development during the Meiji period (1868–1912), for example, Tenrikyō and Konkōkyō.

In support of the first definition it can be claimed that it was only after World War II, with the new constitution and its guarantee of religious freedom, that the great majority of what are today known as new religions registered as independent religious corporations and made their formal debut.

Actually, however, most of these organizations trace their origin to the prewar or wartime years, though it was under the protective umbrella of an officially recognized religious body that they generally carried out their activities. The largest of the postwar new religions, Sōka Gakkai and Risshō Kōseikai, originated before the war. Again, if institutional independence is taken as the criterion, one must also consider as new religions the postwar schismatic groups that split off from long-established organizations. For example, the oldest Buddhist building in Japan, Hōryūji temple, seceded from the Hossō sect in 1950 and became an independent religious corporation, identifying itself as the Shōtoku sect. Yet nobody thinks of Hōryūji as a new religion. In view of these difficulties, it may be concluded that the first definition does not fit the facts.

The second definition, its scope extending back to 1912, represents an attempt to combine two ways of looking at the data: one that stresses formal, institutional emergence and one that takes into account the historical roots of each new religious group. Under the Meiji constitution, effective until 1945, religious organizations had to obtain official recognition from the government in order to acquire the legal right to exist. The government, however, was slow to give this permission. Tenrikyō, for example, was granted recognition only after forty years of petitioning. Unauthorized religious groups were classified as "quasi-religions" (*ruiji shūkyō*) or arbitrarily incorporated as subsects of already authorized organizations. Yet it was precisely these "quasi-religions" from which, in terms of institutional lineage, many of the postwar new religions were born. Ōmoto, for example, gave birth to two sizable organizations: Seichō no Ie and Sekai Kyūseikyō. The majority of Japanese scholars adopt this second definition.

This use of the term "new religions," however, poses certain difficulties. Ōmoto itself, for example, emerged under the influence of Konkōkyō. As a result, scholars who rely on the second definition are generally obliged to refer to Tenrikyō, Konkōkyō, and Honmon Butsuryūshū as "forerunners" of the new religions. Since the forerunners, in their principles of organization and methods of propagation, exhibit characteristics nearly identical to those of the groups that issued from them, it is difficult to see why the lineal descendants should be defined as new religions while the organizations from which they sprang are excluded.

The third definition derives from a perspective that attaches primary importance to the question of genesis. From this point of view all religious organizations that have come into existence since the declining years of the Tokugawa period are new religions. Scholars who frame their definition in this way are able to take into consideration Tenrikyō, Konkōkyō, and other groups which have more in common with their progeny than with the traditional religions.

On the other hand, this method of classification forces into one category religious phenomena that are in fact quite diverse. Under the heading of Sect Shinto alone, for example, there is a world of difference between a group like Ontakekyō, which has a founder and stresses ascetic training and the worship of mountain deities, and one such as Shinto Taikyō, which has no founder and emphasizes moral virtues ideologically oriented to the emperor. Because it tends to blur such distinctions, this definition too is flawed.

It appears, therefore, that all three definitions are questionable. Hence the problem arises of framing a definition that will be less exposed to serious objections.

Since the groups in question are called "new," it is manifestly impossible to frame a definition that overlooks the time factor. Yet no definition which takes time of origin as its sole criterion can avoid the difficulties mentioned above. It is necessary, therefore, to include in the definition a substantive contrast between the new and the traditional religions.

Observation suggests that whereas Shinto and Buddhism are types of religion based respectively on the community and household, the new religions constitute a different type. This type usually arises among the people, has a founder, and actively seeks to enlarge its membership.

In view of these considerations we propose, as a working definition, that the term "new religions" be applied to religious groups that have come into being during or since the closing years of the Tokugawa period, have their spiritual center in the person and purportedly unique teachings of a founder who comes from the people, and are oriented toward the gaining of new members.

General characteristics. Under the heading of doctrine, the first thing to be said is that the new religions are eclectic and syncretistic. The word "new" does not mean they were created out of nothing. The religious traditions of Japan sifted down, over the centuries, into the lives of the people, and it was on this foundation that the new religions took shape. Moreover, over a long period Shinto and Buddhism were amalgamated in practice, so the syncretistic outlook characteristic of the teachings of the new religions is, from this perspective, only to be expected. Thus it is that the founder of Sekai Kyūseikyō could claim at one time to be the Buddhist bodhisattva Kannon and at another the Christian Messiah. Tenrikyō, at the time of its founding, worshiped a mythical Buddhist king, Tenrin'ō, but later a Folk Shinto kami, Tenri Ō no Mikoto. At Seichō no Ie and the Dōtoku Kagaku Kenkyūsho, Jesus, Gautama, Confucius, and Socrates all appear as objects of worship.

A second feature is that these teachings are strongly magical in character. There is probably no new religion that does not claim to rescue people from adversity through essentially magical techniques for restoring health to the sick and happiness to victims of misfortune. The effect of these magical methods of deliverance on the gaining of adherents has been immense. It should be added, however, that syncretism and magical teachings are characteristic not only of the new religions but of many groups among the traditional religions as well. The difference is one of degree.

Still another noteworthy characteristic is the this-worldliness of the new religions. This is not to say they have no concept of a world to come. The new religions affiliated with the Buddhist tradition, in particular, adhere to a belief in other worlds, both past and future. Of overriding importance, however, is concern with this world. The most frequently discussed topics at their meetings are family and health problems—after which comes the problem of how to draw in more members. Life after death is not an issue of central importance. In this respect the new religions differ strikingly from medieval Buddhism, which laid great stress on the next life. People today are too busy to concern themselves with the next world. They have enough problems and anxieties in the present world. The traditional religions, despite their theoretical and largely elite-oriented reforms, have failed to appropriate this changed focus of concern and do not provide concrete help for worldly problems. The this-worldliness of the new religions may be entangled in magical beliefs and practices, but it is an orientation that grew out of the needs of the people. Perhaps for this reason the new religions came to possess a vitality denied the seemingly stagnant traditional religions.

Organizationally, the new religions display two outstanding characteristics: reliance on the laity, and extensive efforts to win new members. Whereas the traditional religions place primary responsibility for attracting new people on the shoulders of the clergy, in the new religions it is the lay adherents who spread the faith. This is one of the main reasons why these religions achieve such impressive results in contemporary society. During the centuries of feudalism, when there was little influence from other cultures and population mobility was low, reliance on religious specialists for spreading the faith may have been effective, but in modern industrial society with its high mobility it is essential to increase the number of people who seek new members. Propagation of the faith is the lifeblood of the new religions. People who join today are urged to bring others tomorrow. Many groups go so far as to link deliverance from adversity to the winning of new members. This has proved a powerful stimulus to lay efforts to draw in more people.

• DISTINCTIVE FEATURES OF THE MAJOR NEW RELIGIONS

The typological problem. Selecting a suitable criterion by which to classify and analyze the distinctive features of the major new religions is not an easy task. The usual procedure is to present them in terms of the tradition in which they stand. Each group is officially classified under the heading of Shinto, Buddhist, Christian, or Other Religions and described with reference to its doctrines, rituals, and line of succession. This is standard procedure at the Ministry of Education's Agency for Cultural Affairs.

But this method of classification is defective in certain respects. Organizations belonging to the same general tradition do not necessarily have the same type of founder, the same principle of organization, or the same magical practices. Conversely, religions that hold these features in common do not necessarily belong to the same religious tradition. Shizensha and P. L. Kyōdan, for example, both stem from Tokumitsukyō, and all three share certain magical techniques. Yet the Agency for Cultural Affairs classifies Tokumitsukyō and Shizensha under Shinto and P. L. Kyōdan under Other Religions. Ōmoto, Seichō no Ie, Sekai Kyūseikyō, and Ananaikyō spring from a common Sect Shinto source and practice the same kind of shamanistic communion with the spirit world, but Ōmoto and Ananaikyō are treated as Shinto groups whereas Seichō no Ie and Sekai Kyūseikyō are classified under Other Religions. Again, Tenrikyō was for many years assigned to the Shinto category, but because of its universal orientation it had its classification changed to Other Religions in 1970. It is evident, therefore, that given the essentially syncretistic and composite character of the new religions, a method of classification that relies on mutually exclusive categories of religious tradition will almost invariably conceal some important correlations and suggest some misleading ones. As a matter of convenience, we propose to discuss the characteristics of the more important new religions under four headings: types of founders, teachings, magical practices, and principles of organization.

Types of founders. Two main types of founders may be distinguished in the new religions: the living kami (*ikigami*) and the human being (*ningen*). As regards the former type, in the great majority of cases the founder believed that a kami had entered into and taken possession of the founder's body. In this type we are confronted with the shaman. To date, whenever the founder was a woman, she has always been of the shamanistic type. Nakayama Miki of Tenrikyō, Deguchi Nao of Ōmoto, Kotani Kimi of Reiyūkai, Naganuma Myōkō of Risshō Kōseikai, Kitamura Sayo of Tenshō Kōtai Jingūkyō, Nagaoka Nagako of Jiu—all are female, shamanistic founders.

Founders of the shamanistic type are by no means limited to one sex.

Among male founders too this type is of great importance. Kawate Bunjirō, the founder of Konkōkyō, believed that the folk deity Tenchi Kane no Kami had entered into him and that he had in fact become Konkō Daijin (the great kami Konkō). Others cultivated the technique of kami possession. Deguchi Onisaburō, cofounder of Ōmoto together with Deguchi Nao, learned from the Shinto priest Nagasawa Katsutoshi how to become possessed by a kami, induced this experience in groups of followers, and made the name of Ōmoto famous. Nakano Yonosuke of Ananaikyō also learned this technique from Nagasawa. Similarly, Okada Mokichi of Sekai Kyūseikyō, as mentioned earlier, identified himself as the bodhisattva Kannon and later as the Christian Messiah. It is evident, therefore, that both male and female founders of the new religions were in many cases shamans who thought of themselves as living kami.

Organizations founded by persons who believed that a kami had entered into them and who regarded their own utterances as expressions of the will of the kami have been exceptionally prone to schism. On the death or retirement of the leader, any member can claim that he or she is the legitimate successor by virtue of a unique experience of kami possession, and the organization has no basis in principle on which to reject such a claim. It was this kind of problem, occasioned by the claims of Ōnishi Aijirō, that caused Tenrikyō to split, the new group taking the name Honmichi.

When the shamanistic founder is a woman, it frequently happens that she takes a man as a spiritual partner. Iburi Izō of Tenrikyō, Deguchi Onisaburō of Ōmoto, Kubo Kakutarō of Reiyūkai, and Niwano Nikkyō of Risshō Kōseikai are examples of such men. In every case these men first worked as organizers for the group, but were soon regarded as more than mere organizers, and came to be venerated as co-founders.

The second type of founder, rejecting the idea of his divinity, affirms that he is only a human being—but a human being who discloses the way of truth. Taniguchi Masaharu of Seichō no Ie, Miki Tokuharu of Hito no Michi and his son Tokuchika of P. L. Kyōdan (the postwar form of Hito no Michi), Kubo Kakutarō of Reiyūkai, Niwano Nikkyō of Risshō Kōseikai, Makiguchi Tsunesaburō, Toda Jōsei, and Ikeda Daisaku of Sōka Gakkai are all examples of this second type.

In the large organizations there seems to be a tendency for a founder of the first type to be succeeded by a cofounder of the second. Thus Nakayama Miki was followed by Iburi Izō and Deguchi Nao by her daughter's husband Deguchi Onisaburō. If the perspective is broadened from founder and cofounders to include subsequent leaders, this tendency to move away from shamanistic qualifications is even more marked. In Tenrikyō since the time of Iburi Izō, for example, shamanistic succession has completely died out. Leadership is now a hereditary matter, leaders being selected from the Nakayama line. In almost all the new religions, succession to the position of leader, after the death of the founder and cofounder, is determined on the basis of lineal descent from the founder. Sōka Gakkai, which does not admit hereditary succession, is a major exception.

It should be noted, however, that no matter whether the founder regarded himself as a living kami or an ordinary human being, in the eyes of his followers he was, in the end, a kami dwelling in a human. Faith in a living kami (*ikigami shinkō*), attaching itself not only to founders but to their successors as well, is a deeply rooted characteristic of the new religions.

Teachings. Great variety is evident in the teachings of the new religions, but for the most part they can be grouped according to standard classifications.

Organizations that worship Shinto kami and observe Shinto ceremonies predominate. In the Shinto tradition there is no such thing as doctrinal orthodoxy, and teachings are almost as numerous as teachers. Generally, however, organizations in this stream advocate shamanism and ancestral rites.

Among the new religions in the Buddhist tradition, those claiming to carry on the teachings of Nichiren are particularly numerous. They are followed by groups perpetuating Shingon and Tendai teachings. The organizations in the Nichiren line all recognize the Lotus Sutra as scripture, and most of them emphasize ritual observances for one's ancestors.

Few new religions have teachings of Christian origin. *Genri Undō* (First Principles Movement), properly named *Sekai Kirisutokyō Tōitsu Shinrei Kyōkai* (The Holy Spirit Association for the Unification of World Christianity), an anticommunist new religion from Korea, is unusual in this respect.

The teachings of groups classified under the heading Other Religions are predictably the most diverse, but even here Shinto ideas are particularly prominent. Typical of the eclecticism of these groups is Seichō no Ie, while the teachings of P. L. Kyōdan, variations on the theme of life as artistry, show the most originality. One bizarre group, now extinct, venerated electricity as its chief object of worship and Thomas Edison as a subordinate deity.

In the midst of this doctrinal diversity one common feature may be discerned: a spirit of protest against the establishment. Tenrikyō, with its slogan of "reform the world" (*yo naoshi*), and Ōmoto, with its call for "reconstruction of the world" (*yo no tatekae*), exemplify this. Repeatedly suppressed by the prewar government, these cries were eventually silenced. But an attitude of protest against unjustified government pressures, representing in effect the voices of those in the bottom ranks of society, has come to constitute a fundamental tradition of the new religions. For this reason it is not surprising that the Federation of New Religious Organizations of Japan (*Shin Nihon Shūkyō Dantai Rengōkai*), together with Christianity, is most sensitive on any issue having to do with freedom of religion.

Magical practices. The essentially magical beliefs and techniques found among the new religions are extremely diverse. In Ōmoto it was formerly believed that healing power resided in a certain kind of ritually qualified dipper, or ladle (*shakushi*). Sekai Kyūseikyō inherited from Ōmoto the idea of magical healing but adopted a different technique. Healing virtue, according to this group, comes from a healer's holding the upraised, open palm near the affected part of the suffering person's body, whereupon a healing ray, the work of a divine spirit, emanates from the palm. In the Tokumitsukyō–Hito no Michi–P. L. Kyōdan line, there can be found a healing technique called *ofurikae* ("transfer"), which allegedly shifts illness from the believer to the spiritual head of the religion. Seichō no Ie claims that sickness will disappear if one achieves the right state of mind. Reiyūkai and its descendant groups maintain that if the ancestors are properly worshiped, sickness and misfortune will vanish. One of these groups, Risshō Kōseikai, has added a form of divination based on the ideographs in one's name. According to Sōka Gakkai, since all misfortunes originate in the sin of clinging to spurious teachings, they will melt away when one bows down before the true object of worship, the mandala attributed to Nichiren. Toda Jōsei, a cofounder of Sōka Gakkai, went so far as to call the mandala "a machine that produces happiness" (*kōfuku seizōki*).

Even this brief résumé may indicate something of the profusion of magical practices. As a general rule, these practices and beliefs are carried over from the original group by the groups that break away. What it has received from its historical progenitor, the splinter group retains, perhaps in altered form, attaching to this heritage an interpretation in accordance with its own teachings.

Principles of organization. The basic organizing principle of nearly all the new religions is the parent-child relationship as it has evolved in Japan. The person under whose guidance one is led to join a new religion takes the position of a parent, and the person so led assumes the subordinate role of a child. Thus the process whereby new members are drawn into the group automatically locates all members in a vertical network of quasi-familial relationships.

In principle this system of organization is independent of geographical limitations. At the institutional level, it could and does happen that a Tokyo group may occupy the child's position in relation to a parent organization located in distant Hokkaido. By the same token, as a subordinate group develops "children" of its own, the parent group increases in strength and influence, and of course the growing subordinate group also rises in status within the organization. The efficacy of this vertical system of relationships in stimulating energetic activity to draw in more and more people has become self-evident. It is no accident, therefore, that the same principle of organization is at work in Tenrikyō, Reiyūkai, Sōka Gakkai, and other major groups.

At the same time, however, this vertical structure develops weaknesses when the organization spreads to remote areas, for then the parent body finds it difficult to provide care and guidance for its offspring, and the ties between them weaken. For this reason, many new religions also employ a separate organizational principle, complementing the vertical, geographically unconfined structure with a horizontal structure organized into geographical districts. It is generally recognized that Sōka Gakkai, for example, owes its immense growth to adroit use of this dual system.

Another weakness in the vertical, quasi-familial system comes into view when internal discord arises. Since more importance attaches to the relationships between spiritual parents and children than to their common commitment to a body of doctrine, when dissension occurs, it may easily turn critical. If a spiritual parent to numerous "children" has a dispute with the leader, he may well summon his followers and form an independent group. Where emotional ties are close and doctrinal ties weak, this risk is probably inevitable. A good example of this kind of fission can be seen in Reiyūkai (founded in 1924), which thus produced Nichirenshū Hōchi Kyōkai (1925), Shōhōkai (1931), Kōdō Kyōdan (1935), Risshō Kōseikai (1938), Shishinkai (1938), Myōchikai (1950), Bussho Gonenkai (1950), Daieikai (1951), Daijikai (1953) Seidōkai (1960), Shōdōkai (1966) and more than a dozen others.

A small number of new religions have chosen not to adopt the parent-child model. Typical of these groups is P. L. Kyōdan. Increase in membership in P. L. Kyōdan, as in the other new religions, is due primarily to the efforts of its lay members, but new members are separated from the members who brought them in and enrolled in their own local chapters. There they come under the guidance of a resident spiritual leader who is assigned to the local group by headquarters and is regularly relocated. This system forestalls the development of close ties between the appointed leader and local followers, thus diminishing the risk of schism.

To stimulate growth, P. L. Kyōdan sometimes holds membership drives in the form of a contest to see which local groups can chalk up the highest scores. In the heat of competition, however, it sometimes happens that groups turn in false figures, so the contests fail, in some measure, to achieve their objective. P. L. Kyōdan may have succeeded in attaining organizational stability, but perhaps at the cost of dynamic growth.

• THE ROLE AND INFLUENCE OF THE NEW RELIGIONS TODAY

Over seventy percent of the Japanese people, recent surveys indicate, do not regard themselves as believers in any religion. Among these people there are many, of course, who on the occasion of a funeral or memorial service ask a priest to come and recite a sutra, who visit a Shinto shrine or Buddhist temple at the turn of the year, and who take their children to a shrine when they reach the age of three, five, or seven. It is a rare person, however, who does these things on the basis of religious faith. For most it is merely a matter of convention. Those who guide their daily lives by the standards of a particular religion constitute only a small minority.

The attraction of the new religions. This is not to say that religion has become unnecessary in contemporary Japan. In modern mass society increasing numbers of people feel frustrated by the lack of human fellowship. Isolated in the midst of thousands, they suffer untold anxieties and are threatened by a loss of identity. In this situation the traditional religions have so far been of little help. Yet this is precisely the situation in which the new religions demonstrate their magnetic attraction.

In contrast to the hesitant, anxious outlook of many people in Japan today, those who belong to the new religions are conspicuous for the sense of confidence they radiate. The new religions are criticized in many ways, accused of being vulgar or encouraging superstition. But no one can deny that it is the new religions which, in very concrete ways, have rescued large numbers of people from distress, given them a sense of purpose and direction, and incorporated them into a community.

Most new religions frequently hold large-scale mass meetings, summoning their members to assemble as local groups and visit the organization's often palatial religious and administrative center. Even more frequent are the small-scale meetings. The stated purpose of these gatherings, large and small, is to provide spiritual training. But they also function as a means whereby different people, allied by virtue of membership in the same religious organization, can experience a renewed sense of identity and belonging. Prior to the urban explosion, this kind of experience was provided by Shrine Shinto, but today the shrines are increasingly unable to perform this function. The new religions have to some extent shouldered this burden, and many uprooted and lonely people find new strength in their meetings.

Underlying the guidance given by the new religions for the conduct of daily life is, in the majority of cases, the traditional Confucian ethic. For people whose sense of values was shaken to the core by the radically new ideas and changes following World War II, there is often a renewed feeling of self-confidence and even a sense of relief that comes from hearing familiar values advocated once again, not apologetically but boldly and confidently. Thus it is that the new religions, though not incapable of producing new ideas, are basically oriented toward reproducing conservative values.

Faith healing vs. medical science. One point where the new religions cause some degree of turmoil in Japanese society is their advocacy of magical practices for the healing of disease. This brings them into direct conflict with modern medical science. True enough, most groups encourage their followers to make use of both medical knowledge and faith-healing methods, but problems arise when some believers, by no means few in number, reject medical treatment because of their conviction that faith healing alone will suffice.

As for science in general, the new religions tend to mingle and confuse science and religion. Some appropriate a few scientific turns of expression and immediately start calling themselves scientific religions. None, however, has attempted to work out, in serious dialogue with science, what kinds of problems belong to the scientific sphere and what to the religious. This careless, compromising attitude that does not differentiate between science and religion can only work to the detriment of both.

When some of the new religions, especially Sōka Gakkai, became mammoth organizations and made their debut in the world of social and political concerns, it caused a great stir among both the long-established

religions and the labor movement. The traditional religions, mortally threatened by urbanization, turned their attention to the new religions in the
hope of benefiting from a study of their organizational principles and techniques. The emphasis on lay movements in Pure Land and Zen Buddhism
appears to be an outgrowth of this endeavor. The sluggishness of the traditional religions in present-day Japan, however, is not simply a matter of
organization. More fundamental is the problem of how to address people
who no longer take any interest in what they have to offer.

This does not mean, however, that the Japanese no longer have any
interest in religion. It means that they are largely indifferent to religion in
its traditional forms, even though they continue to observe the rites and
are counted as adherents. But new religions too can become traditional.
Many of the new religions mentioned above have become outdated for
many Japanese, especially young people. They are attracted to what some
scholars call the "new" new religions, organizations that promise mystic
or occult experience, "inner trips," altered consciousness—even levitation, as in Aum Shinrikyō.[1] Why scientifically educated young people
should find such religions attractive is currently a question of great concern to many Japanese. But it is important to note that thousands and
thousands of Japanese people continue to be drawn to religion, and not
least to the new religions.

1. On the "new" new religions, see chapter 10, "Aspects of the Rebirth of Religion." On Aum
Shinrikyō, see appendix I.

1. A sacred island in the midst of a towering forest, the centuries-old Ise Grand Shrine is the central shrine of the imperial house and the spiritual heart of Japan for many people. Traditionally, the buildings pictured are completely rebuilt every twenty years; at one time on the right-hand site, then on the left.

3. Approaching a shrine for worship, people put some coins in the offering box, clap their hands to invoke the *kami*, pray, and clap again to bid the *kami* farewell.

2. Located in the heart of Tokyo, Yasukuni Shrine was built at the beginning of the modern period as a place for enshrining the spirits of the war dead. The stream of worshipers is endless.

4. In this formal Shinto purification, ritual fire symbolically exorcizes evil spirits, cleanses people from defilement, and restores them to a state of integrity.

5. In front of a Shinto altar a young man and woman, with their parents beside them, exchange nuptial cups. The two presiding priests stand beside the altar while girl attendants assist.

6. *Harae*, a rite of exorcism and purification, is performed by a Shinto priest. Over the bowed heads of those being purified he waves a sacred wand. A highly symbolic act, *harae* effects, according to Shinto teaching, an inward cleansing from all sin and defilement. By extension, this ritual is also believed to rid physical objects of evil influences.

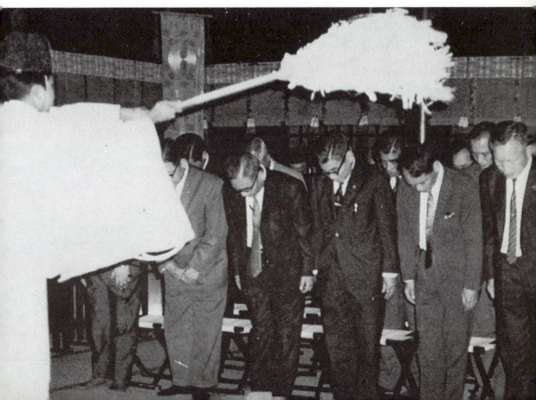

7. A farmer prays to the spirit of a fruit tree, asking for abundant fruit. The straw and specially cut paper, temporarily hung on the tree, show that this is the site of a religious ritual. The axe is a threatening symbol, warning of what will happen if the tree fails to produce.

8. At the office of almost any sizable shrine people may, for a small fee, draw a slip of paper with their fortune printed on it. Many fold the paper and fasten it to a sacred tree on the shrine grounds in the hope that good fortune will come and bad predictions be averted.

9. A magico-religious specialist, wearing special garb and making symbolic gestures, pronounces a curse, using the words of the magical formula laid out before him. The kettle-like object is an inverted bell which the man strikes at certain points in the ritual with a baton, the handle of which may be seen beside the written formula.

10. Christmas decorations at a major department store in Tokyo. Since the end of World War II, as traditional rites became less important, observances connected with Christian culture have found their way into Japanese urban life. This is especially true of Christmas, generally celebrated on Christmas Eve, since Christmas Day is not a holiday in Japan.

11. Valentine's Day became popular in Japan during the 1970s. At this time of year, women crowd around the department store sections where chocolates are sold.

12. The flower Festival (April 8), in addition to being an agricultural rite associated with ancestor worship, is also the day on which the birth of Gautama the Buddha is celebrated. Children are fully involved, bringing flowers and participating happily in the custom of pouring sweetened tea over an image of the Buddha.

13. On November 15, five-year-old boys and girls of three and seven are dressed in festive clothes and taken to the local shrine to pray that the tutelary *kami* of the area will watch over them as they grow up.

14. At annual festivals held in gratitude for past blessings and in the hope of good catches in the year to come, fishermen decorate their boats with gaily colored ribbons and streamers (Tottori Prefecture).

15. Yushima Seidō, Tokyo, is the only remaining Confucian center of learning in Japan.

16. Inside Yushima Seidō formally attired participants hold an observance in which emphasis is placed on propriety. Confucianism is in effect the fountainhead of Japanese ideas of decorum.

17. The oldest Buddhist edifice in Japan, established in 607 by Prince Shōtoku, Hōryūji temple was built both as a place of worship and as a center for Buddhist studies. The pagoda in the foreground is a repository for what are believed to be part of the remains of Gautama. The building on the left is an old lecture hall.

18. At Sōjiji temple, Yokohama, Zen monks, seeking to attain inner enlightenment, sit in concentrated meditation (*zazen*). Each monk is assigned one of the wall cabinets in the photo, keeping his bedding and personal articles there and in effect eating, sleeping, and meditating on one straw pad (*tatami*). The standing monk with the stick whacks the shoulders of those who signal—and sometimes of those who nod off!

19. Something of the aesthetic charm of Buddhism may be sensed in the bodhisattva Maitreya (in Japanese, Miroku Bosatsu) at Kōryūji temple, Kyoto. The bodhisattvas (Miroku, Kannon, and others) are portrayed as merciful figures on whom people can rely for salvation.

20. In the hope of salvation, a priest of the Jōdo Shū recites the phrase *Namu Amida Butsu* ("adoration to Amida Buddha"). With the rosary he keeps track of the number of times he repeats the phrase.

21. At a Buddhist funeral the coffin is incorporated into a five-tiered stand. A photo draped with mourning ribbons identifies the deceased, and around it are placed the traditional funeral paraphernalia. Floral contributions bearing the names of donors flank the stand where a ceremonially attired priest reads a farewell sutra. Immediately beside him are the family and relatives, with friends and associates being seated behind.

22. From all over Japan adherents of the Jōdo Shinshū gathered at Nishi Honganji temple in 1961 to commemorate the 700th anniversary of Shinran's death.

23. A Buddhist altar used by contemporary urban families. In the center is a statue of the Buddha, with mortuary tablets standing on either side. Since World War II the percentage of Japanese households with a Buddhist altar has declined to 59%, according to a 1995 report by the *Asahi Shimbun*, though in rural towns and villages the percentage tends to be higher than 70%.

24. The mother church of Tenrikyō, with the *jiba* at its center, is the focal point of an entire city. As part of its program of lay training and outreach, Tenrikyō welcomes adherents and inquirers who visit the center for short or longer periods of time. Here clusters of pilgrims gather in the spacious grounds.

25. Every year on August 15, the day World War II came to an end, Sōka Gakkai holds a service for the war dead and for world peace. It brings together the president of Sōka Gakkai, Akiya Einosuke (right foreground), bereaved families, and representatives from the Sōka Gakkai youth groups.

26. Middle school members of Reiyūkai. One of the strongest of the new religions, Reiyūkai holds a summer seminar for young boys every year. The photo shows them on the closing day, with arms across each other's shoulders.

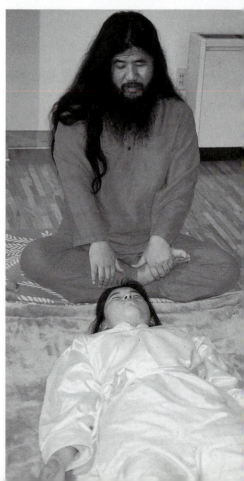

27. Asahara Shōkō, founder of Aum Shinrikyō. Responsible for the sarin gas attack that took place in the Tokyo subway system on March 20, 1995, Aum Shinrikyō caused death to hundreds and injury to thousands of people. The sect was established in 1986.

28. Francis Xavier, S.J., and his companions arrived in Kagoshima on August 15, 1549. This marked the first formal introduction of Christianity to Japan.

29. For approximately a century Christianity grew and flourished. Something of its place in Japanese society may be inferred from this scene of a missionary priest celebrating mass with samurai in attendance at the chapel of the Jesuit residence in Nagasaki. (Detail from a pair of six-panel screens, signed by Kanō Naizen, 1570–1616.)

30. Official Notification

"The Christian faith, as heretofore, is strictly prohibited. Anyone knowing of a suspect shall report to the authorities without fail. The following shall be given in reward:

To an informer on a Father: 300 pieces of silver

To an informer on a Brother: 200 pieces of silver

To an informer on a Retrovert: 200 pieces of silver

To an informer on a Catechist or lay Christian: 100 pieces of silver

Even if the informer himself is a member of a Christian household, he shall be rewarded with goods in the value of 100 pieces of silver. If anybody sheltering such persons is found out by information from others, severe punishment shall be inflicted on him, on his family, on the four other households with which his house is legally bound, and even on the representative of his district."

February, 1711
Office of the Governor

31. A *fumie* (a Christian image to be stepped on). The practice of having suspected Christians prove their innocence by stepping on a *fumie* was instituted early in the Tokugawa period. Gradually the practice spread and was used as a religious test for the entire population. This practice was discontinued in 1858. Note how worn the *fumie* is.

32. This Catholic church near Nagasaki is the site of Father Bernard Petitjean's "rediscovery of the Christians." In 1865, shortly after the reopening of Japan when the church was in the process of construction, a group of peasants entered the building, did obeisance to a statue of Mary, then approached the priest and said "Our hearts are as yours."

33. The austerely beautiful Saint Mary's Cathedral, Tokyo, was designed by the renowned architect Tange Kenzō.

34. Kaigan Church in Yokohama, the oldest Protestant church in Japan, celebrated its first centennial in May 1972.

35. In this conjunction of church and kindergarten an interesting educational enterprise may be seen. The great majority of Protestant churches organize educational facilities of this nature.

THE RELIGIOUS SITUATION TODAY

7

RELIGION AND STATE

Nakano Tsuyoshi

This chapter introduces issues having to do with relationships between Japanese religions and the state as well as the involvement of Japanese religions in politics.

Whether a religious movement, on entering the political arena with the aim of reforming society, becomes a revolutionary movement or merely a political movement has to do not only with its character and goals but also with the degree to which the state itself possesses religious attributes. Depending on how these elements come together, it is possible that a simple movement for social improvement based on religious ideas may turn into a revolutionary political struggle.

In modern Japan the watershed for such issues was defeat in World War II and the Occupation reforms of the Allied powers. It is often said that a distinctive feature of Japan's new religions in their postwar development is the heightening of interest in social and political matters. It should be noted, however, that it was only after the Occupation reforms brought democracy, separation of religion and state, and the guarantee of religious freedom into being that it became possible for new religions to participate in politics.

This chapter, accordingly, will begin by glancing at the prewar and wartime relationship between the state and religion as it existed under State Shinto, then outline the Japanese religious system in its postwar form with particular attention to the matter of participation in political affairs by the new religions, and conclude by discussing postwar religion-and-state controversies.

• STATE SHINTO AND RELIGION UNDER THE IMPERIAL STATE
The Meiji constitution, promulgated on February 11, 1889, established a legislature, a judiciary, and an executive, the last of which was made up of a cabinet of ministers of state. The constitution stated: "The Emperor is the head of the Empire, combining in Himself the rights of sovereignty, and

exercises them, according to the provisions of the present Constitution" (Chapter 1, Article 4). Clearly, the new government took the form of a constitutional monarchy with the emperor as the head of state.

The emperor's right to sovereignty, however, did not derive from the constitution. As an imperial rescript issued at the time of promulgation put it, "the supreme power We inherit from Our Imperial Ancestors." This power, therefore, conferred neither by the citizens nor by the constitution, relied on institutional charisma to perpetuate "the lineal succession unbroken for ages eternal." Article 3 stated, moreover, that "the Emperor is sacred and inviolable," thus vesting him with divine character.

The religious charisma to which the emperor was heir found its practical embodiment in the *kokutai*, an allegedly distinctive and superior form of state organization. Thus the kokutai and its personal embodiment, the emperor, became the wellspring of all authority, whether legislative, executive, or judicial. Until 1945 the national polity was a quasi-religious, patriarchal, centralized state with its axis in the theocratic absolutism of the emperor. The emperor, whose guardianship of the state included secular authority in the form of supreme power over the government and supreme command over the military, also functioned as chief priest of the nation and in this capacity held religious authority. The very structure of the nation was imbued with religious meaning by virtue of the emperor system, and on the basis of this religious ideology the monolithic establishment sought to control even the religious life of the people.

The warrant for this control came from the laws enacted on the basis of the constitution. According to Article 28 of the Meiji constitution, religious freedom was recognized but hedged about with conditions: "Japanese subjects shall, within limits not prejudicial to peace and order, and not antagonistic to their duties as subjects, enjoy freedom of religious belief." The legal basis for government control over religion was spelled out in such laws as the criminal law governing lèse-majesté (1900), the Security Police Law (1900), and the Peace Preservation Law (1925).

In 1939 the Religious Organizations Law (*Shūkyō dantai hō*) was enacted, followed by systematic refinement of the authority to "protect and supervise" religious organizations. This law sought not only to expand government control over religious organizations but also to supervise even more strictly actions that could be construed as interfering with peace, order, or national goals. Also, because the government wanted legally recognized religious organizations to mobilize spiritual support for its aims, it established subsidies to provide such organizations with a solid financial basis.

Given this ideology and structure, any political or social demands based on religious ideas were immediately inspected for their conformity with the ideology of the emperor system. There was little leeway for dealing with such demands on their own terms. Sociopolitical statements and movements initiated by religious organizations could not be considered as mere social or political activities. Instead they were immediately confronted with the whole structure of the state, and this confrontation necessarily took the form of a political struggle. The kinds of political involvement that Japanese religions engaged in under these circumstances can be roughly divided into three main types.

The first type of engagement with the emperor-system ideology was one of compromise and adaptation, even to the extent of becoming zealous in the service of state policies. Shrine Shinto (*jinja shintō*) naturally adopted this stance from the outset, as did most of the traditional Buddhist bodies. Buddhist organizations that had suffered during the anti-Buddhist iconoclasm of the early Meiji period quickly showed themselves willing to collaborate. Responding to the current of rising nationalism, they sought to regain lost ground and increase their influence through energetic cooperation with state policies. Thus when the government, in a change of policy, made State Shinto the de facto established religion, these organizations were quick to proclaim the imperial way and attack Christianity. After the "collision between education and religion" that stemmed from the lèse-majesté charge against Uchimura Kanzō in 1891, mainstream bodies in the Christian world likewise looked to governmental authority for recognition, sought religious freedom within the church alone, and otherwise obediently allied themselves with government policies.

Even among the new religions, adaptation was not unusual. An early example is Tenrikyō. The founder, Nakayama Miki, was adamantly opposed to emperor-system ideology and would permit no compromise with it whatever. But after her death in 1887, Tenrikyō, in exchange for government recognition as an independent body and freedom to propagate its teachings, ingratiated itself with the imperial state by zealously supporting its policies, cooperating both materially and spiritually during the Sino-Japanese and the Russo-Japanese wars. In the early Shōwa period (1926 and following), Seichō no Ie and Reiyūkai stand as examples of the adaptation type.

The second type of engagement is that of nationalistic Shinto radicalism. People of this orientation leveled criticisms at the state on the ground that the nationalistic Shinto recognized by the government had lost not only the form but also the true spirit of the *Kojiki* and the *Nihon shoki*, the two major compilations of myth and early history. This engagement took shape as a movement aimed at a rightist revolution. The classic example is Ōmoto.

The third type of engagement is that of resistance. Members of this type rejected the emperor-system ideology on principle and were consequently viewed as heretical and subjected to persecution. Among the smaller Christian organizations there are some examples of this type, but among the new religions a cardinal example is Honmichi. Its founder Ōnishi Aijirō, on the basis of an independent myth, rejected not only the myths of the *Kojiki* and *Nihon shoki* but also the divinity of the emperor. He claimed that the emperor was not qualified to rule Japan, thus making a frontal attack on the ideology of the emperor-system.

Another example is that of Makiguchi Tsunesaburō, who developed a unique educational theory from the standpoint of empirical rationalism, connected this theory with Nichiren Shōshū faith, and founded the lay organization known as Sōka Kyōiku Gakkai, the forerunner of today's Sōka Gakkai. Makiguchi and his group, in accordance with Nichiren Shōshū teaching, stressed that followers of other religions, including Shinto, were guilty of the sin of abusing the Buddhist law. Because Makiguchi and his group refused to accept or bow before amulets of the Grand Shrines of Ise, the symbolic center of the imperial state, they were charged with lèse-majesté and with violating the Peace Preservation Law—and were persecuted.

• THE CONSTITUTION OF JAPAN AND SEPARATION OF RELIGION AND STATE
On August 15, 1945 the Japanese government accepted the Potsdam Declaration and surrendered unconditionally. During the period from that moment until April 28, 1952, when the San Francisco Peace Treaty went into effect and the country regained its independence, Japan was under the administration of the Allied Powers. Among the policies for administering Japan, religion held a position of key importance. It was within the framework of Occupation institutions that the postwar Japanese religious system was determined.

A clear specification of Occupation policy on religion appears in the directive of December 15, 1945 entitled "Abolition of Governmental Sponsorship, Support, Perpetuation, Control, and Dissemination of State Shinto (*Kokka Shinto, Jinja Shinto*)" (SCAPIN 448), commonly known as the Shinto Directive. This directive lays down three principles for administrative policy on religion: religious freedom, strict separation of religion and state, and eradication of militaristic and ultranationalistic thought. A memorandum of October 4, 1945, popularly known as the Human Rights Directive, dealt with the "Removal of Restrictions on Political, Civil and Religious Liberties" (SCAPIN 93).

One of the purposes spelled out in the Shinto Directive, namely, "to put all religions, faiths, and creeds upon exactly the same basis," was realized when the Religious Corporation Ordinance (*Shūkyō hōjin rei*) took effect after its promulgation on December 28, 1945. The immediate occasion for enacting this ordinance was that the Human Rights Directive had ordered the abrogation of the Religious Organizations Law (*Shūkyō dantai hō*, referred to in the directive as the Religious Body Law). To stop short at mere abrogation, however, would have left religious organizations without a legal basis for owning property. It was essential to provide a temporary legal basis for this right, so on the same day the Religious Organizations Law was abrogated, the Religious Corporation Ordinance was enacted.

According to the previous law, only religious organizations recognized by the government had a legal right to exist. Those recognized, moreover, came under strict government controls. In sharp contrast, the Religious Corporation Ordinance relied not on a recognition system but on the regulation principle. Simply by meeting the prescribed regulations and registering its establishment, a group could become a religious corporation. To satisfy the government authorities concerned, it only needed to notify them of its formation. Beyond these matters, there were practically no supervisory rules. This marked the end of statutes that obstructed the freedom of religious organizations to practice their faith.

Under the old Religious Organizations Law there had been forty-three officially recognized religious organizations: thirteen Sect Shinto, twenty-eight Buddhist, and two Christian (one Catholic and one Protestant). When the Religious Corporation Ordinance took effect, new organizations and newly independent branches registered in such a rush that as of the end of 1949 the number of sects and denominations totaled 430. The number of shrines, temples, churches, etc. that split away from parent organizations and became autonomous corporations came to 1,546.

On January 10, 1946 the government responded to the Shinto Directive and its demand for the abolition of State Shinto (*kokka shintō*). It sent a notice in the name of the Vice-Chairman of the Department of Shrine Affairs (*Jingi'in*) to the chief priests of all government shrines (*kankoku heisha*) advising them that abolition was imminent. On January 31 the Ministry of Home Affairs revised its organization, dissolving the Department of Shrine Affairs and related structures. These changes took effect on

February 1. One of the measures taken to eliminate the State Shinto system was that the Religious Corporation Ordinance was amended on February 2 to open the way for Shinto shrines to register as religious corporations. On February 14, 1946 the Association of Shinto Shrines (*Jinja Honchō*), comprising the great majority of former government shrines, registered as a new religious corporation. In this way Shrine Shinto made a fresh start, this time on the same legal basis as other religious organizations.

Under the 1939 Religious Organizations Law, the government agency with jurisdiction over religious bodies other than the government shrines was the Educational Affairs Bureau (*Kyōgaku Kyoku*) in the Ministry of Education. On October 15, 1945 this bureau was dissolved, and the Religion Department (*Shūkyōka*) that had belonged to this bureau was transferred to the newly formed Social Education Bureau and renamed the Religious Affairs Department (*Shūmuka*). Its task was to protect and promote freedom of religion and to assist in the rebuilding of war-damaged temples and churches.

But the Occupation, desiring to remove every trace of government control over religion, suspected this department might become a seedbed for government exploitation of religion. The department not only decided on special grants of building materials for emergency reconstruction of temples and churches, but also was responsible for the gratuitous return of shrine and temple lands that had been requisitioned by the Meiji government when it made Shinto the state religion. Fearing the activities of this department would, in effect, invite the government to interfere with and regain control over religious organizations, the Occupation authorities inclined more and more toward the view that the Religious Affairs Department should be abolished. Subsequently, however, religious leaders spoke out in favor of the Religious Affairs Department. In the autumn of 1948 Occupation authorities decided on its continued existence, and in May 1949 determined the scope of its jurisdiction. It was to collect and distribute information about religion, serve as a liaison office for religious organizations, and handle clerical work concerning ordinances relevant to religious corporations. It had no authority whatever to supervise or control religious organizations.

This department continues to the present day as the Agency for Cultural Affairs in the Ministry of Education. It has taken on certain new tasks in accordance with revisions of the Religious Corporation Law that will be treated shortly. These tasks include paperwork relating to the certification (*ninshō*) of religious corporations, and clerical work for the

Council on Religious Corporations (*Shūkyō Hōjin Shingikai*). On the whole, however, it continues basically unchanged.

The religious freedom and the separation of religion and state that began with the Potsdam Declaration and was formalized in the Shinto Directive thus involved a number of reforms. But it was in the Constitution of Japan, promulgated on November 3, 1946 and put into effect on May 3, 1947, that the basic principles of Japan's postwar religious system were spelled out.

Article 20 says:

(1) Freedom of religion is guaranteed to all. No religious organization shall receive any privileges from the State nor exercise any political authority.

(2) No person shall be compelled to take part in any religious acts, celebration, rite or practice.

(3) The State and its organs shall refrain from religious education or any other religious activity.

Article 89 states:

No public money or other property shall be expended or appropriated for the use, benefit or maintenance of any religious institution or association . . .

The religious-system reforms begun by the Occupation came to tentative completion in the Religious Corporation Law (*Shūkyō hōjin hō*) enacted and put into effect on April 3, 1951. This law, upholding the principles of religious freedom and separation of religion and state guaranteed by the constitution, compensated for the legal inadequacy of the Religious Corporation Ordinance. It was enacted for two reasons. Religious leaders and the Ministry of Education saw the need to put a stop to the schisms, lawsuits, and fraudulent registrations that had occurred with some frequency under the Religious Corporation Ordinance. Also, Occupation authorities held the position that no restrictions were to be formulated except those absolutely necessary.

The purpose of the Religious Corporation Law, as stated in its preamble, is "to provide religious organizations with the legal capability" to maintain and use property in carrying out their activities and to enable them to engage in profit-making enterprises. For this purpose the law requires that religious bodies applying to become religious corporations meet three regulations: public notification, government certification, and the appointment of legally responsible officers.

The Religious Corporation Law continues the regulation principle of the Religious Corporation Ordinance in the sense that registration of its establishment permits a group to become incorporated. But it differs from the Religious Corporation Ordinance in that before registering, a group must now file a public notice, with precise particulars, identifying adherents and other people who hold a stake in the organization. Moreover, the group must later obtain from the proper government office, within a prescribed period, a certificate confirming the rules it proposes to follow as a religious corporation. In addition, it is now required that each religious corporation have a voting body of no less than three people serving as legally responsible officers.

The religious reforms instituted under the Occupation dissolved, then, the prewar quasi-patriarchal state structure erected on the basis of the unity of government and religion (*saisei itchi*). The structure and religious meaning of the state were fundamentally altered. The "national polity" (*kokutai*) and its embodiment in the emperor system, once held up as the wellspring of authority transcending the legislative, judicial, and executive powers, were eliminated. Separation of powers now became the norm.

When the Constitution of Japan, a secular charter, became the source of authority and the basis of positive law, Japan for the first time became a nation under law in the modern sense of the term. The religious character of the state came to an end. Religious freedom was guaranteed as a fundamental human right. These reforms later produced immense changes in Japanese society and religion.

• Postwar Japanese Society and the Political Involvement of Religious Organizations
The Occupation period. Reform of the Japanese religious system led to an immense increase in the scope available for religious activity in postwar Japanese society. Although socioeconomic modernization had begun in 1868, religious ideas that had been suppressed by premodern and modern restraints were now set free. Moreover, because of the establishment of parliamentary democracy and the resurrection of party politics, both individuals and groups now found it possible to initiate social and political activities based on religious motivations and ideas. In what seemed almost a surfeit of freedom, religious organizations plunged into political involvement immediately after the war. It is important to trace this development.

In April 1946, during the first postwar election for the House of

Representatives, eight candidates from traditional Buddhist organizations stood for election, as well as two legally responsible officers from Tenrikyō, one of the new religious organizations. All were elected. In April 1947, during the first election for the House of Councilors, there were candidates from Nishi Honganji of Jōdo Shinshū Buddhism, from the Sōtō school of Zen Buddhism, and from the United Church of Christ in Japan, not to mention several candidates from new religious organizations. New religions engaged in these elections quite as vigorously as the older established organizations. A large number of candidates, Tenrikyō excepted, stood as independents, especially for the House of Councilors. This reflects the fact that political parties had not yet reorganized.

From the beginning the new religions, with the exception of Konkō-kyō, took an active part in postwar politics. It must be admitted, however, that at this stage neither the established religious organizations, the new religions, nor the candidates who made their living by religion displayed a mature awareness of what political involvement meant. It cannot be denied that for some, political involvement was merely a way of currying favor with proponents of postwar democratization policy.

On September 19, 1945, immediately after the surrender, the heads of the forty-three officially recognized Shinto, Buddhist, and Christian organizations were summoned to the Ministry of Education. The government requested their cooperation in rebuilding the inner strength of the people in the wake of defeat. The political debut of these bodies was, at least in part, a response to this request.

Conversely, the new religious organizations that sprang up in scores after the war were regarded by many as nefarious religions with despicable objects of worship. This was also the attitude of the Government Section of the Occupation's General Headquarters, which ordered the Special Investigation Bureau of the Attorney General's Office to investigate a number of new religions and, in certain cases, had them dissolved.

From the Peace Treaty to the mid-1960s: Active participation in politics and the forming of affiliations. September 1951 saw the signing of the San Francisco Peace Treaty, which was to become effective in April 1952. Anticipating the end of the Allied Occupation, the Japanese religious world looked forward to new developments. Among the new religions, the forming of affiliations proceeded apace, and little by little differences in political position became clear.

One noteworthy development on the part of the new religions is that in October 1951 many groups joined together to form the Federation of

New Religious Organizations of Japan (*Shin Nihon Shūkyō Dantai Rengōkai*, often abbreviated as *Shinshūren*). The establishment of a certification system as part of the Religious Corporation Law, together with advice from William P. Woodard, a staff member of the Religions Division and the officer responsible for drafting the Religious Corporation Law, led the new religions to initiate negotiations with government authorities and resulted in the forming of this federation. Member organizations at the time of founding included Risshō Kōseikai, P. L. Kyōdan, Sekai Kyūseikyō, Seichō no Ie, and others, making a total of twenty-four. In April 1952 this federation was accepted as a member of the more comprehensive Japan Religious League (*Nihon Shūkyō Renmei*), and with this step, new religious organizations, once held in contempt, acquired, at least in form, citizenship in the Japanese religious world. In time this federation came to serve as the matrix from which new religious organizations entered the world of politics, but at this formative stage, when there was as yet no united movement, the member organizations did little more than support their candidates for election singly.

In this context, however, one organization that held strongly to the aim of entering politics and soon developed into a patriotic movement is Seichō no Ie. In 1945 it formed a political society called the Seikyō Club, and in 1953 set up the Seichō no Ie Election Committee. Actively involving itself in rightist movements, in 1958 it began to support a body led by the right wing of the Liberal-Democratic Party: the Citizens Association for Self-Defense (from 1959 known as the Citizens Association of Japan). The goals of this association were: to eradicate war, to oppose revolutionary communism, to establish a system to mobilize emergency assistance, and to do away with biased education. (In this context "biased education" meant liberal democratic education introduced from the United States.) In 1957 Seichō no Ie withdrew from the Federation of New Religious Organizations in order to pursue its own course. In 1964 it formed the Seichō no Ie Political Alliance, and since then has entered into politics in earnest.

Another major change in the Japanese religious world following the San Francisco Peace Treaty was Sōka Gakkai's swift development and political activity. Through the efforts of Toda Jōsei, who was released from prison in July 1945, Sōka Kyōiku Gakkai restructured its organization, changed its name to Sōka Gakkai, and prepared to spread its teachings. On May 3, 1951 Toda formally assumed office as the second president of Sōka Gakkai, succeeding Makiguchi Tsunesaburō, who died in prison in 1944. Under Toda's leadership Sōka Gakkai began a massive membership campaign. By the end of 1954 it had a membership of 160,000 house-holds, and in November of that year established a Cultural Department and began its preparations for entry into the political world.

Early in 1955 over fifty members of the Cultural Department were appointed to stand for the April local elections. Of the starting candidates, fifty-three were successful: one in the Tokyo Metropolitan Assembly, one in the Yokohama Assembly, thirty-three in Tokyo ward and city assem-blies, and eighteen in other city assemblies across the country, marking Sōka Gakkai's arrival in the political arena. In the House of Councilors election held the following June, Sōka Gakkai made its first attempt at the national level. Of six candidates, three were elected.

Toda died in April 1958, and in May 1960 Ikeda Daisaku was installed as the third president of Sōka Gakkai. During this two-year interval, how-ever, Sōka Gakkai did not cease to press for advantage in the political world, tirelessly presenting candidates both for House of Councilors elec-tions and for local elections. In the House of Councilors election of 1959 it presented six candidates, all of whom were successful. In 1962 it saw nine members elected to the House of Councilors and three hundred to local assemblies. In the same year it inaugurated the Political Federation for Clean Government (*Kōmei Seiji Renmei*), and in the House of Councilors election of June 1962 it ran an additional nine candidates, all of whom were elected. With fifteen seats in the House of Councilors, Sōka Gakkai formed its Councilors into a bargaining body named the Clean Government Association (*Kōmeikai*). In these and other ways it continued to make remark-able progress.

Initially Sōka Gakkai's entry into the political world was a matter of sending delegates familiar with the Buddhist spirit of compassion to the House of Councilors and to local assemblies. The aim was to help purify the political world and support political actions that would benefit the people. Eventually, however, a change took place. In May 1964, at the twenty-seventh Sōka Gakkai General Conference, it was announced that the Political Federation for Clean Government would henceforth be a politi-cal party based on Buddhist social ideas. November 1964 saw the inaugura-tion of this religiously oriented political party: the Kōmeitō, or Clean Government Party. Its immediate goal was to elect members to the House of Representatives. It aimed to become a moderate, humanist party with its roots in the masses. The motivation for this movement sprang, in the last analysis, from the religious idea of *ōbutsu myōgō* ("a polity funda-mentally united with Buddhism"). The new political party definitely pos-sessed, then, a strongly religious character.

In the unstable political climate following the peace treaty, new religious organizations participated timidly, but as they entered the decade from 1965 to 1975 their political activism became increasingly clear and pronounced. The factors that gave rise to this state of affairs were Kōmeitō's success in the House of Representatives, the alliance between conservative parties and members of the Federation of New Religious Organizations, and the controversy over state support for Yasukuni Shrine. The Kōmeitō and the previously mentioned Seichō no Ie Political Alliance were formed in 1964. During the following year, the Federation of New Religious Organizations formed its own New Political Alliance of Japan (*Shin Nihon Seiji Rengō*) and joined with P. L. Kyōdan and Bussho Gonenkai Kyōdan to campaign in earnest for election success. Seichō no Ie, though its candidate lost in the previous election, won a seat in the 1965 election, and Reiyūkai, a new religion in the Nichiren Stream, threw itself into national elections for the first time, choosing to back a Liberal-Democratic Party candidate.

One view evident among the new religious organizations at this time was their sense of alarm at the rapid advance of the Sōka Gakkai–Kōmeitō combination in politics. A different view appeared in the ruling Liberal-Democratic Party. Painfully aware of weaknesses in its support base in the wake of the turmoil surrounding revision of the U.S.–Japan Security Treaty in 1960, the Liberal-Democratic Party decided to consolidate its conservative base using the new religions. The coupling of these two views was the chief factor behind the political ardor of the new religious organizations.

Pursuing its own course after forming the Kōmeitō, Sōka Gakkai developed a strong support structure and continued its progress. In the House of Councilors election of 1965, it presented nine candidates, all of whom were elected. Buoyed by this experience, the Kōmeitō began to draft its strategy for winning seats in the House of Representatives. For the national election of January 1967 it put up thirty-two candidates, winning seats for twenty-five. Overnight the Kōmeitō became the number three opposition party. In 1969 it held forty-seven seats, a scale without precedent in Japanese history for a political party of religious orientation. Refusing to enter the religious support system envisioned by the conservative camp, Sōka Gakkai held fast to the path of reform and organized social movements among housewives and university students.

The fear arose, however, that the Sōka Gakkai–Kōmeitō political advance and the pursuit of *ōbutsu myōgō* (which some considered a fascist concept rooted in the Nichiren Shōshū demand that Nichiren Buddhism be established as the state religion) were diametrically opposed to the basic principle of the postwar religious system, the principle of separation of religion and state. It was against this background that issues having to do with freedom of speech and freedom of the press emerged in late 1969 and early 1970. Sōka Gakkai came under heavy fire for obstructing publication of a book critical of its methods and actions. It was also criticized for its involvement in politics via its relationship with the Kōmeitō. At a general meeting in May 1970, head office administrators issued, therefore, a statement of clarification that included the following points:

1. Sōka Gakkai aims at *kōsen rufu* ("to spread and make known [the Buddhist Law]"). It is a Buddhist cultural movement; political advance in and of itself is not its purpose.
2. Sōka Gakkai has long opposed the Nichiren Shōshū demand that Nichiren Buddhism become the state religion and will continue to oppose it.
3. The Kōmeitō exists for the welfare of the public. It has no part in Sōka Gakkai's religious activities or efforts to win people to the faith. Sōka Gakkai is, however, one of Kōmeitō's supporting organizations and will uphold it in elections.
4. In order to make clear the difference between the two organizations, Kōmeitō members of national and local assemblies will be removed from Sōka Gakkai administrative posts.

Another matter that helped clarify the political stance of the new religious organizations was the Yasukuni Shrine issue. As early as November 1952, at a national convention of the Japan Federation for the Welfare of War-Bereaved Families (*Nihon Izoku Kōsei Renmei*), a resolution was passed demanding that state funds be used for Yasukuni Shrine ceremonies to placate the spirits of fallen soldiers. In 1956 the Japan Association of War-Bereaved Families (*Nihon Izoku Kai*) resolved that Yasukuni Shrine should receive state support and started a petition to achieve this goal. The Liberal-Democratic Party, for which this association is an important source of votes, joined it in this campaign. In 1964 the Liberal-Democratic Party established a "Subcommittee on State Support for Yasukuni Shrine" in the Cabinet Section of its Political Affairs Research Council. In 1967 this subcommittee began to draft a Yasukuni Shrine bill and submitted its proposal to the Cabinet Section Committee, which meant that the proposal was now on the party agenda.

In response to these actions, the Japan Religious League (*Nihon Shūkyō Renmei*) issued a declaration opposing the Yasukuni Shrine bill. Coming from such a comprehensive body, this declaration shows most of the religions of Japan opposed the bill. Moreover, in February 1968 the Federation of New Religious Organizations submitted to the government, to the Liberal-Democratic Party, and to all concerned groups an appeal for opposition to the Yasukuni Shrine bill. The government and the Liberal-Democratic Party, however, ignored this appeal from the religious world. In 1969 the bill was submitted to the Diet, and in 1974, it was rammed through the Cabinet Committee of the House of Representatives.

This inflexible stance on the part of the government and the Liberal-Democratic Party concerning Yasukuni Shrine soon led to repercussions among the new religions allied with the conservatives. Rifts appeared within the Federation of New Religious Organizations during discussions about how to cope with the bill. Sekai Kyūseikyō, Bussho Gonenkai Kyōdan, and other flag-waving rightist groups withdrew.

Seichō no Ie, however, which had withdrawn as early as 1957, hardened its nationalistic position. Not only did it actively support introduction of the Yasukuni Shrine bill, it also formed a new right-wing body with groups that had seceded from the Federation of New Religious Organizations, taking a position of leadership in this body. The new body later played an active role in promoting, among other things, a Citizens Council for an Independent Constitution, an Association for Honoring the Spirits of the War-Dead, which calls for official visits to Yasukuni Shrine by the emperor and the prime minister, and yet another council to promote a law that would make legally mandatory the use of emperor-linked era-names.

Konkōkyo decided soon after the end of the war not to participate in politics, and consistently held to this decision. Tenrikyō later made a similar choice. As early as 1946 Tenrikyō had put forth its own ministers as candidates for election to the House of Representatives, and for a time involved itself actively in politics. But the 1950 House of Councilors election was its last. From then on, it gave up the idea of nominating candidates, and around 1956 it clearly took the position that "a staff minister or church head-minister, on becoming a candidate for election, must resign his or her post."

For the period from 1955 to 1975, then, political involvement on the part of new religious organizations took four main forms. The first type entered into no alliances with other religious organizations, but sought entry into the political world by forming its own political party. This is exemplified by Sōka Gakkai. Second is the type that approved the postwar reforms of the religious system, but made its entry into the political world indirectly by joining a comparatively liberal wing of the Liberal-Democratic Party, thus supporting conservative political power. This was true of the member bodies of the Federation of New Religious Organizations of Japan. The third type found it difficult to approve the postwar religious reforms, but upheld such ideas as an independent constitution, legalization of state support for Yasukuni Shrine, and restoration of the rights of the emperor. At the top of the list of the right-wing groups that exemplify this type is Seichō no Ie. Fourth is the type that utterly refused to get involved with politics, for example Konkōkyō and Tenrikyō.

From 1975 to the present: The swing to the right and increased political autonomy. In the House of Councilors election of July 1977 a fierce election battle developed between evenly matched conservative and reform groups, giving rise to the prediction that the ruling party might be overturned. Reflecting the sense of crisis in the conservative camp, the religious vote was mobilized in unprecedented numbers. The high rate of election law violations by new religious organizations at that time is an indicator of their transformation into "vote-collecting machines."

This election, however, represents a turning point in the political involvement of new religious organizations. First of all, fresh awareness of the vote-gathering ability of the new religions soon gave rise to a plan to inaugurate, with representatives of right-leaning new religious organizations and the Liberal-Democratic Party, a body to be known as the Association for Research on Religion and Politics (*Shūkyō Seiji Kenkyūkai*). Secondly, other new religious organizations began to take a more independent political stance and put distance between themselves and the Liberal-Democratic Party. Thirdly, and in consequence of the second result, these new religious organizations increased their support for the Democratic Socialist Party and began to field candidates from among their own members.

The immediate occasion for the new religions to distance themselves from the Liberal-Democratic Party was the Yasukuni Shrine bill. After the Liberal-Democratic Party forced the bill through the House of Representatives in May 1974, the bill went to the House of Councilors, where it was thrown out. This power-play was intended to preserve a cooperative spirit among both supporters and opponents of the bill, but the result was that both sides lost confidence in the ruling party.

This distance became evident in the House of Councilors election held the same year. Risshō Kōseikai, the leading body in the Federation of New Religious Organizations, and Seichō no Ie, the leading body among right-wing religious organizations, separately decided on a policy of supporting candidates from within their own organizations. On their first try, all candidates lost. But the organizations held fast to their policy, and two House of Councilors elections later, with the addition of Sekai Kyūseikyō, they were in a much stronger position.

This movement indicates that religious organizations had become more independent in their methods of coping with political issues. From unconditional adherence to the ruling party, they were now, as a result of the Yasukuni Shrine bill, beginning to raise new questions about the significance of their participation, as religious organizations, in the political process. Having reexamined, moreover, the principles and methods of political participation, several religious organizations chose to move away from direct election-involvement in favor of auxiliary political organizations. In January 1976 P. L. Kyōdan established the Artistic Life Research Association, declaring that its aim was to preserve separation of religion and state and to turn out religiously oriented politicians. In February of the same year Reiyūkai set up the Inner-Trip Ideology Research Center for the purpose of selecting candidates it would support. Risshō Kōseikai, having previously participated in elections via the New Political Alliance (a subgroup of the Federation of New Religious Organizations), formed its own group when the New Political Alliance disbanded because of election-law violations during the House of Councilors election of 1977. The new group was called the Research Association for the Promotion of Promising Political Activities. At first it simply gathered the information necessary to make recommendations at election time, but in 1980 it hammered out a four-point political agenda dealing with peace, political ethics, political reform, and freedom of religion and thought, thus making clear the basis for its participation in politics and the criteria for its selection of candidates.

The 1977 House of Councilors election showed the new religions had not lost their capacity to win votes. Forced to recognize this, and watching, their own voter base beginning to wobble, the government and the Liberal-Democratic Party began new maneuvers to secure this immense block of voters as a base for conservative power. With an eye to more favorable election-district apportionments and the establishment of a major political alliance with the religious world, they launched the Association for Research on Religion and Politics in November 1977. Initially, its member bodies were to select their own candidates for election and cooperate in gathering votes. Eventually, it would serve as the key liaison office for proportional distribution of candidates and votes, for gathering funds, and for encouraging harmonious cooperation in election activities.

When Nakasone Yasuhiro was prime minister (1982–1987), his policy of "bringing the postwar period to an end" and the New Political Alliance under the leadership of right-wing religious organizations seemed for a time to go hand in hand. But the "restrictive listing proportional representation system" introduced during the 1983 House of Councilors election shattered this brittle union. For the new religious organizations, which had gained a more diversified political awareness and autonomy in their disaffection from the Liberal-Democratic Party, introduction of this system negated the selection of candidates by religious criteria. On the contrary, it gave absolute control to the Liberal-Democratic Party. This chain of events proved the new religious organizations were at the mercy of the ruling party. Whether their tactic had been to form an independent political party or develop ties with the conservative ruling party, new religious organizations now began to ask more and more insistently how to reconcile their independence with political involvement.

• THE POSTWAR STATE AND PROBLEMS INVOLVING RELIGION

The postwar reforms established freedom of religion. In this new situation religious organizations could participate in politics and grapple with social issues on the basis of religious principles. It is generally held that separation of religion and state involves three basic principles: (1) the state is prohibited from granting special privileges to a religious organization, (2) religious organizations are prohibited from exercising political authority, and (3) the state and its agencies are prohibited from engaging in religious activities.

These principles have been widely accepted, for people remember how freedom was suppressed under State Shinto before and during the war. But with regard to their interpretation, questions have arisen as to whether "separation" is an absolute or relative term, to be understood as an end in itself or as a means of affirming religious freedom. This section introduces a number of postwar issues having to do with the relationship between religion and the state.

State support for, and official worship at, Yasukuni Shrine. During World War II, Yasukuni Shrine, according to the Allied Powers, was an ultranationalistic institution for promoting hero worship and strengthening the fighting spirit of the nation. The Supreme Commander for the Allied Powers ordered, therefore, that it be stripped of its militaristic elements and completely separated from the state. Consequently, Yasukuni Shrine severed its ties with the government, continuing on the same legal basis as other religious bodies, as one religious organization among others.

But with the Peace Treaty and the restoration of independence, a movement to revive special status for Yasukuni Shrine made its appearance. This is the movement calling for state support for Yasukuni Shrine, as discussed earlier in this chapter. By the end of 1974 the Liberal-Democratic bill supporting the public funding of Yasukuni Shrine had been submitted five times, but each time it failed to pass. These actions did, however, divide the postwar Japanese religious world into pro and con camps.

Those promoting state support for the shrine eventually changed their strategy. Instead of staking everything on passage of the bill, they lobbied for the emperor and state officials to offer worship (*sanpai*) at Yasukuni Shrine in their official capacity, for foreign envoys to pay their respects at the shrine, and for uniformed representatives of the Self-Defense Force to offer formal worship there. In these and other ways they sought to give people the impression that Yasukuni Shrine was already a de facto public institution, a religious institution with special ties to the state. It was in this context that the movement for "official visits" (*kōshiki sanpai*) to Yasukuni Shrine emerged.

The event that particularly drew people's attention was Prime Minister Miki Takeo's visit to the shrine on August 15, 1975, the anniversary of the end of the Pacific War. There had been prime ministers who visited the shrine while in office before, but this visit was especially important; it raised the issue of whether this was a religious action forbidden to the government by the constitution, and involved the difficult question of how to evaluate the war. Prime Minister Miki emphasized that he had visited the shrine in a *private* capacity, but it is undeniable that his worship at the shrine opened the way for subsequent official visits. Thus it was that a later prime minister, Nakasone Yasuhiro, emphatically "ended the postwar period" by making an *official* visit to Yasukuni Shrine on August 15, 1985. He signed the register as "Prime Minister of the Cabinet" and made a donation of ¥30,000 from public funds.

Because this visit provoked an unexpectedly strong barrage of protests from China and other Asian countries, official visits to Yasukuni Shrine ceased for the time being. But it was clear that the visit gave preferential treatment to one religion as if its shrine were a government institution, and allowed a government official, acting in his official capacity, to use public funds for a specifically religious act. The visit also opened disputes about where to draw the line between the public person and the private person, and about whether the donation was a religious act or simply a matter of conventional etiquette.

The jichinsai *and the fallen-soldiers monument.* The question of the extent to which the state may participate in or carry out religious activities leads to the thorny issue of whether the principle of separation of religion and state is to be interpreted as absolute or relative.

A pair of lawsuits having to do with a *jichinsai* and with a *chūkonhi* has resulted in court rulings on these questions. A *jichinsai* is a ceremony held at a construction site before breaking ground in order to offer worship to the kami of the locality and pray that construction may proceed without accidents. A *chūkonhi* is a monument (*hi*) to honor the souls (*kon*) of fallen soldiers who have been loyal (*chū*) to the emperor, or to the state, unto death.

Whether the widely practiced *jichinsai* ceremony is to be regarded as a ritual with unmistakably religious meaning or merely as a social custom or convention is difficult to specify in a culture of religious accommodation that does not draw such boundary lines. In April 1965 an assembly-man of the city of Tsu filed a suit against the mayor of the city. He charged that the mayor had violated the constitutional principle of separation of religion and state when, on the occasion of constructing a municipal gymnasium, he used public funds to pay for a Shinto *jichinsai*. Judgment was handed down by courts at three levels. In the first court the plaintiff lost. He appealed to the Nagoya High Court, which upheld his complaint. The case then went to the Supreme Court, which ruled in 1977 that the use of public funds for a *jichinsai* was not unconstitutional.

The basis for the Supreme Court decision was the judgment that a *jichinsai* is not an unequivocally religious action. It is, rather, a social custom of ambiguous religious significance and therefore does not necessarily violate the constitutional prohibition against religious activity by the state.

Furthermore, based on its idea of relative separation as the proper way to interpret the principle of separation of religion and state, the Supreme Court ruled that "the state is required to be religiously neutral, but this does not mean that the state is forbidden to have anything whatever to do with religion. The purpose and consequence of action that involves religious relationships has to be kept in mind. Such relationships are prohibited only if they exceed the bounds of what is deemed proper and reasonable." Its criterion of judgment was that "action with religiously significant purpose, and with the consequence of supporting, fostering, or promoting religion, or again of oppressing or interfering with religion" is the only kind of religious action forbidden to the state.

Until this Supreme Court ruling, it was generally assumed that the principle of separation of religion and state under the postwar constitution would follow the idea of separation of religion and state laid down in the Shinto Directive, namely, the idea of absolute, or strict, separation. The Supreme Court ruling on the Tsu *jichinsai* case scuttled this approach. This ruling opened the way for the state to permit certain religious ties so long as it did not violate the "purpose and consequence" criterion cited above.

The lawsuit concerning the fallen-soldiers monument, or *chūkonhi*, arose in the city of Minō. In December 1975 the city and the municipal Board of Education, with public funds, moved a monument for fallen soldiers from the grounds of a municipal elementary school to donated public land. Early in 1976 the local Association of War-Bereaved Families, with the cooperation of municipal employees, sponsored an *ireisai*, a Shinto ceremony to propitiate the souls of fallen soldiers. Housewives living near the newly located monument filed a lawsuit in February 1976. They charged that since "the *chūkonhi* is a religious facility for ennobling the spirits of fallen soldiers in accordance with militaristic thought related to State Shinto, and the *ireisai* is a religious activity of the Association of War-Bereaved Families, city support for this venture is in violation of the constitution." Municipal authorities defended their action by claiming the *chūkonhi* was merely "a memorial stone to honor the souls of fallen soldiers." The fact is, however, that both before and during World War II, as part of the process of establishing State Shinto militarism, such monuments were erected throughout Japan and represented "the village Yasukuni."

In the first trial the court upheld the argument of the plaintiffs. It ruled the *chūkonhi* was a religious facility and an object of worship. Taking the position of absolute separation and applying the "purpose and consequence" criterion, the court further held that since the purpose involved strongly religious overtones and the consequence involved the city in public support for the activity of one particular religion, the city had violated the constitution. The Osaka Higher Court, however, overturned the judgment of the lower court. It ruled the *chūkonhi* was nothing more than a secular memorial stone to commemorate fallen soldiers and the city's action did not violate the constitution. The plaintiffs appealed, and the Supreme Court handed down its decision on February 16, 1993. The decision made two points: (1) the *chūkonhi* is a memorial pillar honoring fallen soldiers, not a religious facility; and (2) participation by the chairman of the Board of Education in the *ireisai* was a social formality and did not violate the constitution. In effect, therefore, the Supreme Court upheld the ruling of the Osaka Higher Court.

Other cases. In addition to the two cases cited above, there are many other lawsuits that contest allegedly unconstitutional action on the basis of the principle of separation of religion and state. Most of these lawsuits, however, have to do with issues that grew out of prewar and wartime State Shinto. One issue concerns the extent to which a religious organization is autonomous and the extent to which it is subject to judiciary intervention. Lawsuits like this show clearly that the principle of separation of religion and state introduced by the Occupation has not taken firm root in Japan, and has yet to find a harmonious balance with traditional Japanese culture.

The postwar system that assigned a purely symbolic status to the emperor gave rise to yet another type of debate and lawsuit. In connection with the mourning service (*taisō*) held for the Emperor Showa on February 24, 1989, questions arose as to the degree to which this ought to be a state ceremony. In order to forestall constitutional misgivings, it was decided, in the end, that the *Taisō-no-gi*, a Shinto service of mourning for the emperor, would be carried out as an Imperial House ceremony, but that the *Taisō-no-rei*, a separate Shinto rite, would be carried out as a secular state ceremony.

A similar division was employed on November 12, 1990 when the new emperor's *Sokui-no-rei*, or Enthronement Ceremony, was handled as a state ceremony and the subsequent *Daijōsai*, or Great Food Offering, as a private ceremony based on the Shinto of the Imperial House. The central question in all these matters was the extent to which a rite could be a state ceremony without violating the principle of separation of religion and state.

A closely related question giving rise to intense debate was whether the *Daijōsai* should be paid for with private funds from the Imperial House internal budget (*naiteihi*) or with public funds from the Imperial Palace budget (*kyūteihi*). The government, recognizing the religious character of this rite, decided that it would be an Imperial House ceremony. But the government also recognized the "public character" of this rite and chose to use public funds from the imperial palace budget. This decision struck a balance between upholders of tradition, who wanted it to be a state ceremony, and public opinion, which called for strict application of

8

RELIGION AND EDUCATION

Inoue Nobutaka

Inoue Nobutaka

• THE PREWAR AND POSTWAR SOCIAL CONTEXT

The great reforms that took place under the Meiji Restoration played a major role in shaping post-Restoration religion and education in contemporary Japan. Particularly important are such developments as the formation of the modern emperor system; the re-emergence of Christian mission work; the restructuring of the religious world, not least because of the birth of new religious organizations; and the consolidation of an educational system based on the idea of the priority of the state. The modern emperor system exercised constant and formative influence on the issue of religion and education. Christian mission work, with education as one of its primary concerns, provided a new model for the relationship between religious organization and education. The restructuring of the religious world, including the growth of new religious organizations, stimulated diversity within religious education. The state of affairs since the end of World War II differs sharply from the prewar situation, but is to be understood, nonetheless, as an extension of the line of development that began with the Meiji Restoration.

When considering the formative influences mentioned above, it is important to recognize the difference between the prewar and postwar emperor systems, which is clearly reflected in the area of religious education. Before the war, separation of religion and education was a basic principle of the state. At the same time, however, the state gave a unique position to matters having to do with the emperor system. Because teachings that criticized the emperor or impugned the Japanese Empire were simply not allowed, there were definite restraints on religious education. After the war, these restraints ceased to exist. Private schools are now free to offer religious instruction, and the curriculum may include classes taught from a religious perspective. In these and other ways, the social context for education in postwar Japan is fundamentally different from that of prewar Japan, but noteworthy changes have taken place in both the prewar and the postwar periods.

138

• The Position of Religious Education in the Schools

In order to consider how the position of religious instruction within the educational system has changed, it is useful to divide the time span between 1868 and the present into four periods. The first is from 1868 until about 1890 (the early Meiji period), the second from about 1890 until 1926 (the mid-Meiji through Taishō periods), the third from 1926 to 1945 (the early Shōwa period), and fourth is the postwar period. During the first period, the distinction between religious education and academic education gradually took shape. The second period, with the establishment of the modern emperor system, saw, on the one hand, the imposition of restrictions on religious education and, on the other, the incorporation of obligatory moral education. The third period, unusual because it encompassed a wartime situation, was a time when the idea of education became completely subordinate to purposes of state. The fourth period has three distinctive characteristics: the exclusion of religious education in the narrow sense from public education, the acceptance of religious education in the general sense for private educational institutions, and recognition of the need for moral education, or the cultivation of religious ideals.

Early Meiji period: 1868–1890. The early Meiji period was in many ways a time of trial and error. The position of religious education within the whole was constantly changing. Initially, there were areas in which religion and education were not yet differentiated. The government established a system of appointed Shinto propagandists (*senkyōshi*) in 1869, and in 1872 it set up a "teaching priest" (*kyōdōshoku*) system whereby certain Shinto and Buddhist priests were appointed to teaching positions. These two systems were intended not only to enlighten the citizenry but also to promote the idea of empire based on the emperor system, and protect the country by opposing the spread of Christianity. Enlightenment of the citizenry involved educational functions carried out in place of those performed by the schools. Because some of these Buddhist and Shinto priests were relatively well-educated, the educational activities they performed outside metropolitan centers often provided a substitute for academic instruction. More precisely, the government expected that its system of teaching priests would include three kinds of institutes. The head institute (*daikyōin*) would be in Tokyo; most prefectures would have a provincial institute (*chūkyōin*); and Shinto shrines and Buddhist temples would function as local institutes (*shōkyōin*). In fact, however, this system did not work as planned. The Tokyo institute, because of opposition from the True Pure Land Sect, was dissolved in 1875. Provincial institutes failed to materialize in several prefectures; if a good leader was not available, nothing was done. As for the local institutes, a temple or shrine could receive local-institute status by submitting an application, but if no application was submitted, that was the end of the matter. Moreover, in most cases the lectures offered at the local and provincial institutes were well attended only for the first few sessions.

With the formation of an educational system, separation of religion and education proceeded rapidly. In 1872 the Ministry of Education issued its first set of regulations for a nationwide educational system. (A revised edition was issued in 1873.) These regulations gave clear form to the principle of compulsory universal education. The regulations, seeking to standardize educational arrangements in previously autonomous areas, called for the establishment of eight university districts throughout the nation, with thirty-two middle school districts in each university district, and 210 elementary school districts in each middle school district—an extremely mechanical partitioning. At this stage, however, those in power had given little thought to the idea of separating religion and education. The revised regulations allowed both Shinto and Buddhist priests to serve as teachers. When these regulations were replaced by the Education Ordinance in 1879, it became clear that the separation of education from religion was intended. The Education Ordinance classified schools as elementary schools, middle schools, colleges, normal schools, vocational/professional schools, or miscellaneous schools. Normal schools were to train teachers, vocational/professional schools to offer courses in a specialized branch of study. For education based on religious ideas, only the miscellaneous schools were left. Consequently, schools founded on religious principles came to resemble private classes outside the formal school system. In ordinary schools, religious instruction was taboo, in reaction to the growth of Christianity.

The teaching priest system, which was supposed to enlighten the emperor's subjects, gradually lost its meaning, and in 1884 it was abolished. In one sense this can be understood as the end of the period when religious education and academic education, not to mention adult education, were still undifferentiated. But another purpose of the teaching priest system had yet to be fulfilled, namely, to plant emperor worship and the idea of a Japanese empire in people's hearts and minds. This purpose became even more pronounced during the next few decades. In the educational system from about 1890 on, therefore, the implanting of emperor worship and of the idea of a Japanese empire took on great significance.

The system that limited religious leaders to the communication of religious teachings did not mean that education was completely separated from religion. On the contrary, with the emergence of the claim that Shinto was a secular institution, epitomized in the phrase "the shrine is not a religion" (*jinja wa shūkyō ni arazu*), Shinto ideas came to be introduced more and more forcefully into education. It can be argued, to be sure, that this tendency began in the early Meiji period. But while the early Meiji government was still uncertain about how to treat religion and education, a clear policy gradually emerged from mid-Meiji on.

Mid-Meiji through Taishō: 1890–1926. From about the middle of the Meiji period, the policy of giving priority to education that was oriented to State Shinto values and had its center in the emperor system became increasingly evident. Directive No. 12, issued by the Ministry of Education in August 1899, symbolizes this development. This directive ordered that the educational system as a whole be completely separated from religion. Schools founded by the national government and schools founded by prefectural or local governments, together with all schools from high school down that came under the 1886 School Act, were prohibited from offering courses in religion and from conducting religious ceremonies whether inside or outside the curriculum. At first glance it might seem that this directive called expressly for the separation of religion and education. In fact, however, its real aim was twofold: to make central to education the ideas expressed in the Imperial Rescript on Education, and to obstruct the growth of schools based on Christian principles. Education that followed the Imperial Rescript on Education and inculcated State Shinto ideas and values was defined as non-religious instruction and given a privileged position.

When it issued Directive No. 12, the government also put out a twenty-article ordinance covering private, or non-governmental, schools. This ordinance made Directive No. 12 applicable to all private schools, thus ruling out religious education even in schools operated by religious organizations. Only in schools classified as miscellaneous, which came under the ordinance but not under the directive, was religious instruction possible.

This system did not appear overnight. Between 1885 and 1890 there had already been intense controversy, sometimes referred to as the moral education debate (*tokuiku ronsō*), over the question of what should be central in Japanese morality. During the course of this debate, a decision was taken to make the emperor system the pivot of moral understanding. The Imperial Rescript on Education, drafted by Inoue Kowashi, Motoda Nagazane et al. and promulgated on October 23, 1890, played a critical role in strengthening the influence of the emperor system in the field of education. Based for the most part on Confucian ethics, it emphasized the ruler-subject relationship, the husband-wife relationship, the elder brother-younger brother relationship, etc. Because it was an imperial message, many held that the rescript was to be obeyed absolutely. There also arose a tendency to regard the rescript itself as more important than its message, a tendency to sanctify it. As a result, a conflict between religion and education arose.

In 1891 Uchimura Kanzō, a Christian teacher in a public high school, refused to bow his head before the Imperial Rescript, thus precipitating the lèse-majesté incident associated with his name. Uchimura lost his job, but the next year Inoue Tetsujirō, in an article entitled "Kyōiku to shūkyō no shōtotsu" (The collision between education and religion) in the journal *Kyōiku jiron*, fanned the flames by contending that Christianity was incompatible with the character of the nation. Debates over education and religion continued for about a year. In 1892 a similar incident occurred when Kume Kunitake, a professor at Tokyo Imperial University, was dismissed for publishing an article entitled "Shintō wa saiten no kozoku" (Shinto as an archaic ritual custom in honor of heaven).

The 1890s also saw the convening of students in assembly halls and school grounds to hear edifying talks by the principal, talks that came under the heading of moral education. The emperor system was stressed again in the imperial bestowal of *goshin'ei*, a photograph of the emperor and another of the empress. The first bestowal of such photographs took place in 1874 in response to a request from the president of the Kaisei School. In 1882 similar requests were placed by the heads of the Osaka Middle School, the Tokyo Normal School, and the Tokyo Women's Normal School. Goshin'ei were later bestowed on upper middle schools, and in 1890 on Tokyo Imperial University. By 1912, the end of the Meiji period, nearly one hundred percent of the educational institutions in Japan had received goshin'ei. Thus the policy of instilling the emperor-system ideology into the field of education gradually grew stronger and stronger.

In 1918 the University Act (*Daigaku rei*) was promulgated, allowing private universities to receive official recognition. Seizing this opportunity, many of the private vocational/professional schools founded for reli-

142

gious reasons changed to college or university status. In the Shinto stream Kokugakuin University and Jingū Kōgakkan University came into being. Among Buddhist institutions were Ryūkoku University and Ōtani University (of the True Pure Land Sect), Risshō University (Nichiren), Komazawa University (Sōtō Zen), Mt. Kōya University (Shingon), and Taishō University (Pure Land, Shingon, and Tendai). Nearly all the major sects came to have their own university. The Christian stream includes Protestant institutions such as Dōshisha University, Rikkyō University, and Kansei Gakuin University, and such Catholic institutions as Sophia University. The 1920s and '30s thus saw the establishment of an increasing number of universities sponsored by religious organizations.

Early Shōwa: 1926–1945. The third period, when Japan began to prepare for war, was marked by extreme government intervention in education. This was the time when Japan, as part of its colonization policy for Korea, sought to make Koreans into loyal imperial subjects. It is important to recognize, however, that war was not the only cause of this change. The restorationist tendency that arose in reaction to rapid westernization and the mounting sense of alarm over the swift growth of the socialist movement also need to be kept in mind. Important in this connection are the 1910 high treason case, when hundreds of socialists and anarchists were arrested and twenty-six executed on the trumped-up charge of attempting to assassinate the emperor, and the 1911 textbook case, when historian Kida Sadakichi was censured by the Diet and forced out of his post at Tokyo Imperial University for writing a textbook that questioned the legitimacy of the throne. The national morality movement sparked by these events gave rise to the idea that education of the emperor's subjects should be based on the character of the nation, an idea that necessarily led to a separation between scholarship and education. The view which now came to the fore was that education should not be understood as the scholarly pursuit of truth but as the shaping of human morals.

During the latter half of the 1920s, the criticism arose that school curricula were biased in favor of factual knowledge and neglected the cultivation of ideals. A cry was raised for education that would nurture religious ideals: a sense of awe before mysterious power, a spirit of gratitude and loyalty to the emperor, and dedication to his goals for the nation. Against this background, the Ministry of Education circulated a notice in 1932 as to how Directive No. 12 was to be interpreted. The notice indicated that the prohibition on religious education did not rule out education in religious ideals. In 1935 the Vice-Minister of the Ministry of Education issued another notice, "Points for Consideration in Relation to the Fostering of Religious Sentiments," urging educators to drive home the meaning of the Imperial Rescript on Education and promote the spirit of sacrifice for the sake of the nation. This notice placed even greater stress on the point that even though religious doctrines and rituals were barred from the field of education, the fostering of religious ideals was not. The expectation was, no doubt, that cultivating such ideals would enhance the feelings and motives that loyal citizens ought to hold.

All this is connected with the 1937 movement for the complete spiritual mobilization of Japanese citizens. That year marked the beginning of the war with China, and was a time when State Shinto ideology rapidly grew stronger and stronger. It was also the year in which the Ministry of Education, in order to press home the historical meaning of the Japanese empire, published *Kokutai no hongi* (The fundamental principles of the character of the nation).

During the early Shōwa period, militarism gradually blanketed Japanese society. Religious education, like everything else, was wrapped in militarism's smothering embrace. As war fever mounted, free and unrestrained religious education became impossible. In March 1941 the act that had governed elementary schools was replaced by another act creating "national schools" (*kokumin gakkō*), thus initiating a system intended to produce subjects of a single heart and mind. In detailed regulations, it was laid out from the beginning that the goal of education was to produce loyal subjects for the empire. The very first article emphasized the significance of the Imperial Rescript on Education, asserted that education was the means by which to teach "the way of the empire," and extolled the promotion of belief in the character of the nation. In the same year the Ministry of Education's Department of Education published *Shinmin no michi* (The way of imperial subjects) and distributed it to every school. Bowing in respectful obeisance before the goshin'ei became expected behavior even in the Christian schools.

The postwar period. The fourth period signifies, so to speak, the raising of the curtain on a new age of freedom. The most fundamental changes of the postwar years were the exclusion of sectarian religious education from all public schools and the freedom to offer religious education in private schools.

In October 1945, immediately after the end of World War II, the Ministry of Education issued a new directive on religious education in private schools. Revising the 1899 Directive No. 12, the new directive said that as long as they were extracurricular, religious education and religious ceremonies would now be permitted. To this freedom, however, three conditions were attached: (1) there was to be no interference with the religious freedom of the students, (2) the school rules should state explicitly that the school intended to teach the precepts and observe the ceremonies of a particular religious group, and (3) the school should see to it that in the implementation of these teachings and ceremonies, no unusual burdens, whether physical or spiritual, were laid on the students.

In December 1945 the Supreme Commander for the Allied Powers issued the Shinto Directive, which completely abolished the "special protection" State Shinto had previously enjoyed. The Imperial Rescript on Education was likewise suspended in practice, though its legal invalidation did not take place until 1948.

Basic policy with regard to religious education was spelled out in the Fundamentals of Education Act promulgated in 1947. This act determined the standards for religious education in accordance with the spirit of the Constitution of Japan, particularly Article 20, which guarantees freedom of religion to all and prohibits the state from engaging in religious education or religious activities. Partly because of the soul-searching that followed recognition of the nefarious influence of State Shinto, the declared policy called for the prohibition of religious education from all public education. In Article 9 this act enjoined, with regard to religious education, an attitude of tolerance for religion and respect for the position of religion in society. It also stipulated that schools established by the state or by local public entities must refrain from religious education and from any other religious activities that would benefit a particular religion. On the other hand, it expressly declared that as long as an attitude of tolerance for religion and respect for the place of religion in society was observed, and as long as their teachings were not militaristic, private schools were free to engage in religious education without restriction.

The year 1949 saw the promulgation of the Private Schools Act, which permitted the founders of non-governmental schools to register them, subject to certain conditions, as legal corporations. This system guaranteed that the interests of private schools would benefit society as a whole and that their autonomy would be respected. In addition, the "baby-boom" of the late 1940s gave rise to an urgent need for more private schools to accommodate rising numbers of young people seeking high school and university education. This postwar educational system was utilized to considerable advantage by religious organizations that chose to establish schools in one or more of the prescribed categories.

Not long after the end of the war, the tendency to emphasize the role of education in the fostering of religious ideals reappeared. In September 1945 the Ministry of Education issued its "Fundamental policy for the construction of a new Japan." In 1946 it published its "Guidelines for new education," and in the same year the Diet passed a "Resolution on cultivating religious sentiments through education." All three documents held up the need for education that would foster religious ideals. All three, however, were within the parameters later set out in Article 20 of the constitution and Article 9 of the Fundamentals of Education Act. In 1949 the Vice-Minister of Education circulated a notice on the treatment of religion in primary and middle school education. This notice prohibited public schools from taking pupils to religious facilities for the purpose of participating in worship, religious ceremonies, or festivals. It also indicated that even if a visit was for research or cultural purposes, pupils were not to be compelled to go. With regard to the matter of classroom teaching materials, teachers could use religious materials for research or educational purposes if necessary, but should not give the impression that one religion was better, or worse, than others. Nonetheless, pupils who voluntarily chose to organize a religious group as an extracurricular activity were free to do so. These guidelines did not apply to private schools, where freedom of religious education was guaranteed. This basic policy continues, by and large, to the present day.

In the regulations governing the application of the School Education Act of 1947, it is clearly stated that private schools are free to include religion courses in the curriculum, and that if they do so, the religion courses may take the place of courses in moral education. Many private schools established by religious organizations have taken advantage of this option. Thus there is a marked and growing tendency for public schools and private schools established by religious organizations to diverge in the opportunities they offer for religious education.

Given the restrictions on religious education in the public schools, a call for moral education eventually arose. With the opening of the academic year in April 1958, one hour of moral education per week was established in primary and middle schools, and again the problem of fostering religious ideals raised its head. But in 1965, when the Central Education Council published *Kitai sareru ningenzō* (The model person), it one-sidedly promoted a single set of values and evoked strong reaction in favor of value-pluralism.

It was in this context that universities established by religious organizations proliferated after the war. Some universities grew out of what had earlier been vocational/professional schools, like Tenri University (Tenrikyō), Meiji Gakuin University (Protestant), and Tokyo Union Theological Seminary (Protestant). Many new universities were founded from scratch, including International Christian University (Protestant) and Sōka University (Sōka Gakkai).

• The Educational Activities of Religious Organizations

What is distinctive about the educational activities of religious organizations now is that approximately two-thirds of the schools are Christian. When one considers that Christians represent only about one percent of the population of Japan, this is an astonishingly high proportion. Conversely, the proportion of Shinto schools is exceedingly low. Again, Christian schools tend to be zealous about education for girls and young women, while Buddhist schools focus their efforts on education for boys and young men. Among the Christians, it is noteworthy that many Protestant schools have existed since before the war, whereas many of the Catholic schools have come into being only since the end of the war. Schools founded by new religions have also gradually increased in the postwar period.

The present state of affairs can perhaps best be explained by showing, in historical context, how each of the major streams of religious tradition has involved itself with education.

Christian schools. Schools in the Christian stream range from primary through university, and their number is impressive. The establishment of Christian schools began in the years before 1868, the tumultuous years of Japan's change from feudal to modern society. Because Christian evangelism was legally forbidden at the time, many missionaries founded private academies, especially English-language academies. Many of the schools based on Christian principles were known as "mission schools." The general pattern was for missionaries to start Christian schools or go by invitation to an already existing school and engage in educational work for the purpose of spreading the gospel. As early as 1862, G. H. F. Verbeck had opened a Bible class in Nagasaki, and in 1863 J. C. Hepburn established a private academy in Yokohama. Table 1 summarizes these and other noteworthy developments.

Denominations eager to spread the gospel through education included the Reformed Church in America; the Presbyterian Church in the United States; the Methodist Episcopal Church, U.S.A. and the Methodist Episcopal Church, South; the Church of England; the American Baptist

TABLE 1

Early Christian Schools

Date	Founder	Location	Institution
1862	G.H.F. Verbeck	Nagasaki	Bible class
1863	J.C. Hepburn	Yokohama	Private academy, later joined Brown's academy and a Tokyo seminary to form Meiji Gakuin
1864	S.R. Brown	Yokohama	Yokohama Academy, later joined Hepburn's academy and a Tokyo seminary to form Meiji Gakuin
1870	Julia Carrothers	Tokyo	Academy for girls, later Joshi Gakuin
1871	Mary E. Kidder	Yokohama	Academy for girls, later Ferris Jogakuin
1873	Eliza Talcott	Kobe	Academy for girls, later Kobe Jogakuin
1874	C.M. Williams	Tokyo	Academy for English and Bible, later Rikkyō Gakuin
1874	Dora Schoonmaker	Tokyo	School for girls, later Kaigan Joshi Gakkō and later still part of Aoyama Gakuin
1875	Niijima Jō	Kyoto	Dōshisha
1876	Hara Taneaki	Tokyo	Hara Jogakkō
1876	Sakurai Chika	Tokyo	Sakurai Jogakkō
1878	Sawayama Pōro	Osaka	Baika Jogakkō
1879	Mary Jane Oxlad	Osaka	School for girls, later Poole Gakuin
1879	R.S. Maclay, M.S. Vail	Yokohama	Mikai Shingakkō (theological seminary), the parent institution of what later became Aoyama Gakuin
1879	Elizabeth Russell	Nagasaki	School for girls, later Kwassui Gakuin

Churches in the U.S.A.; and the Southern Baptist Convention.

In 1873, when the public notices proscribing Christianity were removed and Christian evangelism was tacitly permitted, the educational enterprises that had been an important part of missionary activity began to flourish. Japanese translations of the Bible progressed, and as Christians began to spread the gospel in earnest, educational evangelism came to

occupy an important position. Christian schools founded not by missionaries but by Japanese believers include Dōshisha (1875), and three girls'
schools: Hara Jogakkō (1876), Sakurai Jogakkō (1876), and Baika Jogakkō
(1878).

Besides these educational endeavors by mainstream denominations,
the Seventh-Day Adventists established a Japanese-English Bible School
in the Shiba Park area of Tokyo in 1898 and devoted themselves to the
training of evangelists. This school later became the junior college now
known as San'iku Gakuin.

In addition to these forerunners of schools of higher learning, there
were also, during the early Meiji period, schools of the miscellaneous category which later became middle schools. By 1895 a number of such
schools had been established.

During the first half of the twentieth century Christianity went through
a difficult time, and few new schools were established. Since 1946, however, the number of new Christian schools has again increased. One distinctive feature of the postwar years is the prominent number of new
Catholic schools.

In contrast to the Protestants, who began mission activity through
education quite early, the Catholics started their educational work rather
late. The year 1913, when the vocational/professional school that later
became Sophia University received legal recognition, marks the earliest of
the Catholic ventures in higher education. The increase in the number of
new Catholic schools since the end of the war has been spectacular. By
and large, the Christian schools have shown from the beginning a pronounced inclination to emphasize education for women, and this tendency still holds true today.

Buddhist schools. Several Buddhist schools have their antecedents in late
feudal period grammar schools attached to Buddhist temples. Some
started as local institutes (*shōkyōin*) during the early Meiji period under
the "teaching priest" (*kyōdōshoku*) system, but survived as full-fledged
schools even after that system was abolished. It is generally held that the
greatest stimulus to Buddhist educational development had two sources:
the anti-Buddhist iconoclasm (*haibutsu kishaku*) of the early Meiji period,
and the growth of Christianity at about the same time. In order to
demonstrate the legitimacy of Buddhism and prevent the enlargement of
Christianity, an association of Buddhist sects was formed in 1869. At the
same time, a number of Buddhist sects independently established their
own educational facilities. Nishi Honganji and Higashi Honganji, the two

major branches of the Jōdo Shinshū, or True Pure Land Sect, not only sent students abroad to experience conditions in Europe and America but also reformed their training institutes (*gakurin*) and established conventional schools (*gakkō*). The Jōdo Shinshū universities, Ryūkoku University (Nishi Honganji) and Ōtani University (Higashi Honganji), received legal recognition in 1922. Table 2 summarizes the major developments.

Thus, a significant number of Buddhist schools came to be established. One of their main purposes was to train, for specific organizations, successors to those in positions of responsibility. Consequently, there was a pronounced emphasis on education for young men. In 1888, however, a Buddhist school called the Joshi Bungei Gakusha, or Women's Institute for Literary Arts (the present Chiyoda Jogakkō), was established in Tokyo. The next year saw the promulgation of the Act Governing Secondary Education for Women (*Kōtō jogakkō rei*), and a subsequent sharp increase in the number of Buddhist middle schools and high schools for women.

Shinto schools. The prewar and wartime government position that Shinto was not a religion led to its being given preferential treatment as compared to other religions, but also had the unanticipated effect of reducing the number of new Shinto schools. Since the public schools gave classes on the emperor as well as on the two major classics, the *Kojiki* and *Nihon shoki*, it was thought unnecessary to create other schools for education in these subjects. But because of the need to train Shinto priests, a few institutions of higher learning were established (see Table 3).

With the end of the war, State Shinto (*kokka shintō*) was dissolved. Since Shrine Shinto (*jinja shintō*) was now considered one religion among others, most shrines banded together in 1946 to form the Jinja Honchō, or Association of Shinto Shrines. Kōgakkan University and Kokugakuin University are the only Shinto institutions of higher learning which offer training courses for would-be Shinto priests.

Secondary schools in the Shinto stream are limited in number; apart from a high school operated by Kokugakuin University and another operated by Kōgakkan University, only a few exist. Among the middle schools and high schools in the Shinto tradition, some do not even offer classes in Shinto. One example of a school that does emphasize Shinto education is Naniwa Gakuen in Osaka. At this school, classes in Shinto are required, and it is also obligatory for all first-year middle school and high school students to make a group excursion to the Grand Shrines of Ise and participate in *misogi*, purification through bathing in a river.

150

TABLE 2

Buddhist Schools

Date	Sect	Location	Institution
1872	Nichiren	Tokyo	School of religion, later Risshō University.
1873	Shingon	Various places	Local institutes (*shōkyōin*)
1875	Shingon	Various places	Provincial institutes (*chūkyōin*) NOTE: The local and provincial institutes served as primary and elementary schools.
1875	Zen (Sōtō)	Tokyo	Sōtōshū Daigakurin, initially a vocational/professional school. Komazawa University since 1925.
1876	Zen (Sōtō)	Nagoya	Vocational/professional branch school at the primary and elementary level. Now Aichi Gakuin University.
1886	Zen (Rinzai)	Kyoto	Hanazono High School
1886	Pure Land	Chion-in, Kyoto	Institute for Buddhist learning, later Bukkyō University.
1886	Shingon	Mt. Kōya	Kogi Shingonshū Daigakurin ("training institute in the old interpretation of Shingon teachings"), Mt. Kōya University since 1909.
1887	Pure Land	Zōjōji temple, Tokyo	Institute for Jōdo Shū studies, later Taishō University.
1891	Shingon (Chizan and Buzan branches together)	Gokokuji temple, Tokyo	Shingi Daigakurin ("training institute in the new interpretation"), now Buzan University.
1922	True Pure Land (Nishi Honganji)	Kyoto	Ryūkoku University
1922	True Pure Land (Higashi Honganji)	Kyoto	Ōtani University

TABLE 3

SHINTO SCHOOLS

Date	Institution	Location	Description
1882	Kōten Kōkyūsho	Tokyo	Originally to train priests and conduct Shinto research. Later entered into Kokugakuin University (see below).
1882	Jingū Kōgakkan	Ise	First established to train priests and engage in scholarly research into Shinto. Came under jurisdiction of the Ministry of Home Affairs as a vocational/professional school independent of the Vocational/Professional School Act (*Senmon gakkō rei*). Granted university status in 1940. Dissolved in 1946 by Occupation order. Reestablished in 1955 as a private institution, known today as Kōgakkan University.
1890	Kokugakuin	Tokyo	Founded under the aegis of the Kōten Kōkyūsho, but in 1906 the two institutions formed Kokugakuin University.

Schools of the new religions. Educational enterprises begun by new religions are comparatively few as yet, but the number is increasing. Most are middle schools, though some new religions are beginning to establish high schools and universities. At first, their involvement with education was primarily a way to nurture human resources from which successors could be drawn and also as a way of qualitatively improving their followers' children. Konkōkyō, Tenrikyō, Sōka Gakkai, Risshō Kōseikai and other organizations, once they established educational institutions, tended to invest immense energy in the educational enterprise. Before World War II, the only new religions involved in education were Konkōkyō and Tenrikyō. For a bird's-eye view of prewar developments, see Table 4.

Since the end of World War II, while these organizations have continued to strengthen their educational institutions, other organizations have begun to establish new middle schools and high schools. Generally, an

2

TABLE 4

Schools of the New Religions

Date	New Religion	Institution
1894	Konkōkyō	Children's school, legally registered as a middle school in 1898. Now enlarged to include a high school, it is known as Konkō Gakuen.
1900	Tenrikyō	Children's school which in 1908 became a legally registered middle school under the name Tenri Chūgaku. Known today as Tenri Kōtōgakkō, or Tenri high school.
1925	Tenrikyō	Tenrikyō school of foreign languages, founded in connection with Tenrikyō's purpose of winning members outside Japan. Now Tenri University.

organization forms a legally registered educational corporation (*gakkō hōjin*) and establishes a range of schools under its auspices. Thus Risshō Kōseikai, P.L. Kyōdan, Reiyūkai, Benten Shū, and Sōka Gakkai all operate schools extending from primary school through university. One of the Tenrikyō churches, the Tōhon Daikyōkai in Tokyo, has independently established a school known today as Shūtoku Gakuen.

Among the schools established under the auspices of new religious organizations, some devote considerable energy to teaching students about the sponsoring religious body, while others differ little from ordinary schools. Examples of the former would include Tenrikyō and Shōroku Shintō Yamatoyama. Tenrikyō, even at the primary school level, teaches children about Tenrikyō rituals. The Reiyūkai and Risshō Kōseikai schools, though they initially gave admission-preference to children of members, now operate much the same way as standard public schools. The Benten Shū schools give classes on their religion, but only once a week, and even then only to foster religious ideals. In all the schools the most prominent goal is to prepare students for higher education.

• An Overall Picture of Religious Education

In schools founded by religious organizations before World War II, there was a strong tendency to draw on religious ideas. Buddhist schools nurtured young people who could succeed those in positions of responsibility. Among schools of the Shinto tradition, the purpose was to cultivate new priests. In Christian schools, there was a decided emphasis on education as evangelism. The new religions established schools partly to cultivate future leaders, partly to employ qualified members and provide educational opportunities for their children, and partly to win respect in Japanese society.

Since the war, however, the religious fervor of the founding period has waned, and in the schools established after the war, the originally strong religious purpose weakened accordingly. In the middle schools and high schools, classes in religion were held once a week to provide a simple introduction to the religious body or religion. At the university level, courses to train successors for official positions were attenuated, and in some cases theological departments were discontinued. The average student at such universities was for the most part utterly indifferent as to whether their alma mater was sponsored by a religious organization.

By and large, during the decade following the war, there were numerous examples of religious education motivated by strong religious purpose, but gradually less weight was given to education of this kind. Since 1958, when classes in moral education were instituted, the fostering of religious ideals became the main form of religious education.

As a general rule, it is useful to divide religious education into three categories. One is denominational or sectarian education from the standpoint of a specific religion. The second is education in religious knowledge, and the third education that aims to foster religious ideals.

In private schools, where the religious freedom of the students was recognized, all three categories were and are possible. In national, prefectural, and municipal schools, the first category was automatically ruled out. As for education that sought to advance knowledge of religion, no problem existed. When it came to the fostering of religious ideals, however, the general attitude was that such education was permissible if it did not go too far, but there was also opposition to education of this kind. The type of education that gradually received the strongest support was the cultivation of modified, postwar religious ideals: a sense of awe before that which transcends the human, a spirit of respect for human beings, and a feeling of reverence for life.

In terms of religious education, the private schools as they presently exist can be divided into two categories. One type seeks to put religion into practice; the other promotes education and places little emphasis on practical religion. One of the main goals of the latter type, in other words, is to run a viable educational enterprise, to recruit superior students, and to earn a good reputation.

Schools of the first type were comparatively numerous before World War II, but since the war schools of the second type have come to pre-

154

dominate. Most students choose their school on the basis of its rank in relation to other schools, taking little account of whether a religious organization was involved in its founding. Schools that hold religious ceremonies explain their intention to each entering class, but this seems to pose no impediment to entering students. What they consider important is not so much the religious affiliation as the question of what percentage of a school's graduates are admitted to schools of a higher level and the related question of the difficulty of the entrance examination. Most students take the numerical value that results from the calculation of a school's rank as an indicator not only of their own academic ability but also of the degree of difficulty of the entrance examination.

Quantitatively, the number of religious organizations in the postwar period that have undertaken educational enterprises is considerable. When the number of private schools is compared to the total number of schools throughout Japan (primary schools, middle schools, high schools, junior colleges, universities, branch schools and night schools), and the number of schools operated by religious organizations is compared to the total number of schools in 1993, the percentage of private educational facilities, especially at the junior college and university level, is striking. (See Table 5.)

Qualitatively, however, many problems have arisen. According to a recent survey of high schools founded by religious organizations, nearly all such schools give required classes in religion and employ an average of three people, whether full-time or part-time, to teach them. In most cases the educational materials they use have a direct or indirect connection

TABLE 5

1993 DATA ON TYPES OF SCHOOLS

Schools	National	Public	Private	Total	Private/ Total (%)	Religious	Religious/ Private (%)	Religious/ Total (%)
Primary schools	73	24,432	171	24,676	0.7	99	57.9	0.4
Middle schools	78	10,578	636	11,292	5.6	237	37.3	2.1
High schools	17	4,164	1,320	5,501	24.0	358	27.1	6.5
Junior colleges	37	56	502	595	84.4	136	27.1	22.9
Universities	98	46	390	534	73.0	91	23.3	17.0

with the sponsoring religious body. These classes offer instruction about religion in general, but when it comes to the question of whether these classes have a positive effect, the answer is probably not. Young people have little interest in religion, and the task of stimulating religious interest in them is extremely difficult. In an information-saturated society like present-day Japan, religious education involves considerable difficulty for those charged with its teaching.

URBANIZATION, DEPOPULATION, AND RELIGION

Ishii Kenji

• RECENT DEVELOPMENTS

Urbanization is certainly one of the processes involved in modernization, but it is not generally recognized that urbanization and the depopulation which followed it have led to massive structural change in the religions of Japan. This chapter will focus on the long-established forms of religion most influenced by urbanization, namely, the Shinto shrines and the Buddhist temples.

The urbanization of Japan progressed in tandem with the industrialization that occurred after the restoration of imperial rule in 1868. From the Meiji period, when the modern Japanese state came into being, until shortly after World War II, the movement of the population from farm villages to cities was comparatively slow. During this time, the villages and cities coexisted, the villages as traditional communities, and the cities as the places where modern capitalist society was taking shape. Modernization proceeded within the parameters of this two-fold structure.

The most striking feature of Japanese urbanization was the large-scale movement of the population to Tokyo and other major cities beginning in the 1960s. Surging economic development rapidly swelled the demand for labor and swept an avalanche of people from farm, mountain, and fishing villages into the industrial areas in and around the major cities. People who had been primarily engaged in farming, fishing, forestry and the like, usually second and third sons who had graduated from secondary school, were drawn to the cities where they found employment either in the manufacturing and processing industries or in the commercial, transportation, and service industries. Between 1955 and 1970, the populations of Tokyo, Osaka, and Nagoya grew by a total of approximately fifteen million people. If one compares the number of people in agricultural employment for 1960 and 1965, the figures show that even in these five short years, over twenty percent of those who had been doing agricultural work switched to other types of employment. This will give some idea of the abruptness of the population movement and the change in industrial structure which took place at that time.

The sudden depopulation of the agricultural, fishing, and mountain villages, when publicized in a 1965 state of the nation survey, was widely taken up as a grave social problem. According to a 1988 publication issued by the Depopulated Areas Development Office of the Regional Development Bureau in the National Land Agency and entitled "The present state of affairs regarding a counterplan for depopulated areas" (*Shōwa 63 nendo kaso taisaku no genjō*), the number of cities, towns, and villages that had undergone depopulation amounted to 1,157, or 35.6% of the national total, and involved 46.2% of the total land area. "Depopulation" here refers to a condition in which the maintenance of life is threatened by population loss, a condition which includes the related difficulties of inability to rationally exploit available resources and a dramatic decline in the productive functions of a community area. More specifically, depopulation has led to deterioration in education, insurance, disaster prevention and other sectors essential to the maintenance of community. It has also led to a decline in agriculture, forestry, and fishing, and to the problem of imbalance in the age composition of a community because of the departure of the young. Within and around the major cities, moreover, it has given rise to skyrocketing land prices, housing shortages, increase in crime, pollution problems, and still other indications of environmental deterioration.

On top of all this, population movement has exercised immense influence on the structure of the Japanese family as well as on traditional communities and patterns of human relationship. The lineal-descent families typical of farm, mountain, and fishing villages have decreased, while nuclear families composed of husband, wife, and about two children have increased, as has the number of single-person households. City households, moreover, have rapidly subdivided into smaller units. The traditional community based on ties of territory and blood has disintegrated, and mass society made up of anonymous individuals has arisen in its place.

In the midst of these developments and as a result of urbanization and depopulation, the Shinto shrines, which counted the total population of particular local communities as parishioners (*ujiko*), and the Buddhist temples, which took the ancestor-venerating household (*ie*) as their basic organizational unit, have been forced to reconsider their principles and work out new organizational forms.

• BUDDHIST TEMPLES IN DEPOPULATED AREAS

The influence that depopulation exerted on Shinto shrines and Buddhist temples was immense. The Buddhist temples, in particular, suffered serious damage. Because of the sudden population movement, a great number of the Buddhist temples found themselves stranded in depopulated communities. It is helpful to look at the results of surveys conducted by two religious bodies: the Nichiren Shū and the Jōdo Shinshū Honganjiha. The Nichiren Shū survey, edited by the Nichiren Shū Contemporary Religion Research Center and published in 1989, is entitled *Kasochi ji'in chōsa hōkoku: koko made kite iru kasochi ji'in* ("Report on a survey of temples in depopulated areas: The problem of temples in depopulated areas grows worse"). This is a survey of ten areas across Japan. The Jōdo Shinshū survey, edited by the Ryūkoku University Center for Field Research on Temples in Depopulated Areas and published in 1990, is entitled *Kasochi ji'in jittai chōsa hōkokusho* ("Report on a fact-finding survey of temples in depopulated areas"). It is a questionnaire-type survey of Buddhist temples located in depleted communities.

Fukui Prefecture is one area where Nichiren Shū temples have felt the effects of depopulation keenly. Facing the Japan Sea, Fukui Prefecture has traditionally been a Jōdo Shinshū stronghold. At the same time, however, Nichizō (1269–1342), the Nichiren Shū priest who initiated the spread of Nichiren teaching in Kyoto, later devoted himself to spreading Nichiren Shū faith in Fukui Prefecture. Since then, Fukui Prefecture has produced a number of famous priests and maintained a deep and longlasting relationship with Nichiren Shū Buddhism. After World War II, Fukui Prefecture suffered from a slump in the forestry business, and to make matters worse, the rapid economic growth beginning in the 1960s brought a large proportion of younger Fukui natives flooding into the cities.

Two communities in Fukui Prefecture, Imajōmachi and Natashō-mura, were selected by the Nichiren Shū survey. In both communities the Buddhist temples were tottering. Both Imajōmachi and Natashōmura had been designated "depopulated communities." The population of Imajōmachi fell from its 1960 level of 9,299 to 5,711 in 1985. The chief occupation is farm work carried on as a sideline by elderly people. Natashōmura likewise saw its population drop from its 1960 level of 4,391 to 3,141 in 1985. Forestry accounts for 96% of the community's economic activity, but because the snowfalls are so heavy, the young people have moved to the cities. Only the elderly remain. At the present time, there are six Nichiren Shū temples in Imajōmachi and Natashōmura. The average number of supporting families per temple is 14.3, an unusually low figure even for Nichiren Shū temples. The number of supporting families has fallen drastically. Families that long supported their temple are now reduced to members in the upper age-brackets. If a couple dies or goes to the city to live with their eldest son, the temple loses one supporting family. This is the situation these temples faced according to the 1989 Nichiren Shū survey. With the continuing depopulation trend, their situation today is, if anything, worse.

None of the six Nichiren Shū temples in Imajōmachi and Natashō-mura has a successor to take over from the priest in charge. A successor is vital to the maintenance of a temple's religious activities. The first reason the temples have no successors has to do with their difficulty in making ends meet, a difficulty that stems, again, from the decline in the number of supporting families. Two of the six priests hold concurrent positions elsewhere, but even among the temples with full-time priests, several priests rely on pensions or other forms of income independent of temple income. Because of the decrease in supporting families and the advanced age of the families that remain, the priests, unable to live on the meager income that temple activities bring in, are barely able to sustain their own lives. In the second place, there is now a tendency for supporting families with diminished income to look with disfavor on the idea of a full-time priest. If the priest is full-time, the financial burden on each supporting family is that much heavier. Thirdly, because the customs and conventions traditional to everyday life in rural villages are far removed from those of modern life, the younger members of a potential priest's family fear too much interference with their privacy—a generation-gap conflict of lifestyle.

The Nichiren Shū report, after analyzing the present state of affairs, concludes that "in Fukui Prefecture ten or twenty years from now, it is almost certain that there will be an increase in the number of temples without priests, and it is feared that there may be grave consequences for the winning of new Nichiren Shū members in Fukui Prefecture in future."

The Jōdo Shinshū Honganjiha report is based on a questionnaire directed to some two thousand Buddhist temples located in what the Geographical Survey Agency has designated as depopulated areas. Of these two thousand, approximately twenty percent are Jōdo Shinshū Honganjiha temples. In terms of historical development, the Jōdo Shinshū Honganjiha has traditionally won the bulk of its members from people living in farm, mountain, and fishing villages. Geographically, its temple distribution is strongest in the Kinki districts (Kyoto, Osaka, Mie,

Shiga, Hyōgo, Nara, and Wakayama prefectures) and westward. There is considerable overlap between its temple distribution and the areas that the Geographical Survey Agency has designated as depopulated.

Of the Jōdo Shinshū Honganjiha temples in depopulated areas, over 60% are located in remote mountain hamlets, only 26% in flatland communities. The average number of supporting households for the temples in depopulated areas is seventy-five, though some temples have no supporting households whatever. Questionnaire replies show that as compared with the number of supporting households thirty years ago, 77.1% of these temples registered a decline. Only 2.2% of the temples registered a gain. Many priests expect that in years to come the number of supporting households will decline even further and the proportion of household members in upper-age brackets will increase.

This decline in the number of supporting households is having a major effect on the educational activities of the temples. Reports indicate deleterious effects not only in the Buddhist youth groups, children's groups, and Sunday schools but also in the women's groups and men's groups. As for future prospects, one temple in five replied "we can't see any way out." Reports predict a gloomy future for these depopulated communities, for there is almost no prospect of future development.

These examples of depopulation and consequent change in Nichiren Shū and Jōdo Shinshū Honganjiha temples permit a more general statement. Conditions like these arise because of a gap between the temple distribution pattern that existed until now and the recent change in population distribution that accompanied the change in social structure. This problem is not limited to the Nichiren Shū and Jōdo Shinshū Honganjiha, but affects all the schools of Japanese Buddhism. From these Nichiren Shū and Jōdo Shinshū Honganjiha examples, we may draw a more general picture of the process of change in temples located in depopulated areas.

As population declines, the temples experience an immediate backlash in the form of a decline in the number of supporting households. As a result, the financial basis for temple operations and the subsistence of a priest and his family become precarious. In this situation, the priest must choose among three possibilities: (1) he may continue as priest but take a concurrent position as priest, or substitute priest, at another temple; (2) he may continue as priest but seek employment outside Buddhism as well; or (3) he may change his occupation entirely, in which case the temple will have no priest. Among priests who choose either the first or the second possibility, there is a tendency to live away from the temple, and thus there are many temples without a resident priest. With regard to educational activities, it is obvious that major cutbacks are unavoidable. In several cases, the temple has been abandoned and has fallen into ruin. If present trends continue, the 1989 survey predicts, it is expected that the number of Nichiren Shū temples will diminish from five thousand to three thousand.

When it comes to the question of a method by which to bridge the gap between population movement and temple distribution, one idea is for temples in depopulated areas to move to the cities. The rapid increase in the urban population has produced the converse of the problem experienced by depopulated communities: an insufficient number of temples. In order to correct this imbalance, it seems advisable to relocate the temples in accordance with the present distribution of the population. In fact, however, many difficulties stand in the way. The financial straits of temples in depopulated areas find their reverse image in the inflated land prices of the cities, a situation which makes it financially difficult to establish new temples in urban areas. Also, the strong sense of territorial rights among existing urban temples likewise acts as an obstacle to the establishing of new temples. All in all, none of the schools of Japanese Buddhism are making much progress in this regard.

• URBANIZATION AND SHINTO SHRINES

The flow of population into the cities that began with the concentration of industry in urban areas entered a new phase after the oil crisis of the 1970s, when economic growth turned sluggish. Even in this situation, however, urbanization did not slow down; in some cases it actually accelerated. Something of a U-turn occurred during the 1970s, when many people turned their backs on the cities and returned to the country. But the 1980s once again saw a strong flow into the major cities. Even more rural cities with relatively stable populations saw slight increases, but the significant growth took place in Tokyo and other metropolitan centers. What with the enlargement of Tokyo's daytime population, the even greater concentration of urban functions, the increase in land prices and their restabilization at a higher level, the growth of the "doughnut" phenomenon of depopulation in the heart of a city, and the complementary "sprawl" phenomenon of rising population in surrounding areas—all this suggests that urbanization had entered a new stage. Moreover, the emergence of young people so different from their parents as to give rise to the expression *shinjinrui* ("a new type of human being") is an indicator of the degree to which urbanization caused structural changes in daily life and even in the dimension of consciousness.

For Shrine Shinto, as compared to Japanese Buddhism and Christianity, urbanization was a far more serious problem because it affected the fundamental structure of Shrine Shinto. That is to say, Shrine Shinto emerged from the soil of the agricultural village and had grown deep roots in Japanese agricultural traditions. It is closely connected with traditional Japanese culture in attaching great value to the idea of harmony with nature. The shrine parishioners of rural areas, offered strikingly high prices for their land but watching their residential environment deteriorate, moved to the outskirts of the cities. In these urban areas, moreover, clusters of immense apartment buildings went up, and new residents moved in at one sweep. This high degree of population mobility resulted, on the one hand, in a weakening of the awareness of being an *ujiko*, or member of a community under the protection of a common deity, and on the other, in the collapse of shrine-parishioner organizations. In consequence, the shrines in the cities were driven toward a transformation which would shake them to the core.

For the Japanese, New Year's Day (and the next two or three days) is a markedly religious event. With little or no sense of membership in a religious organization, people flock to Shinto shrines and Buddhist temples at this unusual time. According to National Police Agency statistics, the total number of people who visited shrines and temples during the first three days of 1996 came to about 87,660,000, a gain of some 2,450,000 people over the previous year. If we ignore the theoretical possibility that one person may go to several shrines and temples, it turns out that two out of every three Japanese people visit a shrine or temple at New Year's.

These immense numbers of people visiting a shrine or temple for the new year have tended, in recent years, to go to certain well-known shrines in major cities. The weakened sense of identity as an *ujiko* has led to the practice of visiting not the shrine in their neighborhood but one of the big-name shrines. One result of the concentration of population in the cities, then, is a new pattern of shrine visitation whereby people who had once gone to small local shrines at New Year's now flock to a comparatively small number of major shrines.

The harsh environment urbanization has created does not affect the large shrines as much as the small ones. In this scenario of small shrines losing their parishioners as people stream to the big shrines, numerous examples have arisen since the 1980s of local shrines that transfer their religio-economic basis of support from parishioners to something else. An increasing number of these shrines, in order to obtain a sound financial footing, have turned the area under the sanctuary into a parking lot, or converted large sections of the shrine grounds into apartments for rent or building lots.

Ontaké Shrine, located in the Shibuya Ward of Tokyo, was erected during the early part of the Muromachi period (1336–1573) and in later years achieved such prominence that even the Emperor Meiji visited the shrine. It was destroyed, however, during World War II, and even though it later put up a temporary sanctuary, great numbers of its parishioners moved to the suburbs as a bustling business and shopping district developed near the shrine. Some years ago, it began to have difficulty maintaining its dilapidated sanctuary. In 1980 Shibuya Ward, which was searching for a building site for the Chamber of Commerce and Industry, and Ontaké Shrine, which wanted to rebuild its sanctuary, recognized that their interests dovetailed. Their agreement resulted in the erection of a stepped building seven stories high at the highest level, the shrine being relocated on the roof of the three-story level. Thanks to earnings from rents and leases, the shrine has now acquired a secure source of income that guarantees the possibility of semipermanent existence. Ontaké Shrine still continues to hold its annual festival with the help of the few remaining parishioners, but those who shoulder the palanquin, or scaled-down portable shrine (*mikoshi*), are not parishioners but employees of intraparish companies responding to requests from the shrine.

Ontaké Shrine exemplifies the type of shrine that gives priority to sound financial support but is rather passive about coming to grips with urbanization. Another type, however, is that which actively seeks continued existence for an *ujigami jinja*, or shrine that honors the guardian deity (*ujigami*) of a particular territory, by deliberately drawing worshipers from afar. Shrines of this type, instead of relying on parishioners who live within a particular area, try to attract people who will come to worship regardless of their place of residence. In order to achieve this goal, it becomes necessary to claim something unique about the faith of this particular shrine. It becomes necessary, in other words, to dream up a selling point and actively promote it.

Koami Shrine, located in the Nihonbashi Koamichō section of Tokyo's Chūō Ward, is similar to Ontaké Shrine in that it was established during the Muromachi period, but it flourished as a shrine honoring a guardian deity for local craftsmen. With the emergence of the "doughnut" phenomenon in the 1960s, however, the number of parishioners dropped from a thousand households to the current two hundred and fifty. The neighborhood filled up with office buildings, and the sanctuary was buried in their shadow. Because of the decrease in parishioners (despite the increase in the daytime population), it became impossible to hold even such commonplace rituals as the *hatsumiya mōde*, in which a couple presents their recently born child to the *ujigami* and tacitly beseeches his favor and protection, or the mid-November *shichi go san*, in which three- and five-year-old boys and three- and seven-year-old girls are dressed up and presented to the *ujigami* in token of gratitude for their healthy growth.

Confronted by these conditions, Koami Shrine came up with a number of ideas. Taking Chūō Ward as its frame of reference, it proposed a "Pilgrimage to Eight Downtown Shrines" and a "Pilgrimage to the Seven Gods of Good Fortune." Forming eight small shrines into one group and seven others into another, it sought to bring out their individuality and attract worshipers. Again, in order to make its festivals into significant events, it actively recruited the cooperation of business enterprises in the parish. In consequence of such efforts, there was a conspicuous increase in the number of people who came to worship at the shrine during the New Year season, not least because cooperating businesses observed their annual "beginning of work" ritual by having employees make a group visit to the shrine. The participation of these enterprises in the major shrine festivals, moreover, has made them bustling, cheerful affairs. The priest claims that for city shrines it is essential not to have laconic priests with a negative attitude toward what a priest or a shrine ought to be, but priests of individual character who will give clear explanations of the rituals the shrine observes.

For traditional Shrine Shinto, these transformations in the guardian-deity shrines signify a shaking of the foundations. In particular, the metamorphosis in the external appearance of these shrines has shocked the Shinto world. Ontaké Shrine is not the only case in point. Hachikan Shrine (1982) and the Asahi Inari Shrine (1984) in the Ginza district of Tokyo's Chūō Ward are just two examples of the growing number of shrines that have torn down their old sanctuary and built a new one as part of a modern building. It is generally held that one essential condition of a shrine is that the inner sanctuary (*honden*), the dwelling place of the *kami*, be in direct contact with the earth and have nothing above its roof except the sky. Moving guardian-deity shrines into high-rise buildings involves a major change not only in their external appearance but also in their very nature.

The postwar city improvement and road planning carried out by the national and local governments, together with the buying up of land by major investors and the construction of clusters of towering buildings, effected major changes in the shrine environment. As the buildings around them grew higher and higher, the shrines suffered a loss of dignity. What originally gave a shrine its stateliness was that its pillars were larger and its ornamental crossbeams higher than anything found in ordinary residences. But a shrine that finds itself at the bottom of a chasm of high-rise buildings, far from commanding the view, is now looked down on. In addition, there are many shrines that have had to whittle away their grounds in order to accommodate city improvement and road planning arrangements. Urbanization has created an environment which threatens the preservation of the shrine as a sacred space. Moreover, in order to be sure of a secure financial base, many shrines have had to build and rent apartments and offices or undertake the management of parking lots. The shrines have taken secular space into themselves, where they have not transmuted their own sacred space into secular space.

• URBANIZATION AND BUDDHIST TEMPLES

The damage that urbanization inflicted on Buddhist temples in the cities appears to have been less serious than that suffered by Shinto shrines. In contrast to the parishioners of a guardian-deity shrine, the supporting households (*danka*) of a temple do not necessarily reside within a particular area. Nonetheless, as land prices skyrocketed and supporting households moved one after the other to the suburbs, the distance between the temple and its households became too great to sustain a close relationship. In practical terms, the priest found it impossible to pay a monthly visit to the home of each household on the day commemorating a death in the family. As a result, the times when members of supporting families went to the temple came to be limited to *higan*, the equinoctial weeks in March and September when people visit their ancestral graves, and *bon*, the midsummer Feast for the Dead. This led in turn to a weakening of identification with a particular temple.

Brought face to face with the departure of supporting households, the difficulty of initiating new programs for the spread of Buddhist teaching in the city, and abrupt leaps in land prices, many temples, like their Shinto counterparts, have chosen to build parking lots on the temple grounds or construct apartment and office buildings. Since their restrictions on the use of sacred space are less stringent than those of Shinto shrines, in that they are not required by tradition to rest on the earth and have open sky above them, Buddhist temple-building projects tend to be large-scale.

Myōzenji temple, a Nichiren Shū temple located in the Roppongi district of Tokyo's Minato Ward, constructed a large apartment building on its grounds in 1987, using a land-equivalence exchange formula. Myōzenji temple goes back to the early years of the Tokugawa, or Edo, period (1603–1868), but when it became necessary to rebuild the main sanctuary, the temple came up with the idea of erecting an apartment building in order to ease the financial burden on supporting households and establish a sound financial basis for the future. From the street, the temple is invisible. It is only by passing through the entrance to the apartment complex that one arrives at the temple and its graveyard.

Tokyo is not the only place where temples are associated with high-rise buildings. In Kyoto, the Akamon Shōgakuji temple of the Jōdo Shū put up a five-story building in 1989 and rebuilt both the temple and its cemetery on the roof. Since the temple grounds exist in Kyoto's prime commercial district, pressure mounted for the temple to evacuate the premises. The price for 1,200 square meters of temple land went as high as one hundred billion yen (in 1989, approximately 725 million U.S. dollars). The temple chose to remain where it was, but because it could not survive with its small number of supporting households, it was forced to establish its own financial basis of operations. This is why it erected the five-story building, leasing space to a sushi bar, a pub, and boutiques. Akamon Shōgakuji temple has chosen to remain a city temple, and there are other instances of this type as well. But there are also many examples of another type. A number of temples in Kyoto and Osaka, caught between the Scylla of decreasing supporters and the Charybdis of rising land prices, have chosen to move to the suburbs.

If the tendency on the part of many temples to use their land to guarantee their continued existence is characterized as passive, it should also be noted that in the highly mobile urban situation, some temples have undertaken to spread Buddhist teaching actively. Instead of relying on the dead to mediate their ties with the living, instead of depending solely on funerals and graveyards, on *bon* and *higan*, these temples and priests are venturing to establish deeper bonds with living supporters. Some participate in a telephone counseling service known as *Inochi no denwa*, or Lifeline. Some promote Buddhist weddings, heretofore the preserve of Shinto and Christianity. Some sponsor cultural events like art shows and concerts. As yet, however, it appears that these efforts have not been enough to reverse the difficult situation urban temples continue to face.

• URBANIZATION AND NEW RELIGIONS

It was the new religions that blossomed most rapidly in urban centers during the period of meteoric economic growth in the 1960s. Among the new religions, some, like Sōka Gakkai and Risshō Kōseikai, became mammoth organizations. Risshō Kōseikai had 1,410,000 members in 1955, but reported 2,500,000 members in 1965, 4,840,000 members in 1970, and nearly 6,500,000 members in 1993. Sōka Gakkai had 1,500,000 households in 1960, and by 1970 its membership had grown five-fold to 7,550,000 households. It currently reports 8,030,000 Japanese member households, and 12,602,000 individual members outside Japan.

The people who joined new religious organizations had once maintained ties with a Buddhist temple in their home villages, but on moving to the city had formed no new temple connection. In addition they had experienced a weakening of the traditional bonds with their birthplaces and old friends. In short, they formed a "religiously floating population." For these drifting new urbanites learning to fend for themselves in the midst of a society based on anonymous relationships, the new religions offered new life-patterns and ways of thinking. While satisfying their expectations with regard to immediate, tangible benefits, the new religions also provided concrete resources for the overcoming of hardships and a sense of substitute community.

• CONCLUSION

According to a survey entitled *Nihonjin no shūkyō ishiki,* or "The religious consciousness of the Japanese people" (Tokyo: Nippon Hōsō Shuppan Kyōkai, 1984), the more remote a rural town or village is, the more its people tend to be "religious," whereas in the larger metropolitan centers like Tokyo and Osaka people tend to be "non-religious." This trend appears in typical form in the answers to two questions, both of which have to do with religious practices found among Japanese people in general. One question asks whether the respondent makes grave visits at *higan* and *bon,* the other how often the respondent offers worship before the *kamidana,* or household altar to the Shinto kami. The results are shown in Graphs 1 and 2.

In the *Kokuminsei no kenkyū* (Studies of Japanese national character) published every five years by the Institute for Statistical Research, the same trend is clear. Over the years, with few exceptions, there has been a diminishing percentage of people in the six largest cities who answer "Yes" to the question "Do you believe in a religion?" Moreover, even though the answers given by people in the six largest cities have not always ranked lowest, in the two surveys conducted during the last ten years they have been lower than those of any other area. The answers to

GRAPH 1

Grave Visits at *Bon* and *Higan*

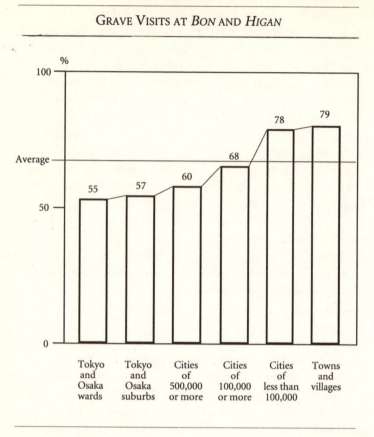

the question "Do you consider religion important?" show the same tendency. The largest cities have become places with the smallest percentage of people who believe in a religion.

Nihonjin no shūkyō ishiki offers two reasons to explain the contrast between the high percentage of people in towns, villages, and small cities who engage in religious behavior and think of themselves as religious, and the low percentage of people in big cities who identify themselves in this way. The first has to do with the relationship between humans and nature. When nature shows that its power far exceeds that of human beings, people become conscious of religion and perform religious acts. This kind of relationship with nature is stronger in towns and villages than in big cities, so the religious tendency is more pronounced among

GRAPH 2

FREQUENCY OF WORSHIP BEFORE THE *KAMIDANA*

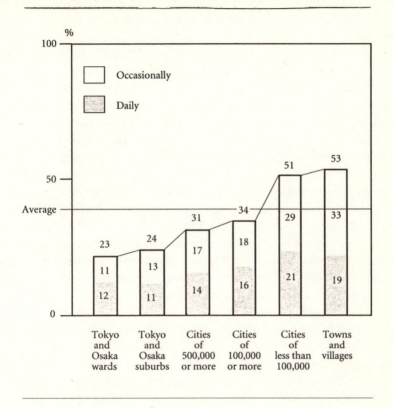

the people in these areas. The second reason has to do with shrine and temple support organizations. The *ujiko soshiki*, or organization of parishioners supporting the Shinto shrine, and the *danka seido*, or organization of households supporting the Buddhist temple, play a stronger and more central role in town and village life than they do in the big cities. These organizations, moreover, not only give meaning to such practices as grave visits and acts of worship before the household *kami* altar but also make them habitual and customary. Generalizing from these two reasons, *Nihonjin no shūkyō ishiki* suggests that for Japanese religion, depending as it does on community and custom, the small town and village provide a more viable climate than the big city.

In consequence of the urbanization that began in the 1960s, people have been cut off from their home temples and now belong to none. By the same token, they have been cut off from the *ujigami*, or guardian deity, that bound them to traditional forms of community, and they now form a religiously floating population. The cities, moreover, are producing day by day an environment that makes it difficult for traditional religion to survive.

Even today, to be sure, people must face the problem of what to do about a grave when a close relative dies, and there are people who, seeking a community where they can enjoy peace of mind, attach themselves to one of the established religions. Among the traditional religions there are some that try to cope with the chronic shortage of cemetery plots by enlarging an existing graveyard or developing parklike cemeteries in the suburbs. In the huge apartment complexes where people born and raised in different areas live side by side, there are some attempts to reintroduce an *ujigami*. There are also attempts to introduce dialogue about Buddhism in a coffee shop setting where people can speak more informally than in a temple. In order to spread the teaching of Buddhism, some people have formed computer networks, others have produced videos, animated cartoons, and comic books. In these and other ways they actively seek to appeal to people through the use of multimedia resources.

In perspective, however, these activities affect only a fraction of the whole. For people in the big cities, interest in religion is growing weaker. Even the ritual acts that bring city dwellers in touch with established religion—praying at a Shinto shrine during the New Year season, taking three-, five-, and seven-year-old children to a shrine for a *shichi go san* ceremony, and visiting the family grave and Buddhist temple at *bon* and *higan*—are losing their religious meaning and tending toward the customary and conventional.

ASPECTS OF THE REBIRTH
OF RELIGION

Shimazono Susumu

• FROM DECLINE TO REBIRTH

The influence of religion has waned in Japanese society, and the chances are that it will continue to wane in future. This was the view that postwar scholars and intellectuals took for granted until the 1970s. In fact, however, the new religions grew spectacularly during the 1950s and 1960s. Sōka Gakkai reported only a few thousand members in the early 1950s, but by 1970 it claimed over 7,500,000 member households. During this period many other new religions also won members at a phenomenal pace. Nonetheless, their growth was not regarded as signifying the rebirth of religion. The prevailing idea was that the new religions were vestiges of the premodern period, to be found only among a small group of people with low incomes and a low level of education. Scholars assumed that the trend of Japanese society was toward the decline of religion.

This view was not entirely mistaken. Public opinion surveys provided strong evidence for the religious decline theory. For example, the Japan Broadcasting Corporation has a Public Opinion Research Division that conducts a survey every five years. One of the standard questions is: "Do you yourself belong to a religion?" The number of people who responded in the affirmative was 35% in 1958, 31% in 1963, 30% in 1968, and 25% in 1973—a steady decline. It is easy to see why this should be so when we recall that this was the period when educational influence grew by leaps and bounds. The number of high school students increased from 1,200,000 in 1948 to 4,230,000 in 1970, and the number of junior college and university students from 120,000 in 1948 to 1,670,000 in 1970. One result of this rapid educational growth was wide dissemination of the world view of rationalistic enlightenment, including faith in the development of modern science and a secular state. During the twenty-five year period following the end of World War II, the spirit of enlightenment-period rationalism inundated Japanese society.

Despite the support it received from educational institutions and the media, this world view had only limited influence. The religious outlook of ordinary people incorporated certain features of the scientific world view, and adopted some new ideas, but it remained basically intact. The growth of the new religions is a manifestation of its survival. Thus it was that until the 1970s, intellectuals and opinion polls continued to confirm the decline of religion in Japan, while the everyday faith of ordinary people, exemplified by the new religions, not only proved tenacious but even showed signs of renewed strength.

This state of affairs seems to have changed from about the middle of the 1970s. By the 1980s, scholars and journalists were making frequent use of terms such as "religious boom," "the return of religion," and "the rebirth of religion." Moreover, as of 1990, it was generally held that this new trend showed no sign of stopping. But is this really the case? If so, what kinds of religion are growing in strength? And what kinds of changes are taking place in the structure of Japanese religion as a whole? These are the questions this chapter will address.

• EVIDENCE FOR THE REBIRTH OF RELIGION

The most important reason why scholars and journalists began to speak of "the rebirth of religion" has to do with public opinion survey results. According to the Japan Broadcasting Corporation's Public Opinion Research Division survey mentioned above, the number of people who replied "I belong to a religion" was a low 25% in 1973, but by 1978 had risen to 34%. Since then it has fallen again to 26% in 1994, but most surveys taken during the 1980s reported percentages in the low thirties. During the 1990s, increasing awareness that a religious organization should not pursue its own advancement to the exclusion of others has led to a decline in the number of respondents who affirm adherence to a specific religion. It should be noted, however, that religious publications—not those of specific religions such as Buddhism, Christianity, or the new religions but those on "religious questions" and "spirituality"—increased dramatically during the 1980s and the first half of the 1990s.

Two or three other survey questions also elicited significant data. One question was "During the past year or so, have you gone to a shrine or temple to pray for your own safety, for prosperity in business, or for success in entrance examinations?" In 1973 only 23.0% gave affirmative answers to this question, but in 1978 the figure rose to 31.2%, in 1983 to 31.6%. The 1994 figure was still a high 31.0%. A separate item asked people whether they could affirm the statement "Nothing I do has any connection with religion or faith." In 1973 15.4% of the respondents agreed. In 1978 the percentage fell to 11.7%, in 1983 to 9.6%, and in 1994 to 6.5% (data from the Institute of Statistical Mathematics and the *Yomiuri Shimbun*). As these data show, people in the 1990s show an increasingly pronounced tendency not to associate themselves with any particular religion. When it comes to religious behavior, however, no such tendency can be observed.

With regard to these ideas about religion and religious behavior, it is interesting to note that percentages are conspicuously high among young people, those who will lead society in the future. In the 1983 survey by the Japan Broadcasting Corporation, one item asked respondents to indicate whether they agreed with the statement: "Souls, or spirits, definitely exist." Of those who agreed, 57% were between ten and nineteen years of age, 36% were in their twenties, 28% in their thirties, 23% in their forties, 27% in their fifties, 34% in their sixties, and 31% in their seventies or above. Properly speaking, the data need to be analyzed not only in terms of the influence of age groups but also in terms of the influence of changes in the times, but even without going into detail, it is clear that young people of recent years show more interest in religion than their elders. On the basis of these statistics, it seems plausible to affirm evidence for the rebirth of religion.

It can be argued, of course, that these results indicate nothing more than a return to the level of about 1960. Yet even so, we still have to ask why there has been so much talk of a "religious boom" and the "return of religion." Surely this is because matters that command the attention of journalists and scholars, especially religious matters relevant to mass media and scholarship, have become increasingly important. It seems that the mass media and academia, after twenty-five postwar years under the influence of rationalistic education, changed drastically beginning in the 1970s and are now inclined to give serious consideration to religion. For this reason, the rebirth of religion looms larger, in the eyes of scholars and journalists, than social trends in general.

If it is accepted that the media have played a major role in the rebirth of religion, the reason for the religious awakening found among young people soon becomes clear. In recent years youth culture has been increasingly led by the ideas and attitudes of the mass media. During the 1970s and 1980s, this closeness between youth and the media seems to have enhanced the process by which a new religious culture took shape. But before taking up this matter, it is important to consider the changes that have occurred both in the new religions that grew so conspicuously during the 1950s and 1960s and in the folk religion from which they sprang.

• "OLD" NEW RELIGIONS AND "NEW" NEW RELIGIONS
In the history of the new religions, the 1970s mark the end of a period. It was from about this time that the leading new religious organizations, which had grown precipitously during the twenty-five years following the end of World War II, reached a plateau. Sōka Gakkai, for example, hit a peak of 7,500,000 households in 1970, but in the years that followed grew very little. In the case of Reiyūkai, Sekai Kyūseikyō, Seichō no Ie, P.L. Kyōdan, and Risshō Kōseikai, it is a little more difficult to infer this change from the statistics, but there is clearly a slowdown if not an outright stagnation in membership. Some languishing groups have even lost members. These membership changes seem to be related to the emerging tendency toward individualism—a matter discussed in some detail below.

On the other hand, however, there are also organizations that recorded conspicuous growth beginning around 1970. Shinnyoen is one example. This group was established in 1936 by Itō Shinjō (1906–1989) and his wife Tomoji (1912–1967). The membership increased steadily and was officially reported as approximately 125,000 in 1965. But by 1975 the membership had increased to 300,000, by 1985 to 1,816,000, and by 1989 to 2,596,000. In this short period of time Shinnyoen had become one of the most prominent religious organizations. Other groups that experienced rapid growth during this period, even though they did not become as large as Shinnyoen, include Sekai Mahikari Bunmei Kyōdan (which split off from Sūkyō Mahikari in 1978 and is generally referred to as "Mahikari"), Agonshū, the God Light Association, Ōyama Nezu no Mikoto Shinji Kyōkai, Reiha no Hikari Kyōkai, Byakkō Shinkōkai, and Kōfuku no Kagaku. Groups that originated outside Japan but, once imported, made rapid strides during this period are Sekai Kirisutokyō Tōitsu Shinrei Kyōkai (The Holy Spirit Association for the Unification of World Christianity) and Jehovah's Witnesses. None of these organizations, however, became as large as Shinnyoen. (As of 1989, Ōyama Nezu no Mikoto Shinji Kyōkai at 779,000 and Reiha no Hikari Kyōkai at 739,000 were the largest.) Compared with the organizations that became powerful between 1945 and 1970, though, these groups remain rather small.

The idea of categorizing these religious groups differently from those whose growth ended about 1970 emerged in the late 1970s or early 1980s among scholars and journalists. They called these groups "new" new religions. This implied that the new religious groups whose period of spectacular growth ended around 1970 were to be considered "old" new religions. Precisely to what extent the new new religions differ from the old and to what extent they exhibit novel characteristics of their own is a matter of dispute. Scholars agree, however, that certain features stand out.

First, some organizations attach importance to mystical performances and to physical experiences involving alteration of the senses or of consciousness. For example, Mahikari has a ritual known as *tekazashi* in which, it is said, the transcendent power of the deity Su is channeled through the palm of a believer into the body and spirit of another person, thus effecting purification and healing. When this mystical light is transmitted to the faithful, many experience an enhanced sense of awareness. In the enactment of this mystical experience, the spirit that dwells within the body takes control of the conscious mind and gives vent to previously suppressed sufferings. Many believers also testify that *tekazashi* is important for the corroboration of faith. In Shinnyoen there is a practice called *sesshin*. There are hundreds of mediums in this organization, and in *sesshin* a medium enters a trance-like state, changes into a being of the spirit world, and communicates spirit-messages to the believer. For many believers, an important goal of the life of faith is to experience this transcendent power through deeper faith, thus achieving the status of a medium. In the God Light Association an important step in the deepening of faith is to recover the memory of a previous life and speak in the language of the person one used to be. Since the previous incarnation spoke a different language, the present-day person must speak in tongues. It is said, for exampie, that one who remembers that her previous existence was in ancient India will be able to speak one of the languages of ancient India.

Second, instead of emphasizing an intimate community of faith and a tightly knit organization, several "new" new religions tend to emphasize the freedom and autonomy of individual adherents. Agonshū, the God Light Association, and Ōyama Nezu no Mikoto Shinji Kyōkai exemplify this tendency. These groups downplay the importance of discussion meetings for believers, relationships between leaders of the faith and their spiritual "children," and giving people positions of responsibility and counting on them to contribute to the administration of the organization. To make up for the tenuous ties between believers, they bind individual adherents directly to the center through the use of mass media such as journals and videos. Here the daily life of adherents involves almost no religious restrictions.

Third, in diametrical opposition to the second point, there are also "new" new religions with extremely close-knit organizations which form communes or the like with distinctive patterns of thought and behavior permeating every dimension of daily life. This tendency is particularly evident in the Holy Spirit Association for the Unification of World Christianity, Jehovah's Witnesses, and Aum Shinrikyō. These three organizations resemble each other in another way too, for they all have a strong sense of imminent eschatological crisis. The Yamagishi Kai is a somewhat different kind of group. Organized in the wake of World War II, it began in farm villages as a movement to promote poultry raising, but developed into a utopian movement. It does not put forward religious ideas as such, but in seeking to actualize utopia through the reform of the human spirit, it bears a close resemblance to a religious movement. During the 1970s and later it attracted quite a number of university students, who left their studies and plunged into communal life. The three groups people came to regard as socially problematic were the Holy Spirit Association for the Unification of World Christianity, Yamagishi Kai, and Aum Shinrikyō. The reasons vary with the group. The Holy Spirit Association for the Unification of World Christianity was believed to use its young people to sell vases and family seals at exorbitant prices with promises of spiritual benefits. The Yamagishi Kai was accused of deceptive solicitation and mind control. Aum Shinrikyō was regarded as a dangerous mix of drug-related methods for attaining enlightenment, violence toward critics and disobedient members, and the threat of terrorism toward society at large. Common to all was intense stress between believer and family, a strained relationship that most Japanese people deem incompatible with a religious organization.

The foregoing characteristics seem particularly prominent in the "new" new religions, but this does not mean that they were completely absent in the pre-1970 new religions. The first characteristic, attaching importance to mystical performances and alteration of consciousness, was conspicuous in Ōmoto until about 1920, in Reiyūkai, founded in 1930, and, for a time, in the post-1945 Sekai Kyūseikyō. The second feature, a weak organizational network and community, appeared in Seichō no Ie in 1930 when it came into being and continued at least into the 1970s. The third characteristic, a closely knit organizational structure and common life, is quite conspicuous in Tenrikyō, Sōka Gakkai, and Risshō Kōseikai. It is impossible, therefore, to regard these characteristics of the "new" new religions as radically different from those of the earlier new religions.

To be sure, these characteristics appear in pronounced form in the "new" new religions. Moreover, because the "new" new religions do not stress the idea of solidarity in hardship and suffering, horizontal bonds among the faithful are weak. In addition, the "new" new religions do not show much regard for rituals or doctrines or ethical practices intended to strengthen human ties. They reflect the religious individualism of contemporary Japanese society. Nonetheless, when one compares the "old" and the "new" new religions with respect to the features they hold in common, these differences become trivial. It is best to consider the "new" new religions as an addition to the list of previously existing new religions. The new religions have become increasingly diverse, but on the whole, there has been no major change in their standing.

• The "Little Gods" of Folk Religion

As mentioned above, the year 1970 or thereabouts signals a change in the new religions, but this change cannot be described as major. The new religions do not play the leading role in what is spoken of as the rebirth of religion. It is among groups that do not take the form of religious organizations, rather, that the substance of the rebirth of religion is to be found.

The phrase "little gods" served as the overall title for a series of articles presented in the *Asahi Shimbun*, a major newspaper, in 1984. It refers primarily to people who work as professional shamans and attract a comparatively small number of followers in obscure corners of major cities. When such a shamanistic leader and his or her followers grow beyond a certain number and formally organize themselves as a group, they naturally form a new religious organization. The term "little gods" has to do with a prior stage. At this stage the group has neither doctrines nor formal organization. It is a contemporary manifestation of folk religion that aims to provide solutions for a limited range of human difficulties and places a high value on direct communication with the sacred. Folk religion is not something that dies out in the cities. On the contrary, it remains extremely active and even continues to develop. The results of various scholars' research into the temples, shrines, and shamanistic groups of Ikomayama, a mountain center with which the citizens of Osaka and neighboring cities have close ties, were made public almost simultaneously and attracted great attention for showing that folk religion is still alive and active. It was research of this kind that gave rise to the term *chîsana kamigami*, or "little gods." The fact that belief in concrete benefits in answer to prayer remains active in folk religion was confirmed both by this research and by the public opinion survey referred to above.

It is probable, then, that the rebirth of religion includes newly active forms of folk religion. But just as it would be a mistake to overemphasize the "new" new religions, so it would also be a mistake to exaggerate the importance of the "little gods." In Japanese religious history belief in such powers has always been fairly strong. Even with the advance of modernization and urbanization after the Meiji Restoration, this did not change. In rural areas it was taken for granted that people suffering from illness would first consult someone with shamanistic powers. Only recently have such people started to entrust themselves completely to medical doctors. In the cities, where medical services were more advanced and regulations governing folk religious practices were more stringent, fewer people looked to folk religion for healing. In these cities, where folk religion was often denigrated as a vestige of premodern society, scholars and journalists paid it little attention.

• THE SPREAD OF INDIVIDUALISTIC RELIGION THROUGH THE MEDIA

To say that the rebirth of religion includes both the rise of the "new" new religions and the revitalization of the little gods is no doubt correct. But the most important component in the rebirth of religion is the individualistic religion that relies on the agency of mass media. More than the established religions or the new religions, it is the growth of this individualistic religion that characterizes Japanese religious history since the 1970s. That this form of religion is not absolutely novel must be admitted at the outset, but in terms of scale, its explosive growth exceeds anything that went before.

Individualistic religion can be roughly divided into two types. One has to do with occult "commodities," things people buy and use that begin as objects of amusement or curiosity and eventually embody a belief in magic oriented to the pursuit of immediate benefits. The other is what should perhaps be called a "Spirit World movement" that relates to the intellectual exploration of the self. There is a close connection between these two types, and they are also closely involved with the "little gods" and the "new" new religions. But for the sake of an overall view, it will be easier to consider the "occult boom," the "Spirit World movement," the "little gods," and the "new" new religions separately.

About the middle of the 1970s, mystical phenomena and superhuman powers became wildly popular in television, movies, magazines, cartoons, and videos (see Nishiyama Shigeru et al., eds., *Gendaijin no shūkyō* [Tokyo: Yūhikaku, 1988]). After the American magician Yuri Geller demonstrated his spoon-bending techniques on television, a number of Japanese children appeared on television to show that they too had spoon-bending power—which became a widespread conversation topic. Among movies, "The Exorcist" (1974) and "Poltergeist" (1982) exemplify this trend, as do such occult magazines as *Mū* and *Twilight Zone*, founded in 1979 and 1983 respectively. In 1980 the movie actor Tanba Tetsurō published a book called *Tanba Tetsurō no shisha no sho* (The Book of the Dead according to Tanba Tetsurō) in which he gave an account of the reality of life after death. The book became a bestseller. In 1987 he made a movie entitled "Daireikai" (The Spirit World) that gave him considerable notoriety as a star of the occult. Throughout the 1980s, trade in occult amusement commodities was a brisk and growing industry.

But occult commodities did not stop at amusement. In many cases they were used to fulfill desires and solve various problems. Young people with an interest in superhuman powers, eager to win the favor of a friend or succeed in university entrance examinations, pinned their hopes on the occult. The divination page in comic books and the fortune-telling booths in department stores no doubt gave comfort to young people anxious to be accepted by their peers. Movies about life after death undoubtedly strengthened people's faith in the reality of the spirits of the dead and the existence of an afterlife. Occult products function in much the same way as folk rituals or the magic and animism of the new religions.

The term *seishin sekai*, or spirit world, came into widespread use in 1978 when a Tokyo bookstore set up a special display section labeled "books of the spirit world." Before long, many bookstores had permanent sections on "books of the spirit world" that threatened to eclipse the religious books section. Although it is among these "books of the spirit world" that books on the occult are to be found, most of the books are of a higher intellectual level. Many have to do with meditation or mysticism. The works of Fritjof Capra, the founder of New Age Science, and other leaders or promoters of the New Age movement such as Krishnamurti, Shirley MacLaine, and Rudolf Steiner are located here. What Europeans and Americans call "New Age" and what the Japanese call the "Spirit World" are different manifestations of a worldwide movement.

In the broad sense, "books of the spirit world" are concerned with religion. But because they cannot be fitted into the framework of organized religions like Buddhism or Christianity, and because they tend to be critical of established religions, they require a separate category. The readers of these books of the spirit world are not studying the doctrines or ideas or history of a particular religion. They are exploring, one might say, their own inwardness. The term "spirit world" suggests mystical phenomena, but it also suggests the inner space of the heart. It is widely held that the search for a higher self or a unique state of consciousness in the depths of the individual heart is part of the goal of human existence.

The readers of these books do not form a community. Their commitment depends on the mass media and on communication with a small number of friends. Because their goal is to avoid restricting the individual, they think of their "networks" as ideal ways of establishing connections between people. We have spoken of this phenomenon as a "movement," but it has no central organization to propel it. There is simply a cumulation of diverse and separate actions in a convergent direction.

The channels of this Spirit World movement are not limited to specific commercial products like books, thematically related tape recordings, or videos. Lectures and seminars also play a major role. Some of these lectures and seminars, moreover, are enterprises undertaken by organized corporate entities. The Human Potential movement is a representative example. During the late 1980s, iBD, Forum (est), Life Dynamics (ARC International) and similar enterprises came to Japan from America, and their seminars were extremely popular. Participants paid the equivalent of as little as a few hundred dollars or as much as several thousand dollars to receive group training that drew heavily on psychotherapeutic techniques. They learned how to change passive thinking to active, and how to liberate the self diminished by fear of or hostility toward others. The people who took these seminars learned how to live as self-reliant individuals, but they did not form an ongoing community whose members would learn together and help one another live together cooperatively. Some participants shared in the administration of the seminars, to be sure, but they were few in number. In general, the Spirit World movement is an extremely individualistic movement that aims at the reform of the self. What connects the individual participants even more than personal communication is the mass media.

The Human Potential movement stems from group psychotherapy (sometimes called "encounter groups" or the like). As this suggests, psychotherapy is a key element in the Spirit World movement. Books on psychotherapy are generally included in the category of "books of the spirit world"; works by Carl Jung and his followers are highly rated. Another school of thought, still in the process of formation, is transpersonal psychology, which should probably be characterized as the theology of the New Age movement. When religion becomes a matter of exploring the inner self, it approaches the realm of psychology and psychotherapy. As systems of thought and practice for the healing of mind and body, religion, psychology, and psychotherapy overlap.

Psychology and psychotherapy belong to science, but in the Spirit World movement, points of convergence are taking shape not only between religion and psychology but between religion and science in general, especially between religion and natural science. In physics, biology, sociology, anthropology, and particularly in the field of religious studies, many scientists and scholars have considerable sympathy for the Spirit World movement. These intellectuals regard the Spirit World movement not so much as a religious movement as one of thought, an academic undertaking. Supporters of the Spirit World movement tend to be intellectually accomplished, and often of high social status. Although the movement spans the globe, it should be noted that the New Age movement and the Spirit World movement are popular in relatively few advanced countries, and draw their support from people of high educational achievement.

• AN OVERALL VIEW OF THE RELIGIOUS SITUATION IN JAPAN SINCE 1970
The term "rebirth of religion," made popular by scholars and journalists, contains a degree of exaggeration. The fact remains, however, that since 1970 religion has grown in strength in several areas. This may be confirmed by the results of public opinion surveys. In which areas, then, has religion become more vigorous?

The established religions, whether Shinto, Buddhist, or Christian, display few signs of new strength. In the new religions, certain shifts of energy have occurred. In the Shinto stream, there is some effort to use New Age language to link new and old. In the Christian stream, especially in Okinawa, the pentecostal movement has been active recently. But on the whole, the older new religions exhibit little evidence of new growth. As opposed to the "old" new religions which face the threat of stagnation, the "new" new religions, manifesting a number of characteristic features, have grown remarkably. These "new" new religions, however, do not differ radically from their predecessors. Considered as a whole, the new religions have not grown as much in the years since 1970 as they did during the twenty-five years following World War II, but they have not lost ground either. A certain degree of reinvigoration is also evident in folk religion, which seeks concrete benefits through prayer to the "little gods."

But the new religious energy that grew most remarkably during this period, developing outside all the above categories, is that of individualistic religion spread through the mass media. Individualistic religion has two aspects: the occult as pleasurable diversion, and the Spirit World movement toward the intellectual exploration of the self. Both types reflect the individualistic lifestyle of a complex, diversified, and affluent society. The fact that similar phenomena may be observed in the United States and other advanced countries suggests their social environments have much in common, and that reciprocal cultural influence has assumed immense importance.

A glance at the history of Japanese religion during the past century shows that from the closing years of the nineteenth century until 1970 the established Buddhist organizations waned while the new religions grew and flourished. During this period, Shinto underwent a momentous change in status from state religion to one religion among many, but the major religious shift, whether for households or individuals, was a unilateral move away from established Buddhism toward the new religions. The new religions attached great importance to the establishment of lay communities, but in emphasizing personal decision in choosing a religion, they reinforced the tendency toward individualism. Since 1970, the conspicuous growth once characteristic of the new religions has slowed. The development of individualistic religion through the agency of the mass media is ascendant today. But with regard to the strengthening of individualistic tendencies, it should be noted that this is a continuation of what began before 1970 during the shift from established Buddhist organizations to the new religions.

It is a simple matter of fact that one who looks at the history of the new religions will see that the organizations in which the individualistic tendency is prominent are the ones growing in strength. Among the "new" new religions, there are a few organizations that form tightly knit communities in apparent resistance to this trend. In the "new" new religions as a whole, however, the individualistic tendency is predominant. It appears, therefore, that the years before and after 1970 show a consistent pattern of change from community religion to individual religion.

In conclusion, I should like to say a word about how we are to understand this "rebirth of religion." As mentioned above, during the twenty-five year period following World War II, the dominant philosophy was one of rationalistic enlightenment. In fact the influence of this way of thinking can be traced back even further. Despite a period of reaction, this has been one of the chief currents of thought in modern Japan ever since the end of the feudal period and the beginning of the Meiji Restoration. Scientifically grounded secular knowledge coupled with the power of the state and of corporate enterprise to put this knowledge into practice gave rise to a widely held hope for rapid progress in attaining a happy human life. Since 1970, this hope has lost its power. Conversely, religions that were left behind by enlightenment ideas have made a comeback. This change, moreover, is not limited to Japan. The rebirth of religion in Japan, stemming primarily from loss of faith in the nation-state and in the secularized modern civilization that provided its support, is one aspect of a "rebirth of religion" phenomenon of world proportions.

In many parts of the world, however, this rebirth takes the form of the recovery and expansion of traditionally organized religion. Islam in areas from Southeast Asia to North Africa and Christianity in Eastern Europe, South Korea, and China exemplify this pattern. On the other hand, in advanced countries where secularism and capitalism have thoroughly permeated society as is the case in Japan, this kind of recovery by traditional religion is not much in evidence. Even such modern religious movements as cults and new religions tend more toward stagnation than growth. In these areas individual spiritual energies and disgust with modern civilization are shaped by the mass media, as in the New Age or Spirit World movements.

11

INTERNATIONALIZATION IN JAPANESE RELIGION

David Reid

• WORD AND REALITY

Religions have been crossing political boundaries for centuries. Why, then, the recent emphasis on *kokusaika*, or the "internationalization," of Japanese religion? How is the term to be understood? What does it signify?

Modernization, industrialization, urbanization, secularization, and most recently globalization are portfolio terms that point to social, political, economic, and cultural changes of regionally disparate character but worldwide significance. "Internationalization" is a similar term. It suggests expansion across national boundaries. In the case of religious organizations and movements, it suggests propagation that begins in one country and spreads to others.

The term "Japanese religion" is commonly taken to refer to religious organizations that originate in Japan. If this definition were adopted, only Shinto and the new religions would qualify, for Buddhism, despite its nearly 1,500 years in Japan, began as a foreign import. As used here, therefore, the term "Japanese religion" will mean any religious organization that exists in Japan. "Internationalization," accordingly, becomes a two-way street. It includes not only religious organizations that move outward from Japan but also those that originate outside Japan and move inward.

Tables 1 and 2 give some idea of this inward and outward movement. Table 1 shows some of the religious organizations that entered Japan between 1859 and 1992. Table 2, indicating some of the religious groups that spread outward from Japan, gives a bird's-eye view of the scope of the phenomenon between 1873 and 1995.

This chapter will sketch the pre- and post-1945 history of this centripetal and centrifugal diffusion, look for patterns in the post-1945 situation with particular reference to Japanese religions overseas, and conclude with a few remarks on the significance of this phenomenon. The aim is to form a general picture rather than to trace the activities of specific religious organizations.

TABLE 1

START OF WORK BY NON-JAPANESE RELIGIOUS ORGANIZATIONS IN JAPAN, 1859–1992

Year	Organization	Country of Origin	Year	Organization	Country of Origin
1859	Presbyterian Church in the U.S.	U.S.A.	1892	Women's Auxiliary, C. of England	Canada
1859	Protestant Episcopal Church	U.S.A.	1895	United Brethren in Christ	U.S.A.
1859	Reformed Church in America (Dutch)	U.S.A.	1895	Free Meth. Church of N. America	U.S.A.
1859	Sociète des Missions Etrangères	France	1895	Salvation Army	England
1860	American Baptist Churches	U.S.A.	1896	Trappist Order (men)	France
1860	American Seamen's Friend Society	U.S.A.	1896	Seventh-day Adventists	U.S.A.
1860	Southern Baptist Convention	U.S.A.	1898	Franciscaines Missionnaires de Marie	India
1861	Holy Orthodox Church in Japan	Russia	1898	Trappist Order (women)	France
1869	American Board of Commissioners for Foreign Missions	U.S.A.	1901	Latter-day Saints (Mormons)	U.S.A.
			1901	Young Women's Christian Assoc.	England
1869	Congregational Church	U.S.A.	1905	Church of the Nazarene	U.S.A.
1869	Church Missionary Society	England	1907	Ordo Fratrum Minorum	Italy
1871	Wesleyan Methodist Church	Canada	1907	Societas Verbi Divini	Germany
1872	L'Institut des Sœurs de l'Enfant	France	1908	Missionskongregation	Holland
1872	Methodist Episcopal Church	U.S.A.	1908	Societas Jesu	France
1873	Methodist Church of Canada	Canada	1908	Societas Sacratissimi Cordis Jesu	France
1873	Finnish Missionary Society	Finland	1910	Apostolatus Orationis	France
1873	Methodist Church of Canada	Canada	1913	Missionary Band of the World	U.S.A.
1873	Meth. Woman's Missionary Society	Canada	1914	Baha'i	Hawaii
1873	Society for the Propagation of the Gospel in Foreign Parts	England	1915	Society of Saint-Vincent de Paul	France
			1917	Church of Christ, Scientist	U.S.A.
1874	Edinburgh Medical Mission	Scotland	1918	American Wesleyan Mission	U.S.A.
1874	United Presbyterian Church	Scotland	1920	Community of the Epiphany	England
1875	National Bible Society of Scotland	Scotland	1920	Kongregation der Franziskanerinnen	Germany
1876	British and Foreign Bible Society	England	1921	Sœurs de la Charité	France
1876	Evangelical Church of N. America	U.S.A.	1923	American Friends Service Committee	U.S.A.
1877	Congrégation des Sœurs de l'Enfant	France	1925	Congregacion de Religiosas	Philippines
1877	Cumberland Presbyterian Church	U.S.A.	1925	Franciscan Sisters of Annunciation	Canada
1878	Baptist Missionary Society	England	1926	Maryknoll Sisters of St. Dominic	U.S.A.
1879	Reformed Church in U.S. (German)	U.S.A.	1926	Pia Societas sancti Francisci Salesii	Italy
1880	Methodist Protestant Church	U.S.A.	1926	Les Sœurs Missionnaires	Canada
1880	Young Men's Christian Association	England	1927	Liebenzeller Mission	Germany
1883	Christian Church (Disciples of Christ)	U.S.A.	1927	Ordo Santi Benedicti	Italy
1885	Evang.-Prot. Missionsverein	Germany	1927	Watch-Tower (Jehovah's Witnesses)	U.S.A.
1885	Religious Society of Friends (Quakers)	U.S.A.	1928	Congregación de Adoratrices	Spain
1885	Presbyterian Church in the U.S. (South)	U.S.A.	1928	Opus Dei	Spain
1885	Wesleyan Missionary Society	England	1929	Istituto delle Figlie di Maria	Italy
1886	Methodist Episcopal Church, South	U.S.A.	1929	Student Christian Movement	England
1887	America Christian Convention	U.S.A.	1930	Ordo Fratrum Minorum	Italy
1887	La Société de Marie	France	1930	St. Benedict's Priory	U.S.A.
1887	Unitarian Association	U.S.A.	1931	Congrégation Romaine de Dominique	Italy
1888	Christian and Missionary Alliance	U.S.A.	1931	Les Sœurs des Saints Noms	Canada
1888	Plymouth Brethren	England	1932	Congrégation de Notre Dame	Canada
1890	Church of Christ	U.S.A.	1932	Fratres Scholarum Christianarum	France
1890	Missionary Society, Ch. of England	Canada	1933	Maryknoll Missioners	U.S.A.
1890	Universalist General Convention	U.S.A.	1933	Society of St. John the Evangelist	U.S.A.
1892	Evangelical Lutheran Church (South)	U.S.A.	1933	Sœurs Missionnaires du Christ-Roi	Canada

186

TABLE 1—*Continued*

Year	Organization	Country of Origin	Year	Organization	Country of Origin
1934	Ancillae Sacratissimi Cordis Jesu	Spain	1953	Ancillae Divini Cordis	Spain
1934	Pia Societas Sancti Pauli Apostoli	Italy	1953	Apostolic Faith Mission	U.S.A.
1934	Les Sœurs de l'Assomption	Canada	1953	Brethren in Christ Missions	U.S.A.
1934	Sœurs de Sainte Anne	Canada	1953	Church of God	U.S.A.
1935	Christian Evangelistic Church	U.S.A.	1953	Religiosas Concepcionistas	Spain
1935	Congrégation de Notre Dame	France	1953	Scandinavian East Asia Mission	Norway
1936	Ordre de Ste-Ursule	Canada	1953	Sœurs de la Charité de Québec	Canada
1938	Orthodox Presbyterian Church	U.S.A.	1954	Free Will Baptists	U.S.A.
1946	Missionsbenediktinerinnen	Germany	1954	Ordre de Moniales Cisterciennes	Belgium
1947	Congregatio Immaculati Cordis Mariae	Belgium	1954	Fraternité des Petites Sœurs de Jésus	France
1947	Ordo Saecularis Carmelitarum	Spain	1955	Catholic Mission Sisters	U.S.A.
1948	Clerics of St. Viator	Canada	1955	Religiosas de Maria Immaculada	Cuba
1948	Congregatio Missionariorum	France	1956	Congregation of Sisters of St. Joseph	U.S.A.
1948	Franciscan Friars of the Atonement	U.S.A.	1956	Instituto de Santa Maria de Guadalupe	Mexico
1948	Missionsgesellschaft Bethlehem	Switzerland	1956	Our Lady's Missionaries	Canada
1948	Scarboro Foreign Missionary Society	Canada	1956	Petits Frères de Jésus	France
1948	Societas Sancti Columbani	Ireland	1957	Franciscan Sisters of the Atonement	U.S.A.
1949	Congregatio Missionis	France	1957	Religiose della Passione	Italy
1949	Evangelical Lutheran Church	U.S.A.	1958	Association des Prêtres du Prado	France
1949	Gideons International	U.S.A.	1958	Institutum Saeculare Missionariarum	Italy
1949	Misioneras Eucaristicas	Mexico	1959	Ordinis Societatis Mariae	France
1949	Mennonite Central Committee	U.S.A.	1959	Rama Krishna Mission	India
1949	Sweden Mission	Sweden	1959	Società Missionarie di Maria	Italy
1949	Tendō Sōtendan	Taiwan	1959	Subud (Islamic mysticism)	Indonesia
1950	Church of the Foursquare Gospel	U.S.A.	1959	Unification Church	Korea
1950	Free Christian Mission	Norway, Denmark	1961	Gospel Fellowship Mission	U.S.A.
1950	Ordo Scholarum Piarum	Spain	1970	Frateres Caritatis	Belgium
1950	Philadelphia Church Mission	U.S.A.	1971	Hare Krishna Movement	India
1950	Societas Missionariorum	France	1972	The Family	U.S.A.
1950	St. Benedict's Priory	U.S.A.	1974	Transcendental Meditation	India
1950	Suore Pie Discepole	Italy	1975	Evangelical Baptist Churches	Canada
1950	Swedish Holiness Union	Sweden	1975	Sri Sathya Sai (Sai Baba)	India
1951	Apostolic Christian Church	U.S.A.	1975	Rex Hubbard World Outreach	U.S.A.
1951	Christian Reformed Church	U.S.A.	1976	Silva Method	Mexico
1951	Deutscher Diakonissenerband	Germany	1977	Verbum Dei Apostolic Institute	Spain
1951	Evangelical Orient Mission	Norway	1979	Pure Gospel Church	Korea
1951	Figlie della Carità Canossiane	Italy	1979	Petites Sœurs de l'Évangile	France
1951	Filiae Iesu	Spain	1979	Senten Taidō Nihon Sōtendan	Taiwan
1951	Frères de l'Instruction Chrétienne	France	1980	P.T.L. Club	U.S.A.
1951	Grey Sisters	Canada	1980	Raelian Movement	Switzerland
1951	Hospitaller Brothers	Spain	1984	Jimmy Swaggart Ministry	U.S.A.
1951	Institut des Sœurs des Missions	France	1985	Church of Scientology	U.S.A.
1951	Ordo Carmelitarum (men)	Italy	1985	Siddah Meditation	India
1951	Les Petites Filles de St. Joseph	Canada	1989	Wiccan	U.S.A.
1952	Congregatio Passionis Jesu Christi	Italy	1992	Baptist Union of Denmark	Denmark
1952	Religious of the Assumption	Philippines	1992	Japan Free Evangelical Mission	Norway
1952	United Pentecostal Church	U.S.A.	1992	Volunteer Youth Ministry	U.S.A.

Data drawn from direct communications and from Ono Yasuhiro et al., eds., *Nihon shūkyō jiten* (Tokyo: Kōbundō, 1985), the *Nihon kirisutokyō rekishi daijiten* (Tokyo: Kyōbunkan, 1988), the *Japanese Journal of Religious Studies*, vol. 18, nos. 2–3 (1991), and Inoue Nobutaka et al., eds., *Shinshūkyō kyōdan • jinbutsu jiten* (Tokyo: Kōbundō, 1996). Only organizations for which a specific date is available are listed. To save space, some names have been abbreviated.

TABLE 2

Overseas Work by Japanese Religious Groups, 1873–1995
(The year indicates the formal or informal beginning of overseas work)

North America		Latin America		Asia		Australia, Africa, Europe, and Russia	
Canada		*Argentina*		*China*		*Australia*	
1905	Juō Shinshū	1964	Sōka Gakkai	1873	Jōdo Shinshū	1964	Sōka Gakkai
1915	Nichiren Shū			1895	Tenrikyō	1973	Risshō Kōseikai
1934	Tenrikyō	*Brazil*		1898	Nichiren Shū	1976	Sūkyō Mahikari
1963	Sōka Gakkai	1914	Jōdo Shinshū	1904	Nihon Kirisuto	1978	Sekai Kyūseikyō
1964	Seichō no Ie	1923	Japanese Catholic		Kyōkai	1980	Tenrikyō
1970	Shinnyoen		priest Nakamura	1905	Jōdo Shū	1995	Kōfuku no
1975	Reiyūkai		Chōhachi	1905	Zen (Rinzai)		Kagaku
1986	Konkōkyō		arrives to serve	1907	Konkōkyō		
1995	Kōfuku no		emigrants	1908	Izumo	AFRICA	
	Kagaku	1923	Japanese Anglican		Yashirokyō	*Congo*	
			priest Itō Yasoji	1908	Zen (Sōtō)	1962	Tenrikyō
U.S.A.			arrives to serve	1908	Shingon Shū		
California			emigrants	1911	Kurozumikyō	*Ghana*	
1896	Tenrikyō	1926	Ōmoto	1913	Nihon Seikōkai	1965	Sōka Gakkai
1897	Zen (Rinzai)	1929	Tenrikyō	1915	Honmon	1974	Seichō no Ie
1898	Jōdo Shinshū	1932	Seichō no Ie		Hokeshū		
1906	Nichiren Shū	1934	Shingon Shō	1915	Nihon Kumiai	*Kenya*	
1912	Shingon Shū	1955	Sekai Kyūseikyō		Kirisuto Kyōkai	1969	Sōka Gakkai
1930	Konkōkyō	1957	P.L. Kyōdan	1917	Holiness Kyōkai		
1934	Zen (Sōtō)	1960	Sōka Gakkai	1919	Nihon Methodist	EUROPE	
1936	Jōdo Shū	1964	Konkōkyō		Kyōkai	*England*	
1954	Sekai Kyōseikyō	1971	Risshō Kōseikai	1930	Jōdo Shinshū	1910	Tenrikyō
1960	P.L. Kyūdan	1974	Sūkyō Mahikari			1961	Sōka Gakkai
1969	Gedatsukai	1975	Reiyūkaiō	*Hong Kong*		1978	Reiyūkai
1973	Reiyūkai	1981	Shūyōdan	1900	Jōdo Shinshū	1995	Kōfuku no
1980	Sōka Gakkai		Hōseikai	1961	Sōka Gakkai		Kagaku
1982	Shinnyoen	1982	Tendō Sōtendan				
1984	Shūyōdan	1988	Tenshō Kōtai	*India*		*France*	
	Hōseikai		Jingūkyō	1969	Nihonzan	1963	Sōka Gakkai
1984	Honmichi				Myōhōji	1979	Reiyūkai
1995	Kōfuku no	*Chile*		1977	Daijōkyō	1985	Shinnyoen
	Kagaku	1932	Zen (Sōtō)	1981	Reiyūkai		
						Germany	
Hawaii		*Columbia*		*Indonesia*		1956	Jōdo Shinshū
1893	Jōdo Shū	1969	Tenrikyō	1961	Sōka Gakkai	1963	Sōka Gakkai
1897	Jōdo Shinshū						
1898	First Shinto shrine	*Cuba*		*Korea*		*Holland*	
1901	Nichiren Shū	1968	Sōka Gakkai	1877	Jōdo Shinshū	1980	Yamakage
1904	Zen (Sōtō)			1881	Nichiren Shū		Shintō
1908	Izumo Yashirokyō	*Dominican Republic*		1893	Tenrikyō		
1908	Tenrikyō	1966	Sōka Gakkai	1897	Jōdo Shū	*Italy*	
1914	Shingon Shū			1897	Shinrikyō	1972	P.L. Kyōdan
1918	Tendai Shū	*Mexico*		1901	Zen (Sōtō)		
1922	Japanese	1961	Tenrikyō	1902	Konkōkyō	*Scandinavia*	
	Salvation Army	1963	Sōka Gakkai	1904	Kokuchūkai	1963	Sōka Gakkai
1925	Konkōkyō	1977	Reiyūkai	1904	Shingon Shū	1967	Shinnyoen
				1911	Church of Christ		
					in Japan		

TABLE 2—Continued

North America		Latin America		Asia		Australia, Africa, Europe, and Russia	
1936	Seichō no Ie	*Panama*		1911	Japan Congrega-	*Spain*	
1941	Kegon Shū	1968	Sōka Gakkai		tional Church	1984	Reiyūkai
1951	Tenshindō			1924	Ōmoto		
1953	Sekai Kyūseikyō	*Paraguay*		1925	Shinshūkyō	*Switzerland*	
1954	Tenrikyō	1961	Tenrikyō	1925	Kurozumikyō	1967	Sōka Gakkai
1955	Tenshō Kōtai	1961	Sōka Gakkai	1927	Fusōkyō	1974	Sūkyō Mahikari
	Jingūkyō	1983	Reiyūkai	1927	Jikkōkyō		
1957	Risshō Kōseikai			1927	Ontakekyō	*Russia*	
1960	Sōka Gakkai	*Peru*		1928	Hito no Michi	1887	Jōdo Shinshū
1963	P.L. Kyōdan	1903	Jōdo Shū	1934	Reiyūkai	1917	Jōdo Shū
1963	Shinreikyō	1938	Zen (Sōtō)	1936	Seichō no Ie	1992	Aum Shinrikyō
1965	Spirit of Jesus	1965	Seichō no Ie	1976	Zenrinkai		
	Church	1979	Reiyūkai	1982	Risshō Kōseikai		
1968	Nihonzan						
	Myōhōji			*Laos*			
1968	Honmon			1970	Tenrikyō		
	Butsuryūshū						
1970	Shinnyoen			*Malaysia*			
1973	Shūyōdan			1935	Jōdo Shinshū		
	Hōseikai			1974	Sōka Gakkai		
1974	Benten Shū						
1976	Sūkyō Mahikari			*Philippines*			
1977	Ijun			1903	Zen (Sōtō)		
1979	Tenshinkyō			1919	Jōdo Shinshū		
1994	Kōfuku no			1961	Sōka Gakkai		
	Kagaku						
				Singapore			
Seattle Area				1893	Zen (Sōtō)		
1901	Jōdo Shinshū			1971	Tenrikyō		
1915	Nichiren Shū						
1919	Konkōkyō			*Taiwan*			
1927	Tenrikyō			1895	Zen (Sōtō)		
				1896	Jōdo Shinshū		
Washington, D.C.				1897	Tenrikyō		
1981	Tenshō Kōtai			1899	Nichiren Shū		
	Jingūkyō			1900	Zen (Rinzai)		
				1901	Konkōkyō		
Other Locations				1975	Ōkan Michi		
1960	Sōka Gakkai			1974	Sūkyō Mahikari		
1970	Shinnyoen			1976	Ijun		
1995	Kōfuku no			1985	Shinnyoen		
	Kagaku						
				Thailand			
				1906	Jōdo Shū		
				1966	Shinnyoen		
				1979	Reiyūkai		
				Vietnam			
				1961	Sōka Gakkai		

Data from direct communications and from Inoue Nobutaka et al., eds., *Shinshūkyō jiten* (Tokyo: Kōbundō, 1990), Ono Yasuhiro et al., eds., *Nihon shūkyō jiten* (Tokyo: Kōbundō, 1985), Inoue Nobutaka, *Umi o watatta Nihon shūkyō* (Tokyo: Kōbundō, 1985), Nakamaki Hirochika, *Nihon shūkyō to nikkei shūkyō no kenkyū* (Tokyo: Tōsui Shobō, 1989), the *Japanese Journal of Religious Studies*, vol. 18, nos. 2–3 (1991), and J. Gordon Melton and Constance A. Jones, "New Japanese Religions in the United States," in Peter B. Clarke and Jeffrey Somers, eds., *Japanese New Religions in the West* (Sandgate, Folkestone, Kent: Japan Library, 1994). Only organizations for which a specific date is available are listed. To save space, some names have been abbreviated.

• Religious Internationalization Before 1945

Centripetal diffusion. In historical perspective, the first religion of foreign origin to establish itself in Japan was Buddhism, which formally entered Japan in the sixth century C.E. The second was Christianity, which arrived in the sixteenth century, was outlawed in the early seventeenth century, and reentered Japan around the middle of the nineteenth century.

A distinctive feature of the way Buddhism took root in Japan is that it began, so to speak, at the top. From the sixth century, when Buddhism entered Japan, until nearly the end of the twelfth century, when it began to take hold among ordinary people, Buddhism found its chief supporters among the nobility. Only with what has come to be called Kamakura Buddhism (Pure Land, True Pure Land, Zen, and Nichiren Buddhism) did Buddhism start to attract commoners in significant numbers. One catalyst for this growth was the publication of "comic books" that vividly depicted the pleasures of paradise (*gokuraku*) and the torments of hell (*jigoku*). Another was the widespread belief that the final period of history was about to come to an end and that people should prepare for this denouement. Still another was the merging of Buddhism with ancestral rites, which allowed many to believe faithful performance of the rites would not only help the spirits of departed loved ones but also protect the living from malignant spirits.

However fitful, this growth continued until Francis Xavier brought Christianity to Japan in 1549. For nearly a century, Christianity competed with Buddhism for followers, but pressures to ban Christianity and close off Japan from contact with the West reached a climax with the Christian revolt at Shimabara in 1637–38. For the next two hundred and fifty years, the government required all Japanese households to register as supporters of their local Buddhist temple and obtain from the temple priest annual certificates that they were innocent of association with Christianity. This system changed the nature of the relationship between Buddhism and the Japanese people. Before its establishment, people came to Buddhism voluntarily. Under the new system affiliation became a legal requirement. To be sure, even under this system some people were attracted to Buddhist thought and the Buddhist way of life as a matter of principle. For the great majority, however, the temple was a locus of formal connection, not of religious conviction. The government-imposed system, though rescinded in 1871, laid a deadening hand on traditional Japanese Buddhism, from which it has still not fully recovered—though new religions in the Buddhist stream offer an alternative that has proved attractive to many.

Nineteenth-century Christianity first entered Japan from the United

States, which was then expanding westward and seeking trade partners in Asia. Japan was in disorder, still reeling from the shock of Commodore Matthew C. Perry's having forced the shogunate to open Japanese ports in 1854. The ensuing conflict between pro-shogunate and pro-imperial factions resulted in an imperial victory and the formation of the Meiji government. It was during this time of sociopolitical disorientation, power struggle, and reorganization that Christianity reentered Japan. The first Protestant and Catholic missionaries arrived in 1859, the Russian Orthodox missionary Nikolai in 1861.

The foreign religion proved attractive to two groups of people: samurai and young women. The interested samurai were not those in government, who generally opposed Christianity, but members of former pro-shogunate factions, now excluded from government. Many of them hoped the ethical rigor of Christianity and its connections with western technology would help them contribute to the building of a modern Japan. Young women found Christianity attractive because of the mission schools, which made higher education available to them for the first time. If people connected with positions of power are regarded as standing at the center of society, these two groups must be understood as marginal. The fact that Christianity has historically attracted people on the margins of Japanese society goes a long way toward accounting for its slow growth.

Centrifugal diffusion. The expansion of Japanese religions to overseas areas began in the late nineteenth century. It will be useful to look at this expansion in four regions: Hawaii, the United States mainland, Brazil, and Korea.

The first ship carrying Japanese emigrants to Hawaii left Yokohama in 1868 with about one hundred and fifty passengers. Their reasons for leaving Japan are not recorded, but the power struggles that attended the end of the shogunate and the formation of the Meiji government can hardly be unrelated. Hawaii, then an independent kingdom, was in urgent need of laborers for its sugarcane plantations and signed a treaty with Japan for this purpose. By 1894, the year of the last shipload of Japanese emigrants, approximately thirty thousand people had moved from Japan to Hawaii. In 1893 Queen Liliuokalani was deposed, and in 1898 Hawaii was annexed by the United States, becoming a state in 1959.

Individual Buddhist priests, motivated partly by a desire to serve the spiritual needs of Japanese emigrants in Hawaii and partly by fear of their coming under the influence of Christianity, began their work in Hawaii in 1889. The first Japanese Buddhist organization that formally established itself in Hawaii was the Jōdo Shū, or Pure Land sect. This was in 1893, and other Buddhist organizations soon followed suit: the Honganjiha (Nishi Honganji) wing of the Jōdo Shinshū, or True Pure Land sect, in 1897, the Nichiren Shū in 1901, the Sōtō branch of Zen in 1904, and the Shingon Shū in 1914. Of these organizations, the largest is the wing of the True Pure Land sect known as the Jōdo Shinshū Honganjiha (Nishi Honganji). A Japanese language school was opened as early as 1902, primarily to offer instruction to the children of those who had come from Japan.

Emigration from Japan to the United States mainland dates from 1869, when a small contingent of refugees from the political power shift in Japan arrived in San Francisco. Not until 1890, however, did emigration begin in earnest. Japanese labor was in demand for railroad construction work, mining, and especially farm work. Tenrikyō, then classified as a Sect Shinto organization, began its work in California in 1896, twelve years before starting in Hawaii.

The first Japanese Buddhist organization to formally begin work in California was the Jōdo Shinshū, or True Pure Land sect, particularly the Honganjiha (Nishi Honganji) wing, which established its first church in San Francisco in 1898. (Buddhist institutions that would be called "temples" in Japan are called "churches" in America.) Within five years it had established churches in Oakland, San Jose, Fresno, and Seattle, and during its first forty years opened forty-four churches, primarily in California. Zen Buddhism also made a start about the same time, but did not draw many members until the 1960s.

Nearly all these churches were located in areas where people of Japanese origin were living. The services they performed were chiefly funerals and memorial rites, though the churches also served as ethnic community centers where people could mingle, play games, and communicate with one another in Japanese. In both respects there was a clear affinity between the services these bodies offered and the needs of the people they served.

The isolationist spirit in the United States after the end of World War I had many consequences, one of which was the United States Exclusion Act of 1924. Its quota system effectively put an end to new Japanese immigration. Religious organizations that formally initiated work in Hawaii at about this time include esoteric Buddhist bodies such as the Tendai Shū and new religions such as Tenrikyō and Konkōkyō.

The first ship carrying Japanese emigrants to Brazil arrived in 1908 with some eight hundred passengers. It was not until the 1950s, however, that the Jōdo Shinshū and other bodies formally began their work among expatriate Japanese in Brazil. Nationalism and initial resistance from the Catholic Church was one reason for this delay, but another reason concerned the nature of the work Japanese migrants were doing at that time. Forced by financial need to move from one coffee plantation to another, they did not really have fixed residences until the end of World War II. Industrialization and urbanization got under way in the 1960s, and it was from the latter half of this decade that a number of Japanese new religions made headway in Brazil. Particularly noteworthy are Seichō no Ie, P. L. Kyōdan, Nichiren Shōshū, Sekai Kyūseikyō, and Sūkyō Mahikari, but of them all, the most influential is Seichō no Ie, which will be considered in the next section.

The Korean peninsula, perhaps because it is so easy to reach, was the first place in Asia to which Japanese religions spread. The first Japanese religious organization to work in Korea seems to have been the Jōdo Shinshū, for a missionary of the Higashi Honganji wing started work in Pusan as early as 1877. He was followed by a Nichiren Shū missionary in 1881, a Tenrikyō missionary in 1893, a Jōdo Shū missionary in 1897, etc. By 1910, when Japan annexed Korea, the Japanese religious organizations active in Korea included, besides those listed above, Konkōkyō and Shinrikyō in the Sect Shinto stream, the Shingon and Zen forms of Buddhism, and the Nihon Kumiai Kirisuto Kyōkai, or Japan Congregational Church. A State Shinto shrine, Chōsen Jingū, was established in Seoul in 1925. Though specific dates are not yet available, it is known that between 1910 and 1945, the number of Sect Shinto groups expanded to include Izumo Ōyashirokyō, Fusōkyō, Shinshūkyō, Jikkōkyō, and Ontakekyō. Tendai and Kegon arrived from the Buddhist stream, and Christian groups increased to include the Nihon Kirisuto Kyōkai, or Church of Christ in Japan, the Nihon Mesojisuto Kyōkai, or Japan Methodist Church, the Kiyome Kyōkai, or [Japan] Holiness Church, and others. For the most part these groups served the needs of Japanese people working abroad. The most prominent exception to this rule was Tenrikyō, which from the beginning sought to serve and win non-Japanese people as well.

Immediately after 1945, most Japanese religious organizations pulled out of Korea, Manchuria, Taiwan and other areas that had been de facto Japanese colonies. As Japan rejoined the community of nations and its economy began to recover, however, a number of groups resumed or initiated mission work in Asia. Chief among these groups were Tenrikyō and Sōka Gakkai.

• INTERNATIONALIZATION SINCE THE END OF WORLD WAR II

The centripetal dimension. A glance at table 1 will suffice to show that the vast majority of religious groups that entered Japan before World War II were Christian. It should be noted here that during the years immediately preceding and following the Meiji Restoration, treaty agreements stipulated that Christian worship services could be held only for non-Japanese foreigners resident in Japan. Thus American Protestant missionaries were to serve American residents, French Catholic missionaries were to serve French residents, etc. In fact, however, Christian missionaries soon ignored these restrictions. In their view the Christian message could not be restricted to members of a particular nationality. From the outset they sought to communicate the Christian message to the Japanese, to win them to the community of believers, and paradoxically, to serve their needs in such fields as health and education quite apart from the question of conversion. Perhaps because of this orientation, most of the Christian mission groups, barred from Japan during World War II, were quick to return to Japan after the war. As a matter of mission strategy, some groups focused strictly on preaching the gospel while others decided to add education or social service. All in all, however, theirs was a mission to and for Japanese people. The major difference between pre- and post-war forms of the Christian mission in Japan is that before the war, missionaries of mainstream denominations tended to be in positions of institutional leadership and Japanese Christians in subordinate positions, whereas after the war, the positions were reversed.

This reversal did not take place immediately, to be sure. The Japanese economy was devastated by the war; for a number of years Christian programs in Japan were dependent on overseas resources, and hence on the priorities of mission board directors and administrators. Even during these years of financial dependence, however, Japanese Christian leaders functioned actively in their various posts, and missionaries from overseas, though warmly welcomed, were expected to serve under their Japanese colleagues. This tendency became even more pronounced as Japanese Christian groups grew stronger financially, beginning in the 1960s when the Japanese economy as a whole began to recover.

Exceptions to this tendency do exist. Japanese Christian institutions have not hesitated to elect qualified foreigners to positions of leadership. The general pattern, however, is the one described above.

The period since the end of World War II has also seen a number of religious groups entering Japan for the first time. Several are mainstream Christian groups, both Catholic and Protestant. The remaining groups come primarily from Korea, North America, and India. Some are difficult to classify in terms of religious affiliation, but can generally be regarded as depending, whether positively or negatively, on Christianity (Unification Church, Children of God, Family of God, Rex Hubbard World Outreach, Jun Fukuin Kyōkai [Pure Gospel Church], P.T.L. Club, and Jimmy Swaggart Ministry), on Indian tradition (Hare Krishna Movement, Transcendental Meditation, Rama Krishna Mission, and Siddah Meditation), or on New Age thought (Scientology, Raelian Movement).

Like the Christian mission, none of these groups is ethnically limited. All seek to win not merely Indians, Koreans, or Americans in Japan but primarily Japanese supporters. In terms of ethnic orientation and institutional leadership, however, the Unification Church tends to bind its members to large-scale rituals held in Korea and to place only people of Korean background in key positions. As for the other groups, the information published to date is too sparse to permit generalization.

The centrifugal dimension. Japanese religious groups that have undertaken overseas work since 1945 belong almost entirely to the new religions (see Table 2). The work of Seichō no Ie in Brazil may be taken as a clue to larger patterns. But the larger patterns will emerge more clearly if we first consider the role of ethnic orientation in overseas work.

If ethnic orientation is used to differentiate organizational types, it becomes clear that the word "internationalization" means two different things. On the one hand, it relates to organizations that send people abroad for the primary purpose of serving Japanese emigrants and their descendants. On the other, it refers to groups that send people abroad primarily in order to serve the people of the country to which they go.

Before and during World War II, most Japanese religious groups abroad fell into the former category. Tenrikyō is the chief exception; in Korea and Taiwan, where it has gained most of its non-Japanese adherents, it sought from the beginning to communicate its message to the indigenous people. After World War II, there was an increase in groups that fall into the latter category. Chief among them are Seichō no Ie, Sekai Kyūseikyō, P.L. Kyōdan, Sūkyō Mahikari, and Sōka Gakkai.[1]

Seichō no Ie, the largest of the Japanese religious organizations in Brazil today, initially drew most of its members from people of Japanese heritage and developed a firm foundation there, but since the 1960s it has

---

1. Sōka Gakkai overseas organizations go by a variety of names. Here they will all be treated under one name.

won many non-Japanese members as well. This is not to say that reaching out to non-Japanese people is a guarantee of successful growth. Ōmoto did precisely that in Brazil before the 1960s, but was overwhelmed by Catholic opposition, government suppression, and the death of missionaries. Seichō no Ie, however, found itself in a different religious, political, and economic climate in the Brazil of the late 1960s. The dominant Catholic Church had adopted a more generous attitude toward the non-Christian religions, government suppression had ceased, and Japan's economic recovery made it, for a time, an attractive model. The question of what elements drew Brazilian people to Seichō no Ie is not a simple one, but one element appears to have been its magical practice of chanting from the sacred scriptures as a means of benefiting the spirits of the ancestors. This in turn suggests that non-Japanese Brazilian members who find Seichō no Ie attractive tend to come from the uneducated strata of the population. At the same time, however, the founder of Seichō no Ie, Okada Mokichi, is also noted for his cultural refinement and clear teachings, a circumstance that has greatly facilitated translation into Portuguese and thereby attracted literate Brazilians.

• PATTERNS OF DOCTRINE AND MAGIC

This characteristic combination of magic ritual and sophisticated doctrine is repeated in other successful centripetal religions, regardless of location. Three patterns emerge.

Sekai Kyūseikyō and its offshoot Sūkyō Mahikari teach that the healing power of their deity's light is transmitted through the palm of the hand, so that if a person has a headache, for example, a believer may help by holding his or her hand a short distance from the painful area and focusing the palm's energy. The founder of Sekai Kyūseikyō, Taniguchi Masaharu, was not only an artistically sensitive person but also a prolific writer with a gift for logical and lucid explanation. Paradoxical though it may seem, the Sekai Kyūseikyō pattern combines magic and logic.

The founder of Sūkyō Mahikari, Okada Kōtama, does not fit this pattern. In somewhat obscure writings dotted with tendentious plays on words, he held that human civilization was on the verge of collapse and reported what he claimed were divine revelations prophesying the spiritual civilization that was to come and showing people how to win spiritual renewal for life in the twenty-first century. Where Sekai Kyūseikyō combines magic and logic, Sūkyō Mahikari combines magic and eschatological prophecy.

P.L. Kyōdan too has a magical dimension. It teaches *migawari*, which means that the head of the organization, when sought out by a suffering member, will vicariously accept the member's grief or suffering as his own. There is also an incantation, *oya shikiri*, the utterance of which is said to give a person kami-like power and thus release from present problems. P.L. Kyōdan also offers, however, ethical instruction for daily life. This instruction is said to go into great detail and to bring to the believing member a sense of calm and mental stability of great value in navigating the jungle of urban life. The pattern here, then, is a combination of magic and practical ethical instruction.

Sōka Gakkai, like the groups named above, includes a magical practice: reciting the words *Namu myōhō rengekyō* morning and evening before the sacred *gohonzon*, or mandala, a copy of the original inscribed by Nichiren. The literal explanation for this practice has nothing to do with magic, to be sure. The first word of the chant means "devotion to" or "praise to," and the rest of the phrase is simply the Japanese title of the Lotus Sutra. But a certain "magicalizing" of the Buddhist concept of cause and effect is evident in that reciting these words is supposed to activate the believer's innate Buddha-nature: the words are to the Buddha-nature as cause is to effect. At a more mundane level, believers often testify that regular observance of this practice has led to improvement in health and human relationships and to prosperity in business. But Sōka Gakkai doctrine, however difficult it may seem to the uninitiated, is logically consistent, theoretically sophisticated, and based on a Buddhist tradition that goes back many centuries. In North America today, not to mention Korea, Sōka Gakkai is one of the most successful of the Japanese religions. In this context it represents a reappearance of the pattern that combines magic and a logically presented body of doctrine.

There is a sense, however, in which Sōka Gakkai differs from all the rest, for it is the only organization that demands exclusive loyalty of its members. Each of the other groups named above supports religious pluralism in the sense that it encourages members not only to participate actively in its own rituals and programs but also to do the same in whatever other religious group or groups they may belong to. Only Sōka Gakkai, claiming that other religions are wrong and that it alone is right, demands that a person cut all ties with other religious groups when becoming a member of Sōka Gakkai. Its pattern, therefore, involves not only magic and a logically presented body of doctrine but also an exclusivism which, if offensive to some, is obviously no deterrent to many.

Among these patterns, then, the only constant is magical practice. Though widely decried, magical beliefs and practice exist all over the world. A religious organization, even if alien, will not seem so alien if it comes equipped with magical teachings and practices that people can easily adopt. Conversely, religious groups that take a strong stand against magic would seem to be at a disadvantage. It may be that this kind of stance needs to be taken into account in order to explain why Risshō Kōseikai, for example, having rigorously rooted out its former magical practices, has been rather unsuccessful abroad.

Other patterns no doubt remain to be discovered. One would expect, as the Ōmoto example shows, that political and economic conditions, both in the host country and in the country of origin, would have to correlate favorably in order for a religio-cultural mission to succeed.

Perhaps enough has been said, however, to show that the major groups that have been most successful as they spread from Japan to other countries in the postwar period are to be found among the religious organizations referred to as new religions. The traditional religious groups, whether Shinto or Buddhist, are still forces to be reckoned with. Their influence is by no means negligible. But the growing edge, for the present at least, appears to lie with the new religions.

• CONCLUDING REMARKS

The internationalization of Japanese religion is part of a much larger phenomenon. Generally increasing urban populations, incremental increases in information-flow, decreased travel costs and the growth of a world economy lead some scholars to suggest that we are now seeing the dawn of an era of globalization. As part of a worldwide movement of cultural exchange, religious internationalization will doubtless continue to grow and challenge traditional religious affiliations.

It has long been acknowledged that religion serves to integrate society and legitimize the establishment. Where society is relatively stable and homogeneous, there is little reason to dispute this view. But the picture changes when alien religions enter the scene. For better or worse, religious internationalization entails a degree of social destabilization.

Reactions to perceived threats to stability take two main forms: religious and political. Both tend to polarize. Religious reactions divide people into fundamentalist or liberal camps, while political reactions cluster either around a conservative pole favoring traditional values understood as culturally homogeneous or a progressive pole favoring cultural pluralism.

For centuries Japan has held to the conservative pole. This is still the case today. Cultural homogeneity in Japan is widely regarded not as an ideal but as an indisputable fact. Religions, whether of foreign or native origin, are allowed to exist so long as they conform to accepted norms, and those that challenge or violate these norms attract few members.

In recent decades Japan has been increasingly attracted to internationalism. In the world of Japanese religion, this often meant little more than initiating mission work in a foreign country. But sensitive interaction with people of other cultures and values can hardly fail to have a rebound effect. The more this happens, the more likely it is that the treasured value of cultural homogeneity will be modified by religious internationalization.

12

RELIGIOUS ORGANIZATIONS IN JAPANESE LAW

Kawawata Yuiken

• GOVERNMENT NEUTRALITY AND RELIGIOUS AUTONOMY

The Japanese constitution of 1946 guarantees religious freedom to all citizens, regardless of their faith (Article 20). The constitution likewise guarantees freedom of thought, conscience, assembly, association, speech, press, and other basic rights (Articles 19, 21). It also adopts the principle of separation of religion and state (Article 89). The state neither supports nor interferes with religious organizations; its basic attitude is one of neutrality.

Religious organizations may become legal corporations under the 1951 Religious Corporation Law. The purpose of this law is defined in a preamble "giving legal capacity to religious organizations in order to facilitate their owning establishments for worship and other properties, maintaining and operating them, and also carrying on business affairs and enterprises for the achievement of their purposes."

The law further asserts that "freedom of faith guaranteed in the constitution must be respected in all phases of government. Therefore, no provision in this law shall be construed as restricting any individual, group, or organization from disseminating teachings, observing ceremonies and functions, or conducting other religious acts on the basis of the said guaranteed freedom." In accordance with this law the executive branch of government involves itself in the administration of religious corporations to the minimum extent necessary for the maintenance of public order and the prevention of unlawful acts, honoring the principle of respect for the autonomy and self-determination of all religious bodies.

Government acknowledgment of this principle represents a significant departure from the way Japanese governments have customarily regarded religious organizations. From 701, when the law of the land was first codified, until 1945, the end of World War II, the basic principle of government religious policy was to supervise religious organizations in the interests of the state. Religious bodies recognized by the government came under government control and protection. Unauthorized religions were not free to disseminate their teachings and received no tax exemptions. This practice was confirmed, rather than relinquished, with the move toward modernization in the Meiji era.

• LEGAL DEVELOPMENTS LEADING TO THE PRESENT SITUATION

Nationalized Shrine Shinto and private religious organizations. The Constitution of the Empire of Japan, or Meiji constitution, issued on February 11, 1889, guaranteed freedom of religion in Article 28: "Japanese subjects shall, within limits not prejudicial to peace and order, and not antagonistic to their duties as subjects, enjoy freedom of religious belief." But the Meiji constitution failed to provide a clear definition of the boundaries between religion and state, and because the police and the judiciary interpreted freedom of religious belief narrowly and its limitations broadly, this guarantee proved weak.

Early on, the Meiji government adopted Shrine Shinto for the service of the state. For administrative purposes, Shrine Shinto was not to be considered a religion, thus avoiding any conflict with religious freedom. In contrast to Buddhist temples, Christian churches, and the various sectarian religious organizations, Shrine Shinto was to maintain a separate existence both administratively and legally.

On the administrative level this was achieved by establishing two distinct government agencies, one to supervise Shinto, the other to supervise the religious organizations. Thus in 1900 the Shrine Bureau (*Jinja Kyoku*) was established under the Ministry of Home Affairs, while in the same year and under the same ministry, a separate Religions Bureau (*Shūkyō Kyoku*) was also instituted. In 1913 the Religions Bureau was transferred to the Ministry of Education, further clarifying the administrative distinction between Shinto and the religions. In 1940 even the parallelism in titles was eliminated when the Shrine Bureau was renamed the Department of Shrine Affairs (*Jingi'in*).

Legally, the status of the Shinto shrines and of what the government regarded as religious organizations depended on the issue of corporations. Article 28 of the Civil Code Enforcement Law of 1899 specified that Shinto shrines, Buddhist temples, shrines of Sect Shinto, and independent Buddhist chapels could not become corporations under the Civil Code. But the intention of this restriction was to enable them to attain this status under a law that had yet to be written. Article 28 was therefore interpreted to mean that these four types of organizations, and by extension all

religious organizations, could become corporations. Shrine Shinto organizations were defined as being corporations.

Yet while both the shrines and the explicitly religious organizations
might thus be or become corporations, their status in law was not identical. Shrine Shinto organizations came under a Ministry of Home Affairs
ordinance (Ordinance No. 2 of 1913) and were classified as public corporations. The legal position of religious organizations, on the other hand,
was stipulated by the Religious Organizations Law (*Shūkyō dantai hō*,
Law No. 77, which went into effect on January 1, 1940). This law designated Buddhist temples as private corporations and permitted Christian
and Sect Shinto organizations to apply for and receive this status subject
to government authorization. In effect, the organizations recognized under
the Religious Organizations Law were the thirteen Sect Shinto groups,
twenty-eight Buddhist sects (consolidated, under government pressure,
from the original fifty-six), and two Christian organizations: the Roman
Catholic Church and the United Church of Christ in Japan, the latter
being a federation of thirty-four Protestant denominations and sects.

On the positive side, the Religious Organizations Law, by enabling
religious bodies to incorporate as private corporations, presented authorized groups with certain advantages. Not only did the incorporated
groups then occupy a clearly defined position within the legal structure,
they were also in a stronger position as regards corporate ownership and
disposition of property. Moreover, under this law Christian organizations
were for the first time given a legal status equal to that of Buddhist and
Sect Shinto organizations. But this law also put into the hands of the state
a battery of regulations for supervising and controlling the organizations
it authorized. In applying the law, government authorities did not hesi-
tate to interfere in the internal affairs of these organizations. As a result
the Religious Organizations Law became an instrument for obstructing
religious freedom.

The turn to neutrality. With the end of World War II, a fundamental
change was effected in governmental administration of religious organizations. On October 4, 1945, not long after the Occupation began, a directive entitled "Removal of Restrictions on Political, Civil, and Religious
Liberties" was issued under the authority of the Supreme Commander
for the Allied Powers. In accordance with Article 10 of the Potsdam
Proclamation (July 26, 1945), which decreed that "freedom of speech, of
religion, and of thought, as well as respect for the fundamental human
rights, shall be established," this directive ordered the abrogation and

immediate suspension of application of "all laws, decrees, orders, ordinances, and regulations which establish or maintain restrictions on freedom . . . of religion," thought, association, and speech. The directive explicitly named the suppressive Peace Preservation Law (*Chian Iji Hō*, Law No. 46 of 1925) and the Religious Organizations Law as enactments to which this order was to be applied. Accordingly, these laws were rescinded on December 28, 1945. On the same day, the Religious Corporation Ordinance (*Shūkyō Hōjin Rei*, Imperial Ordinance No. 719) was promulgated.

The Religious Corporation Ordinance was little more than a stopgap measure. It prescribed a few working rules that enabled any religious organization to maintain or receive corporate legal status simply by filling out a registration form and filing it with the proper government office. As for the state, the ordinance contained no provisions that might allow government authorities to supervise religious groups with regard to doctrines, rituals, or other internal matters. With this ordinance the right of religious corporations to self-determination was not only recognized but given broad scope.

Shrine Shinto denationalized. Occupation policy with regard to nationalized Shrine Shinto was set forth in a directive entitled "Abolition of Governmental Sponsorship, Support, Perpetuation, Control, and Dissemination of State Shinto" (December 15, 1945), commonly referred to as the Shinto Directive. Despite its title, the directive did not limit itself to State Shinto but took into account Japanese followers of "all religions, faiths, sects, creeds, or philosophies." It not only ordered the denationalization of Shinto but also laid down three basic principles: (1) eradication of militarism and ultranationalism, (2) establishment of religious freedom, and (3) separation of religion and state. Thus State Shinto came to an abrupt end, but in denationalized form Shrine Shinto was permitted to survive.

Complying with the Shinto Directive, the Japanese government repealed all laws and ordinances linking Shinto to the state and made arrangements to treat Shrine Shinto organizations like other private religious bodies. The Department of Shrine Affairs in the Ministry of Home Affairs was dissolved. The Religious Corporation Ordinance was amended on February 2, 1946 to make it possible for shrine organizations to register as religious corporations, and responsibility for this matter was assigned to the Ministry of Education, which was already handling the registration of other religious bodies. Shrine Shinto made a fresh start, this time on the same legal basis as Sect Shinto, Buddhism, Christianity, and other religious movements.

On November 3, 1946 the Constitution of Japan was announced to the public, and on May 3, 1947 it went into effect. The new constitution clearly affirmed the principles of religious freedom and separation of religion and state. Thus ended a thousand-year tradition of state control over religious organizations.

Need for a new law. That the government needed a new law by which to administer religious organizations as corporate entities was evident from two angles. First, the Religious Corporation Ordinance, by making corporate status a simple matter of registration, had opened the door to a number of abuses. Secessions from parent organizations and the birth of new groups were everyday occurrences. Religions of every description, some quite nebulous if not downright fraudulent, sprang into being and in many cases faded just as quickly. In practice, therefore, the ordinance proved inadequate.

Second, a new law was needed to correct the abnormal legal situation that existed in Japan during the occupation. According to Japan's legal system, administrative ordinances and regulations are created to implement laws already enacted by the legislature. With Japan's surrender in 1945, however, effective sovereignty passed from the Japanese government to the Allied Occupation. When the Occupation authorities, in issuing the Shinto Directive, nullified the Religious Organizations Law, the Religious Corporation Ordinance filled the vacuum. This ordinance was an emergency measure authorized by the Occupation, but since it had no law behind it, it existed outside the framework of Japanese law. During the years of the Occupation, this state of affairs was unavoidable. In 1951, however, the San Francisco Peace Treaty was signed, and the end of the Occupation was imminent. To restore normality to the legal system with specific reference to religious organizations, the government had to take its Civil Code into account. According to Article 33 of the Civil Code, corporate status can be granted to an organization either in accordance with the Civil Code itself or, exceptionally, through enactment of a specific law. The Religious Corporation Ordinance, however, depended on neither of these possibilities, and if carried over into the post-Occupation period, would have had an ambiguous legal foundation.

In view of these two circumstances a careful study was made and a new law drawn up. On April 3, 1951 the Religious Corporation Ordinance was set aside in favor of the Religious Corporation Law.

• THE PRESENT LAW

Purpose and provisions. The Religious Corporation Law (*Shūkyō hōjin hō*), is based on the principles of religious freedom, separation of religion and state, and respect for the uniqueness and autonomy of religious corporations, and clarifies the responsibilities of such bodies both to their adherents and to the public. Its aim, as indicated earlier, is to provide religious organizations with the legal capacity not only to possess, maintain, and dispose of worship facilities and other properties but also to engage in business enterprises for the achievement of their purposes. The law explicitly prohibits government officials from demanding information about or interfering with religious teachings, rituals, or any other matters properly belonging to the religious domain.[1]

It is not obligatory for a religious organization to become a religious corporation. Any religious body, whether or not it chooses to seek this status, is free to carry on its activities. But if it wishes to apply for religious corporation status and obtain the advantages of corporate property ownership and exemption from certain taxes, it must meet the requirements specified in the Religious Corporation Law. These requirements, formulated in view of the oppressive use to which the Religious Organizations Law had been put, are intended to introduce democratic principles into the organization and legal administration of religious bodies. The requirements can be reduced to three essential points: (1) government certification of information submitted by the applicant, (2) establishment in each corporation of a board of legally responsible officials, and (3) public announcement of proposed important changes.

A religious group desiring religious corporation status must submit to the competent governmental authority certain legally specified types of information. This information includes the organization's purpose, name, address, organizational offices and their terms, business enterprises, and an inventory of property holdings. On obtaining government certification of

---

1. Minor revisions to this law were made in 1951, 1952, 1962, 1963, 1966 and 1968. Because of the March 1995 sarin gas attack in the Tokyo subway system as well as other crimes allegedly committed by Aum Shinrikyō, the Diet enacted major revisions on December 8, 1995. Key points include the following: (1) a religious corporation that operates in more than one prefecture will come under the jurisdiction of the Ministry of Education rather than the governor of the prefecture where the group first registered; (2) all religious corporations will have to submit lists of their senior officials and financial assets to competent authorities every fiscal year; (3) members of the corporation and other interested parties will be allowed to inspect the documents submitted to the authorities; and (4) in cases where suspicions lead to calls for a group's dissolution, authorities now have the right to demand reports and question corporation officers after receiving permission from a Ministry of Education panel.

this information, the applicant may formally register as a religious corporation. Subsequent changes in the information submitted, including mergers or a decision to dissolve the corporation, must also be reported to the competent governmental authority and be authenticated by it.

The legally responsible officials constitute the highest decision-making body of a religious corporation. Only the decisions taken by this board are recognized as the will of the religious corporation. The law requires that an incorporated religious organization have at least three legally responsible officials. Of these, one is to be selected to represent the corporation in all legal matters and to preside over its affairs.

The present law requires public notification to adherents and other interested parties at least one month in advance of a substantive change. Such notification is obligatory when, for example, an incorporated religious organization plans to dispose of or mortgage real estate or other inventoried property, to borrow or give surety, or to construct, move, or demolish a principal building on its grounds. This provision, in combination with the other two, is intended to assure just and open practices by religious corporations.

The law in practice. Religious organizations incorporated under the old Religious Corporation Ordinance were allowed eighteen months, beginning April 3, 1951, the date of the promulgation of the Religious Corporation Law, to apply for incorporation under the terms of the new law. Those that failed to do so within the time specified lost their legal status as religious corporations. The number of organizations that applied for and received religious corporation status under the 1951 law came to more than three hundred and seventy. Local temples, shrines, and churches desiring this status were also required to make the change at this time, but some either failed to apply or could not meet the requirements of the new law. These institutions ceased to exist as legally incorporated bodies.

Religious corporations *(shūkyō hōjin)*, it should be mentioned, are not the same as the incorporated nonprofit foundations *(zaidan hōjin)* or the incorporated social service associations *(shadan hōjin)* permitted by Article 34 of the Civil Code (Law 89 of 1896). Like them, however, religious corporations are considered public service corporations and are exempted from corporation tax, real estate tax, and registration tax.

Clearly, government administration of religious organizations has undergone a major change since the end of World War II. This transformation has its basis in the principles of religious freedom and separation of religion and state. Of necessity this freedom is not absolute, and this

APPENDICES

AUM SHINRIKYŌ

Ishii Kenji

On March 20, 1995, the deadly nerve gas sarin was planted in five subway cars on three lines in the Tokyo subway system, killing or injuring more than five thousand people. Rumors linked the attack to Aum Shinrikyō. Two days later, police searched Aum Shinrikyō's offices at twenty-five locations across Japan on suspicion of the sect's involvement in the abduction and illegal confinement of a notary public. On April 14, 120 Aum Shinrikyō facilities throughout Japan were raided simultaneously. On May 16, in connection with the sarin gas attack, Aum Shinrikyō's founder, Asahara Shōkō, was arrested on suspicion of murder.

That a religious organization would use nerve gas for mass slaughter and paralyze an entire city has profoundly shaken Japanese society. The attack has given the world a horrible demonstration of a new terrorism, in which chemical weapons are the latest deadly threat.

• ASAHARA SHŌKŌ AND AUM SHINRIKYŌ

Aum Shinrikyō is the creation of Asahara Shōkō. Asahara was born on March 2, 1955, in the Kumamoto Prefecture city of Yatsushiro. He began life as Matsumoto Chizuo, the fourth son in a family of five brothers and two sisters. His father made tatami mats, and the family was poor. Congenitally afflicted with glaucoma, the boy could see almost nothing with his left eye, and his right eye was extremely weak. Midway through his first year at the local primary school he transferred to a prefectural school for the blind. For fourteen years, through primary school, middle school, high school, and a specialized course of study, he lived in school dormitories. The specialized course qualified him as a master of acupuncture and moxibustion, and he subsequently worked at an acupuncture and moxibustion clinic in the city of Kumamoto for two months.

In 1977 Asahara went to Tokyo. He practiced acupuncture and moxibustion in Funabashi, Chiba Prefecture, near Tokyo, and took the entrance examination for the University of Tokyo, which he failed. In January 1978 he married twenty-year-old Matsumoto Tomoko, the eldest daughter of schoolteachers in Kisarazu, Chiba Prefecture. After graduating from the Kisarazu prefectural high school, Tomoko took examinations for entrance to university, but was unsuccessful. It was while commuting to a preparatory school that she met Asahara.

Asahara started a business in Funabashi in 1978, calling it the Chinese Herbal Medicine Asia Hall Pharmacy. In 1981 he opened the BMA Pharmacy, a store specializing in health foods and herbal medicines. In June 1982 he was arrested on suspicion of having violated the Pharmaceutical Affairs Law by misrepresenting the efficacy of herbs he sold and taking money under false pretenses. Summarily indicted, he was fined ¥200,000.

Asahara's interest in religion began after his arrival in Tokyo. He studied inner energy (*kigaku*) and fortune telling, and devoted himself to the new religion known as the God Light Association. In 1981, through the practice of yoga, he experienced a Kundalini awakening, an arousal of vital or sexual energy said to transform body, mind, and emotions and lead to spiritual development. In 1982 he joined Agonshū, and from this new religion received influences that would shape much of his subsequent religious activity.

In 1984, however, he left Agonshū and opened his own yoga training center in Shibuya, one of Tokyo's main commercial centers. The following February, he claimed to have had a levitation experience, and in the same year, while visiting the Miura coast in Kanagawa Prefecture, he reported a revelation in which a kami commissioned him to build an ideal world, the kingdom of Shambhala. In March 1986 he published his book *Chōnōryoku "Himitsu no kaihatsuhō"* (The secret of developing extraordinary powers), and in April he founded the Aum Shinsen no Kai. There were about fifteen original members. From this time on he wrote one book after another, and in 1987 began publication of the monthly journal *Mahāyāna*. In February 1987 he met the Dalai Lama. He visited India in July 1987, and there, in the Himalayas, he is said to have attained ultimate deliverance. In the same month he changed the name of his organization to Aum Shinrikyō, and quickly stepped up the pace of its activities.

Aum Shinrikyō applied for religious corporation status in August 1989, and became an independent religious corporation (*tanritsu shūkyō hōjin*) under the jurisdiction of the Tokyo metropolitan government. Its head office was in Tokyo, with branch offices in major cities throughout Japan, a general headquarters and training center in Fujinomiya, Shizuoka

Prefecture and, a short distance from Fujinomiya, land with a dozen buildings in the Yamanashi Prefecture village of Kamikuishiki.

• TEACHINGS AND RITUALS

Changes in Aum Shinrikyō's teachings and rituals have kept pace with its expanding activities. At the time the organization was formed, the focus of its activities fell, first, on the achievement of superhuman powers through yoga practices, leading to the experience of Kundalini enlightenment and levitation, and second, on consequent miraculous healing experiences. Later it placed emphasis on clarifying the doctrine of enlightenment that stemmed from primitive Buddhism, and extreme ascetic practices intended to lead to enlightenment. According to Aum Shinrikyō, the idea of rejecting this world and separating oneself from it is bound up with the experience of meditation; the sect claims that young people, having lost interest in the affluent society, find this teaching very attractive. Progress along the path to enlightenment and salvation is accelerated if the adherent follows the esoteric rituals devised by Asahara Shōkō, for example, plunging into a tank of water and remaining submerged for as long as possible, or entering a metal container that is then buried, staying underground for a week. This teaching has given rise to a kind of salvation-faith, and in turn to a series of ad hoc initiation rites.

As people who attained Kundalini enlightenment became more numerous, a new, stratified cosmology and different types of yoga were established. Going beyond simple yoga, the sect turned to the world of the occult. It taught that on the far side of this phenomenal world there is an astral or causal world, and that above the causal world is the realm of Mahāyāna, or Mahānirvana. After 1989, in addition to the doctrine of salvation for humankind, eschatological thinking came to the fore, and repeated emphasis was placed on Armageddon and the prophecies of Nostradamus. Again, Aum Shinrikyō teachings came to include the doctrine, supposedly legitimated by the Tantra Vajrayāna, that it was proper to punish or even kill people or groups that interfered with the organization. The end result was a teaching utterly different from either Buddhism or Hinduism.

At its peak, Aum Shinrikyō had two major offices in Tokyo (Minami Aoyama and Kameido), its general headquarters in Fujinomiya, and approximately twenty other bases throughout Japan. Overseas it had opened branches in New York, Bonn, Sri Lanka and Moscow. Japanese adherents numbered approximately 10,000, of whom some 1,100 had left their families. Russian adherents are said to have numbered 30,000. Since the

Tokyo subway attack, the number of Japanese adherents has dropped sharply, while in Russia, where the government ordered the sect to suspend operations, there is practically no activity at all.

• SOCIAL FRICTIONS

After its incorporation, Aum Shinrikyō grew rapidly, and rapidly developed a controversial reputation, especially with the families of members. When members renounced the world and dedicated themselves to the sect, they were no longer allowed to communicate with their children and families. They were also required to donate everything they owned to the organization. For these and other extreme policies, the sect became the target of criticism. Only two months after Aum Shinrikyō became a religious corporation, the widely read journal *Sunday Mainichi* raised the issue of the sect's antisocial character, and began a campaign of criticism that ran for seven issues. In October 1989, a number of people who regarded themselves as victims of Aum Shinrikyō formed an organization. In November, a Yokohama lawyer named Sakamoto Tsutsumi, one of those who had supported this victims' group most earnestly, disappeared together with his wife and child. When suspicions arose concerning a connection between their disappearance and Aum Shinrikyō, the police summoned Asahara for questioning, but no provable relationship came to light.

For the 1990 Lower House election, Asahara and twenty-five others from his Shinritō, or Truth Party, stood as candidates, but all were defeated. In April of the same year, Asahara predicted that there would be a major earthquake and held a seminar at Ishigakijima which drew over a thousand people, but the earthquake did not occur. In October, police went to the organization's camp in the Kumamoto Prefecture village of Namino, to the general headquarters at Fujinomiya and to twelve other places throughout Japan, carrying search warrants based on the suspicion that Aum Shinrikyō had violated the Act for Planning the Utilization of National Land by building a residence on land zoned as forest land. It was also charged with issuing and circulating false statements in attested public documents. Several leaders were arrested, but Aum Shinrikyō prevailed in court.

In 1992 a branch was opened in Moscow, apparently on the assumption that it would be easy to win Russian members because of social unrest. Access to weapons may also have been a factor. Aum Shinrikyō representatives gave lectures at a number of universities in Russia, and with Russia as a strategic base, the organization began an aggressive campaign to spread its teachings.

An earlier sarin attack in the city of Matsumoto occurred in June 1994, but when suspicions pointed to Aum Shinrikyō, the organization claimed to have been the victim of a sarin attack itself. (Police suspect an accident caused leakage of sarin on Aum Shinrikyō grounds in Kamikuishiki.) In July 1994 residents of the village of Kamikuishiki complained of a foul smell coming from Aum Shinrikyō buildings. In September of the same year, an innkeeper in Miyazaki Prefecture filed a complaint against Aum Shinrikyō, alleging that he had been abducted and held against his will. In February 1995 a notary public, Kariya Kiyoshi, was abducted, and Aum Shinrikyo's involvement made headlines. The sarin attack in the Tokyo subway system followed on March 20, 1995. On June 30, the Tokyo Public Prosecutor and the Tokyo Metropolitan Government, which has at once land survey responsibility and jurisdiction over its religious corporations, petitioned the Tokyo District Court to order the dissolution of Aum Shinrikyō because of the grievous injury it had caused to public welfare. Moving with unusual speed, the Tokyo District Court handed down its decision on October 30. It acknowledged the justice of the petition and ordered the sect to disband. Aum Shinrikyō appealed to the Tokyo High Court, but on December 19 its appeal was rejected and the dissolution order based on the Religious Corporation Law was upheld. The organization thus ceased to be a legally recognized corporation and lost the tax privileges that had applied to its operations. The Tokyo District Court, responding to applications from victims and their families, declared Aum Shinrikyō insolvent and ordered its assets frozen on December 14. On the same day the national government decided to invoke the Antisubversive Activities Law against Aum Shinrikyō. If this law is applied, Aum Shinrikyō adherents will be free to believe in the organization's teachings as individuals but will be forbidden to support or promote the organization in any way.

• MEDIA FRENZY

The intense press coverage of the Tokyo attack brought Aum Shinrikyō into every home in Japan. Special news programs on Aum Shinrikyō's shocking crimes won universally high audience ratings. Some viewers accepted the media slant, but others had doubts and criticisms.

News programs gave Aum Shinrikyō executives daily TV exposure, allowing them to deny involvement without challenge and grabbing high ratings for the networks. Executives of the sect, appearing on TV day after day to explain its position, became so popular that fan clubs sprang up. Journalists and reporters encamped outside the Aum Shinrikyō office in

Minami Aoyama competed for space with an endless stream of sightseers. During the consecutive holidays on May 3, 4 and 5, huge crowds of curiosity seekers gathered outside the center in Kamikuishiki.

• SOCIO-CULTURAL IMPACT
The Aum Shinrikyō case has had a great impact on contemporary Japanese society. A religious organization that should be expected to benefit people has released poison gas with the intent to commit mass murder. It amassed a huge arsenal of weapons and even planned to overthrow the state. It used drugs in its rituals, blurring together hallucination and religious awakening.

What most Japanese find incomprehensible is that the believers are largely young people. Why were they attracted to a cult leader of dubious reputation who capitalizes on occult powers? How could elite graduates of long-established and highly ranked schools like the University of Tokyo and Kyoto University have lent themselves to the production of sarin and the kidnapping and confinement of members?

That Aum Shinrikyō was born in postwar Japan comes as no surprise. The status of religious organizations in the postwar legal system, the problem of ethics and moral instruction in the postwar school system, the growing mistrust of a government with no clear vision of a prosperous economic future, the legal change from the system of linked households to the nuclear family together with the emergence of one-child families— all these problems of postwar Japanese society come to bear on the case of Aum Shinrikyō. The organization and the crimes it committed have become matters of concern not only to media representatives and scholars but also to great numbers of Japanese people and have given rise to an immense body of publications. Some writers ask whether Aum Shinrikyō has any similarity to the Branch Davidians, many of whom died a fiery death in Waco, Texas, in 1993, or to the Order of the Solar Temple, members of which committed what appears to have been a ritual suicide in Switzerland and Canada in 1994 and in the French Alps in 1995. More broadly, the question is raised as to the reason why cults are springing up around the world as we approach the end of this millennium.

• REVISION OF THE RELIGIOUS CORPORATION LAW
On April 20, 1995, the Religious Corporation Council, an advisory body to the Minister of Education, took up the matter of Aum Shinrikyō. It set June 20 as the date for the first meeting of a special committee to consider the Religious Corporation Law and how the system might be improved.

The special committee's report, presented in September, contained three points: (1) the law should be revised so that religious corporations operating in two or more prefectures will be under the jurisdiction of the Minister of Education, (2) religious corporations should be required to present annual reports documenting their financial condition, and (3) the governmental authority with jurisdiction over a religious corporation should have the right to interrogate its officers if it is ordered to suspend a profit-making enterprise or if its certification is canceled. At an extraordinary session of the Diet in the autumn of 1995, discussions began on the matter of revising the Religious Corporation Law, the most important of the issues to come before this Diet.

In public opinion surveys conducted in 1995 by the *Asahi Shimbun*, *Yomiuri Shimbun* and other newspapers, the majority of respondents were in favor of revision, but in the religious world Sōka Gakkai, the United Church of Christ in Japan, the Kyoto Buddhist community, and many other bodies have voiced their opposition to revising the Religious Corporation Law. Again, after the Religious Corporation Council submitted its report, several Council members called for reconsideration of the findings. As a result, considerable confusion surrounded the issue until December 8, 1995 when the Diet enacted into law a bill revising the Religious Corporation Law.

The revisions adhere closely to the September recommendations of the Religious Corporation Council. Key points include the following: (1) jurisdiction over a religious corporation operating in more than one prefecture will shift from the governor of the prefecture where the group first registered to the Ministry of Education; (2) each religious corporation will be required to submit to the competent authority an annual report documenting its financial assets and listing its senior officials; (3) members of the religious group "and other interested parties" will be allowed to inspect the documents presented to government authorities; (4) if suspicions lead to calls for a group's dissolution and if a Ministry of Education panel grants permission, authorities have the right to demand reports from the religious corporation and to question its leaders.

The revised Religious Corporation Law, by requiring religious groups with corporate status to submit reports on their financial assets every fiscal year, gives government authorities greater control over such bodies. It is to be expected that religious organizations exercising political influence, Sōka Gakkai in particular, will come under pressure from ruling parties seeking to weaken the Shinshintō, or New Frontier Party, reportedly a beneficiary of Sōka Gakkai backing. Confrontation between those in favor

II

STATISTICS

- PROBLEMS OF COMPILATION AND INTERPRETATION

The Agency for Cultural Affairs of the Ministry of Education compiles statistics on the religions of Japan from reports submitted to government offices by religious corporations at the end of each calendar year. Though the validity of these figures is open to question due to certain difficulties which will presently be discussed, they are nevertheless the only official statistics available and are widely used. It is important, therefore, to know what degree of reliability they actually possess.

In compiling these statistics, the Agency for Cultural Affairs encounters three main problems. First, due to the changed relationship between religious organizations and the state since the end of World War II, it is now more difficult to obtain reliable figures. Before the war, the government could easily gather information and statistics by demanding reports from religious bodies on the basis of legal enactments such as the *Naimu hōkoku soku* (Regulations governing reports to the Ministry of Home Affairs [Ministry of Home Affairs Ordinance No. 20, 1888]), *Shinbutsu dōkyō shūha jimu hōkoku soku* (Regulations governing administrative reports by Shinto and Buddhist organizations [Ministry of Education Ordinance No. 6, 1914]), and *Kyōha, shūha oyobi kyōdan no hōkoku ni kansuru ken* (Matters relating to reports from Sect Shinto, Buddhist, and Christian organizations [Ministry of Education Regulation No. 10, 1940]). With the occupation, however, all such ordinances and regulations were rescinded. Until recently, the agency relied solely on the voluntary cooperation of religious organizations. This is still the basic principle for statistics of a general kind.

Second, different organizations have different understandings of the categories of information sought. Even apparently straightforward terms like shrines and temples (*shaji*), churches (*kyōkai*), clergy (*kyōshi*) and adherents (*shinja*) are defined differently by different groups. This matter will be treated in more detail below. The point to be noted here is that the only unambiguous classification is the number of religious corporations. Yet one can hardly form an accurate statistical picture of the Japanese religious world on the basis of this one figure. Meaningful reading of Japanese religious statistics depends on independent knowledge of the organizations in question.

The third type of problem is occasioned by the existence of religious organizations that are not religious corporations. The constitutional principle of religious freedom prevents government administrators from making direct, official contact with such organizations. Only if an unincorporated religious organization is affiliated with a comprehensive incorporated organization can government compilers gain access, through the reports of the latter, to statistical data about the former.

In view of these three fundamental difficulties, it will be evident that statistics published by the Agency for Cultural Affairs present only a suggestive sketch of the different religious groups.

• STATISTICAL CATEGORIES

Religious organizations. The main distinction to be drawn between different kinds of religious organizations is the line between *tan'i shūkyō dantai,* or "local religious bodies," and *hōkatsu shūkyō dantai,* or "comprehensive religious organizations." The former classification applies to local shrines, temples, churches, etc. These are often, though not invariably, members of larger organizations. The latter classification refers to these larger groupings, which often have authority over their constituent local units in such matters as doctrine, hierarchical organization, personnel and the like. The Sōtō Sect of Zen Buddhism and the Roman Catholic Church in Japan are examples of comprehensive religious corporations.

This twofold classification is suggested by Article 2 of the Religious Corporation Law.

> In this law "religious organizations" (*shūkyō dantai*) means the organizations mentioned below, the primary purposes of which are the dissemination of religious teachings, the conduct of ceremonies and functions, and the education and nurture of believers:
> (1) shrines (*jinja*), temples (*ji'in*), churches (*kyōkai*), monasteries (*shūdōin*), and similar organizations possessing facilities for worship;
> (2) denominations (*kyōha*), sects (*shūha*), federations (*kyōdan*), churches (*kyōkai*), orders (*shūdōkai*), dioceses or districts (*shikyōku*), and similar organizations which comprehend the groups mentioned in the preceding category.

Of the local religious bodies, over ninety-five percent belong to comprehensive religious organizations and are therefore identified as "comprehended religious organizations" (*hi hōkatsu shūkyō dantai*). Conversely, some local bodies are unattached to any comprehensive organizations and are incorporated as "independent religious organizations" (*tanritsu shūkyō dantai*). Yasukuni Shrine, located in Tokyo, and the Tokyo unit of Sōka Gakkai, for example, are independent religious organizations.

The governmental offices responsible for registering and receiving the reports of religious corporations differ for local bodies and comprehensive organizations. A local religious body, if it operates in only one prefecture, comes under the jurisdiction of the governor of its administrative area, whereas comprehensive religious organizations register with and submit reports to the Agency for Cultural Affairs.

Clergy. The clergy classification is less precise. For the most part it refers to people who belong to a particular religious organization and devote themselves full time to its operations. But religious organizations decide for themselves what qualifications they want in their clergy, and their reports count clergy members in accordance with standards they themselves have established. Some require seminary training after graduation from a university. Others, especially lay movements that emphasize a life of faith within the secular world, require no more than a few weeks of leadership training. The traditional Buddhist organizations, moreover, distinguish priests (*sōryo*) from teachers (*kyōshi*), whereas in other groups the clergy classification includes both. Thus, for example, the disproportionately large number of clergy given for Buddhist organizations in Table 1 reflects the fact that Sōka Gakkai registers as teachers of religion all who successfully complete its catechismal program. This number currently amounts to nearly one and a half million.

Adherents. Even more problematic from the viewpoint of statistical tidiness is the adherent classification. The names that different organizations use to designate adherents include supporters (*danto*), believers (*shinto*), members (*kai'in*), comrades (*dōshi*), parishioners (*ujiko*), worshipers (*sūkeisha*), seekers (*kyūdōsha*), companions (*dōnin*), followers of the way (*dōjin*), etc. But terminological diversity is only the tip of the iceberg. More important is the conceptual diversity as to what qualifications an adherent should possess. Each organization sets its own standards. There is no uniform definition.

As noted by many observers, the total number of adherents far exceeds the population of Japan, while conversely, over two-thirds of the Japanese people say they believe in no religion. This apparent paradox is a natural consequence of the syncretistic orientation espoused by the traditional religions together with their long-established custom of counting all the households of a given parish or community when computing membership.

Illustrative of this syncretistic orientation is the widespread practice of having in the same home not only a Shinto altar for the worship of the kami but also a Buddhist altar for remembering the ancestors. A member of such a household will be aware that he is counted both as a parishioner of a Shinto shrine and a supporter of a Buddhist temple. Dual adherence of this kind is not at all uncommon. To complicate matters further, it frequently happens that members of the new religions not only take part in the activities of these particular organizations but also rely on a traditional Buddhist temple for funerals, memorial rites and cemetery upkeep, while at the same time participating in the annual ceremonies, rites of passage, and community festivals sponsored by the local Shinto shrine. Since many people adhere to two or even three religious organizations, duplication in the counting of adherents is unavoidable. Christianity and a few of the new religions demand exclusive membership, but this is exceptional.

In the counting of adherents, the basic unit, traditionally, has been the household, not the individual. Shinto shrines and Buddhist temples have an organizational structure that for all practical purposes prevents them from counting the individual as the basic unit. In order to cooperate with government and other agencies that request membership figures in terms of individuals, they generally count the number of households in the community or parish, multiply by the average family size, and give the resultant figure as their number of adherents. Some organizations count as members all who subscribe to their periodical, while still others count everybody who purchases one of their talismans. Given these multiple memberships and irreconcilable methods of counting adherents, it is hardly surprising that Japanese people are sometimes judged as possessing only a weak sense of individuality and, depending on one's viewpoint, a lax or generously tolerant attitude in matters of religion. Statistically, the result of this syncretistic overlapping and methodological disparity is that it is next to impossible to produce order out of the chaos that lurks behind the neat rows of figures. At most, the numbers given under the "adherents" heading may be understood to represent those who have some spiritual sympathy or institutional affiliation with a given religious organization.

Using common sense one can, by comparing the various traditions in terms of number of organizations, clergy and adherents, gain a rough idea of their strength. It should not be assumed, however, that the statistics available at the present time can be used to form an accurate comparative assessment of their social influence or of the number of people they can mobilize. The complexities inherent in the statistics merely reflect the complexities of the Japanese religious situation.

Religious traditions. The Agency for Cultural Affairs tabulates religious statistics by dividing religious traditions into four broad classifications: Shinto, Buddhist, Christian, and Other Religions. The decision as to which classification applies to a given religious organization is made on the basis of its origin, history, scriptures, rituals, and annual celebrations.

Shinto is divided into three groups: Shrine Shinto, Sect Shinto, and New Sect Shinto (made up of organizations that have come into being since 1945); Buddhism into seven: Tendai, Shingon, Pure Land, Zen, Nichiren, Nara, and Other; and Christianity into two: Catholic and Protestant. The Other Religions classification covers organizations that do not fit into Shinto, Buddhist, or Christian categories.

• PRINCIPLES EMPLOYED

It is important to remember that the fundamental principle of organization employed in the compilation of the statistical tables is that the basic unit of tabulation is not the individual adherent but the organization as a religious corporation. Since the groups covered are in the final analysis voluntary religious organizations with overlapping memberships, it follows that the total number of adherents can and does exceed the total population—125,034,000 as of December 31, 1994.

The arrangement within the table is from large to small, from summary to detail. Table 1 presents an overall view. In the clergy columns, figures in parentheses refer to non-Japanese people.

TABLE 1
Statistics on Religious Organizations as of December 31, 1994

Classifications	Religious Organizations (Incorporated and Unincorporated)					Religiou	
	Shrines	Temples	Churches	Meeting Places, etc.	Total	Shrines	Temple
TOTAL	81,423	77,404	34,272	38,329	231,428	81,328	76,109
SHINTO	81,387	12	6,561	2,739	90,699	81,299	8
Shrine Shinto	79,466	—	446	413	80,325	79,435	—
Sect Shinto	102	4	5,175	1,131	6,412	64	—
New	55	—	420	894	1,369	46	—
Undifferentiated	1,764	8	520	301	2,593	1,754	8
BUDDHISM	9	77,362	3,060	8,787	89,218	8	76,077
Tendai	7	4,408	477	219	5,111	6	4,051
Shingon	1	12,426	918	1,984	15,329	1	11,977
Pure Land	—	29,792	302	395	30,489	—	29,649
Zen	—	21,012	25	29	21,066	—	20,907
Nichiren	—	6,929	970	5,704	13,603	—	6,778
Nara	—	266	56	149	471	—	228
Other	—	18	—	10	28	—	12
Undifferentiated	1	2,511	312	297	3,121	1	2,475
CHRISTIANITY	—	6	6,574	2,755	9,335	—	—
Catholic	—	—	880	1,228	2,108	—	—
Protestant	—	1	4,399	1,289	5,689	—	—
Undifferentiated	—	5	1,295	238	1,538	—	—
OTHER RELIGIONS	27	24	18,077	24,048	42,176	21	24

SOURCE: *1995 Shūkyō nenkan* (Religions yearbook), Ministry of Education, Agency for Cultural Affairs, pp. 30–31, 46–49.

NOTE 1. The classification "Undifferentiated," unique to this book, represents the total of: (1) the number of religious organizations registered with a metropolitan or prefectural government, (2) the number of religious organizations which, though not religious corporations themselves, have one or more religious corporations under their organization, and (3) the number of independently incorporated religious organizations. Since

Organizations			Clergy			Adherents
Churches	Meeting Places, etc.	Total	Men (Aliens)	Women (Aliens)	Total (Aliens)	
25,100	1,336	183,873	337,866 (2,809)	308,146 (1,099)	*684,997 (3,908)	219,838,67
4,082	279	85,668	58,884 (46)	31,197 (70)	90,081 (11)	117,378,185
241	41	79,717	23,037	4,693	27,730	95,879,519
3,230	50	3,344	26,032 (1)	17,450	43,482 (1)	4,686, 692
140	52	238	2,620	3,263	5,883	1,090,281
471	136	2,369	7,195 (45)	5,791 (70)	12,986 (115)	15,721,693
1,480	437	78,002	159,500 (124)	98,763 (72)	*297,248 (196)	89,828,502
183	3	4,243	10,954	8,317	19,271	2,718,934
315	55	12,348	27,460 (19)	28,201 (10)	*57,306 (29)	13,687,354
212	215	30,076	50,776 (2)	10,821 (2)	61,597 (4)	19,777,022
18	3	20,928	5,903	637	*23,305	3,322,509
514	15	7,307	19,727 (2)	10,423	*50,725 (2)	25,350,431
11	—	239	700 (5)	922 (5)	1,622 (10)	717,414
—	—	12	38 (1)	35	73 (1)	80,509
227	146	2,849	43,942 (95)	39,407 (55)	83,349 (150)	24,174,329
3,665	307	3,972	12,631 (2,548)	4,014 (880)	16,645 (3,428)	1,519,396
67	159	226	1,814 (812)	—	1,814 (812)	447,639
2,564	33	2,597	6,626 (1,191)	2,606 (474)	9,232 (1,665)	527,408
1,034	115	1,149	4,191 (545)	1,408 (406)	5,599 (951)	544,349
15,873	313	16,231	106,851 (91)	174,172 (77)	281,023 (168)	11,112,595

these numbers are essential to the overall totals but cannot be divided into the classifications that precede them, they are lumped together here under the heading "Undifferentiated."

NOTE 2. The sign — means "not applicable."

NOTE 3. The sign * identifies a clergy total greater than the sum of the figures for men and women clergy. The reason is that some organizations reported a figure for the clergy total but did not differentiate between men and women.

NOTE 4. The total population of Japan as of December 31, 1994 was approximately 125,034,000.

III

CHRONOLOGY

TUMULUS PERIOD (c. 250–500 C.E.) ~~~~~~

c. 3rd century A Chinese book, the *Wei Chih*, tells of the people of Wa (Japan) and the female shaman Pimiko, or Himiko.

c. 5th century Yamato establishes superiority over other clans; special sites are set aside for ruler-performed rituals.

EARLY HISTORY (500–1185) ~~~~~~

ASUKA PERIOD (500–710)

513 Confucian scholars come from Korea.

538 (or 552) Official introduction of Buddhism from Korea.

604 Prince Shōtoku issues the Seventeen-Article Constitution.

607 Construction begins on Hōryūji temple.

625 Jōjutsu and Sanron schools introduced to Japan by the Korean priest Hui-kuan (Japanese, Ekan).

630 Dispatch of imperial envoys to Chinese imperial court begins.

646 Proclamation of the Taika Reforms.

657 Asuka Temple holds Japan's first *bon* ceremonies.

661 Hossō school brought from China by Dōshō.

n.d. Kusha school and second wave of Hossō doctrine introduced by two Japanese priests, Chitsū and Chidatsu.

685 Beginning of the system of alternating the sites of the Grand Shrines of Ise, rebuilding every twenty years.

701 The penal (*ritsu*) and administrative (*ryō*) code of Emperor Tai-hō promulgated, including provisions regulating the ranks assigned to Buddhist monks and nuns.

NARA PERIOD (710–794)

712 Completion of the *Kojiki*.

720 Completion of the *Nihon shoki*, or *Nihongi*.

736	Kegon doctrines introduced by the Chinese priest Tao-hsüan (Japanese, Dōsen).
740	Kegon school founded in Japan by the Korean priest Shen-hsiang (Japanese, Shinjō).
741	A system of state-supported provincial temples (*kokubunji*) and nunneries (*kokubun niji*) is established with Tōdaiji temple (Kegon sect) in Nara as the parent temple.
749	Completion of the Vairocana (Japanese, Birushana) statue for Tōdaiji temple.
n.d.	Compilation of the *Manyōshū*.
754	Ritsu discipline introduced by the Chinese monk Chien-chên (Japanese, Ganjin).
788	Saichō, before going to China, establishes Enryakuji temple on Mt. Hiei.

HEIAN PERIOD (794–1160)

805	Saichō returns from China and founds Tendai school.
806	Kūkai returns from China to found Shingon school.
816	Kūkai establishes Kongōbuji temple on Mt. Kōya.
c. 828	Kūkai completes the *Jūjūshin ron*.
894	Japan stops sending imperial envoys to China.
927	The *Engishiki*, embodying a code of Shinto rituals, brings Shinto into the legal system.
981	Armed struggles among groups of Buddhist priests.
c. 1052	Eschatological ideas (*mappō shisō*) prevail.

TAIRA PERIOD (1160–1185)

1175	Hōnen finds enlightenment in Amida pietism, begins to teach "the one way left," and founds the Pure Land sect.

MEDIEVAL PERIOD (1185–1868)

KAMAKURA PERIOD (1185–1333)

1191	Eisai returns from China and founds the Rinzai sect of Zen.
1194	Practice of Zen suppressed.
n.d.	Chu Hsi Neo-Confucianism introduced in early Kamakura period by Zen priests returning from Sung China.
1200	Kamakura shogunate bans the practice of Amida pietism.
1224	Shinran completes the six-volume *Kyōgyōshinshō* (Teaching,

practice, faith, and attainment) and founds the True Pure Land Sect.

1227   Dōgen returns from China and introduces Sōtō Zen.

1253   Nichiren founds the Nichiren sect.

1272   Nichiren exiled to Sado Island.

MUROMACHI OR ASHIKAGA PERIOD (1336–1573)

1484   Yoshida Kanetomo (1435–1511) establishes Yoshida Shinto at Yamashiro, Kyoto.

1487   Peasant followers of the True Pure Land Sect stage a rebellion in the Kaga area (*Kaga ikkō ikki*) and temporarily establish an autonomous government.

n.d.   Wang Yang-ming Neo-Confucianism introduced in late Muromachi period, possibly by Ryōan Keigo (1425–1514).

1549   Christianity formally introduced to Japan with the arrival of Jesuit Francis Xavier and companions in Kagoshima.

1570–80 Ishiyama Honganji temple, former head temple of the True Pure Land Sect, clashes with Oda Nobunaga.

1571   Oda Nobunaga razes the buildings of Enryakuji temple.

MOMOYAMA OR AZUCHI-MOMOYAMA PERIOD (1573–1603)

1587   Edict issued banning Christianity and expelling the Jesuits.

1597   Twenty-six Christians martyred at Nagasaki.

TOKUGAWA OR EDO PERIOD (1603–1868)

1608   Hayashi Razan becomes Confucian tutor to the Shogun.

c. 1608–18   Regulations governing the relationships between head and branch temples are formalized.

1614   Ieyasu begins suppression of Christianity.

1622   Construction of new Buddhist temples is prohibited.

1635   Inspectorate of temples and shrines (*Jisha Bugyō*) established.

1637–38 Christian revolt at Shimabara.

1638   *Danka seido* established as a nationwide system.

1639   Beginning of Japan's two centuries of seclusion.

1657   Work begins on the *Dai Nihon shi* (History of great Japan) under the Mito school of Confucianism.

1662   Establishment of nationwide system requiring annual temple certificates (*terauke seido*).

1778–98 Motoori Norinaga publishes studies on the *Kojiki* (*Kojikiden*).

1811	Hirata Atsutane (1776–1843), a Shinto restorationist influential in the nineteenth-century antiforeign movement, publishes his *Kodō taii* (Threshold of the ancient way).
1814	Kurozumi Munetada founds Kurozumikyō.
1838	Nakayama Miki founds Tenrikyō.
1854	Perry demands a treaty. Japan emerges from seclusion. Tokugawa Shogunate totters.
1859	Christianity reintroduced by Protestant and Roman Catholic missionaries. Kawate Bunjirō founds Konkōkyō.
1861	Nicolai founds the Holy Orthodox Church in Japan.
1865	Petitjean's "discovery of the Christians."

MODERN PERIOD

Meiji Era (1868–1912)

1869	Meiji government revives ancient *Jingikan* (Department of Shinto Affairs) and disestablishes Buddhism.
1871	Climax of anti-Buddhist iconoclasm. Rescinding of the *danka seido* law. Iwakura delegation to the West.
1873	Removal of public notices prohibiting Christianity.
1877	Bureau of Shinto Shrines and Buddhist Temples established in the Ministry of Home Affairs.
1889	Promulgation of the Meiji constitution.
1890	Imperial Rescript on Education.
1891	Uchimura Kanzō provokes furor by refusing to bow before the Imperial Rescript on Education.
1892	Deguchi Nao founds Ōmoto.
1900	*Jinja Kyoku*, or Shrine Bureau, and *Shūkyō Kyoku*, or Religions Bureau, separately established.

Taisho Period (1912–1926)

1913	*Shūkyō Kyoku* transferred from the Ministry of Home Affairs to the Ministry of Education.
1925	Peace Preservation Law. Kubo Kakutarō founds Reiyūkai.

Showa Period (1926–1988)

1929	Taniguchi Masaharu founds Seichō no Ie.
1930	Makiguchi Tsunesaburō begins Sōka Kyōiku Gakkai.
1932	Religious education proscribed in public schools.

228

1939   Religious Organizations Law.

1941   Formation of the United Church of Christ in Japan.

1945   Allied Occupation begins. Land reform. Peace Preservation Law, Religious Organizations Law, etc. are rescinded. Occupation authorities issue the Shinto Directive, and the government promulgates the Religious Corporation Ordinance.

1946   Emperor formally rejects the idea he is a kami. Establishment of the Association of Shinto Shrines. New constitution.

1947   New family law written into the Civil Code, abolishing the traditional family system.

1948   Diet pronounces Imperial Rescript on Education invalid.

1951   Religious Corporation Ordinance replaced by Religious Corporation Law. San Francisco Peace Treaty.

1952   Allied Occupation ends.

1964   Sōka Gakkai sponsors establishment of the Kōmeitō, or Clean Government Party. Government sponsors a requiem service for the war dead at Yasukuni Shrine.

1967   Kōmeitō candidates elected to House of Representatives.

1970   The first World Conference on Religion and Peace opens in Kyoto.

1971   Okinawa reverts to Japan. Incorporated Okinawan religious organizations, including registered Shinto shrines, are recognized as religious corporations under the Religious Corporation Law of 1951.

1986   Asahara Shōkō founds the Aum Shinsen no Kai, changing its name to Aum Shinrikyō in 1987.

HEISEI PERIOD (1989–)

1991   Nichiren Shōshū expels Sōka Gakkai.

1995   Aum Shinrikyō founder and key followers are arrested for murder in connection with sarin gas poisoning. The Religious Corporation Law is revised to give government authorities greater control.

1996   Political parties and religious bodies debate whether the Antisubversive Activities Law should be invoked in order to outlaw Aum Shinrikyō.

INDEX

butsumetsu 仏滅, 83

California, Japanese religions in, 191
Chian iji hō 治安維持法. *See* Peace
Preservation Law
chinju 鎮守. *See* Kami, as area guardian
Christianity
Catholic, 67–70, 189, 221
crucifixions to eradicate churches
of, 67–68
distribution of, 70, 72, 190
Dōkai 道会, 72
educational institutions of, 70,
74–75, 137, 142, 146–148, 153
emperor system and, 23, 73
foreignness of, 63, 64, 65
growth of, 22–23, 24, 63, 65–68,
76, 190
hidden Christians (*kakure kirishitan* 隠れキリシタン), 69–70
human rights and, 75
indigenization of, 76–78
influence of, 24, 68, 74–76
insider/outsider distinction in, 66
intolerance toward, 65, 68
introduction of, 22, 67, 71, 189–
190, 194
Japanese (*Nihonteki kirisutokyō*
日本的キリスト教), 76
missionaries and mission work of,
67, 68, 71, 74, 77, 137, 193
motivation of converts to, 71, 75–
76, 190
Nonchurch (*Mukyōkai* 無教会),
72–73
opposition to spread of, 138, 140
Orthodox, 70–71, 190
and other religions, 76, 77
and principle of religious freedom,
73–74
prohibition of, 67–68, 73, 147
Protestant, 71–73, 189–190, 221
and social classes, 65–67
and social justice issues, 77
socialist movement and, 75
social work of, 70, 75
and the state, 23, 24, 64, 67, 68, 138
as subversive religion, 64, 68, 69
weddings of, 78
chūkonhi 忠魂碑, 133–135
chūkyōin 中教院, 138
Coming of age (*seijin shiki* 成人式). *See* Rites

Confucianism, 18, 25, 60, 110
Constitution
Constitution of Japan (1946), 118–
122, 132, 133, 134, 135, 144, 199
Imperial Constitution of the Great
Empire of Japan, or Meiji consti-
tution (1889), 25, 28, 74, 115–
116, 200
Seventeen-Article Constitution
(604), 18
Corporations, religious (*shūkyō hōjin* 宗教
法人), 199, 200–201, 204, 205, 210.
See also Religious Corporation Law;
Religious Corporation Ordinance;
Religious Organizations Law
Council on Religious Corporations
(*Shūkyō Hōjin Shingikai* 宗教法人審
議会), 121

Daigaku rei 大学令. *See* University Act
Daijōsai 大嘗祭. *See* Great Food Offering
daikyōin 大教院, 138
danka 檀家. *See* Buddhist temple, supporting households of
danka seido 檀家制度, 47, 60, 69, 169
Death. *See* Rites, mortuary
Deguchi Nao 出口なお (1836–1918),
104, 105
Deguchi Onisaburō 出口王仁三郎
(1871–1948), 105
Dengyō Daishi 伝教大師. *See* Saichō.
Depopulation, surveys on effects of
by Jōdo Shinshū Honganjiha 浄土
真宗本願寺派, 159–160
by Nichiren Shū 日蓮宗, 158–159
Divination, 92, 93, 107
Dōgen 道元 (1200–1253), 21, 55
Dōkai 道会, 72
dōsojin 道祖神. *See* Kami, at entrance to
village
dōzoku 同族, 79, 94
Drumming out of noxious insects
(*mushi okuri* 虫送り), 86

Eclecticism, 102, *See also* Syncretism
Education
and emperor system, 137, 138, 139,
141, 142
moral, 138, 140, 145
religious, 137, 138–146, 152–155
in religious ideals, 142, 145, 153

Magic (*majinai* 呪い), 47–48, 51, 52, 92–93, 102–103, 107, 195–197
Mahikari 真光, 174, 175. *See also* Sekai Mahikari Bunmei Kyōdan; Sūkyō Mahikari
majinai 呪い, 92–93
Makiguchi Tsunesaburō 牧口常三郎 (1871–1944), 105, 118, 124
Mandala (*gohonzon* 御本尊), 107, 196
mappō 末法. *See* Eschatology
Marriage (*konrei* 婚礼). *See* Rites, marriage; Weddings
matsuri 祭. *See* Festivals
matsurigoto 政, 15
Media, mass, 173, 175, 180, 182, 183, 213–214
Meditation, 56, 211
Mediums, 175. *See also* Possession
Meiji constitution. *See* Constitution
migawari 身代わり, 196. *See also* Magic
Miki Takeo 三木武夫 (1907–1988), 132
Miki Tokuchika 御木徳近 (1900–1983), 105
Miki Tokuharu 御木徳一 (1871–1938), 105
mikoto mochi 命持ち, 41
Militarism, 118, 131, 134, 143, 144, 202
Ministry of Education, 120, 139, 140, 142, 143, 145, 202, 214, 215
misogi 身滌, 149
Misogikyō 禊教, 30
Miura Ayako 三浦綾子 (1922–), 78
Modernization, 60, 75
mono no aware 物の哀, 59
Moonviewing (*tsukimi* 月見), 87
Moral education debate (*tokuiku ronsō* 徳育論争), 140
Mori Arinori 森有礼 (1847–1889), 73
Mortuary tablets (*ihai* 位牌), 97. *See also* Rites, mortuary
Motoda Nagazane 元田永孚 (1818–1891), 141
Motoori Norinaga 本居宣長 (1730–1801), 35
Mountain ascetics (*yamabushi* 山伏 · *shugenja* 修験者), 98
mukaebi 迎え火. *See* Fire
Mukyōkai 無教会. *See* Christianity, Nonchurch
mushi okuri 虫送り. *See* Drumming out of noxious insects

Naganuma Myōkō 長沼妙佼 (1889–

1957), 104
Nagaoka Nagako 長岡良子 (1903–1948), 104
Nakamura Keiu 中村敬宇 (1832–1891), 73
Nakano Yonosuke 中野與之助 (1887–1974), 105
Nakasone Yasuhiro 中曽根康弘 (1918–), 131
Nakayama Miki 中山みき (1798–1887), 104, 105, 117
National polity (*kokutai* 国体), 116, 122
National schools (*kokumin gakkō* 国民学校), 143
Nature, importance of in Shinto, 32
Namu myōhō rengekyō 南無妙法蓮華経, 196
Nenbutsu kō 念仏講, 95, 98. *See also* Associations, voluntary religious
nenchū gyōji 年中行事. *See* Folk religion, yearly round of observances
Neutrality. *See* Separation of religion and state
New Age, 179, 181, 183, 194. *See also* Occult; Spirit World
New religions (*shin shūkyō* 新宗教), 25–26, 62
    conservative values of, 110
    definition, 100–102
    educational institutions of, 146, 151–152, 153
    general characteristics, 102–103
    growth of, 171, 182, 197
    magical practices of, 107, 195–197
    "new" (*shin shin shūkyō* 新新宗教), 174–177, 181, 182
    in politics, 123
    principles of organization, 108–109
    reliance on laity, 103
    role and influence of, 109–111, 167
    teachings of, 106–107
    types of founders in, 104–106
    urbanization and, 166–167
    winning new members in, 103
New Year (*shōgatsu* 正月), 84, 162
New Year's Eve (*joya* 除夜), 88
Nichiren 日蓮 (1222–1282), 21–22, 56–57
Nichiren Shōshū 日蓮正宗, 118, 126. *See also* Sōka Gakkai
Nichiren Shū 日蓮宗, 158, 191
Nichizō 日像 (1269–1342), 158